Compliments of

Oakland and Surroundings Illustrated & Described

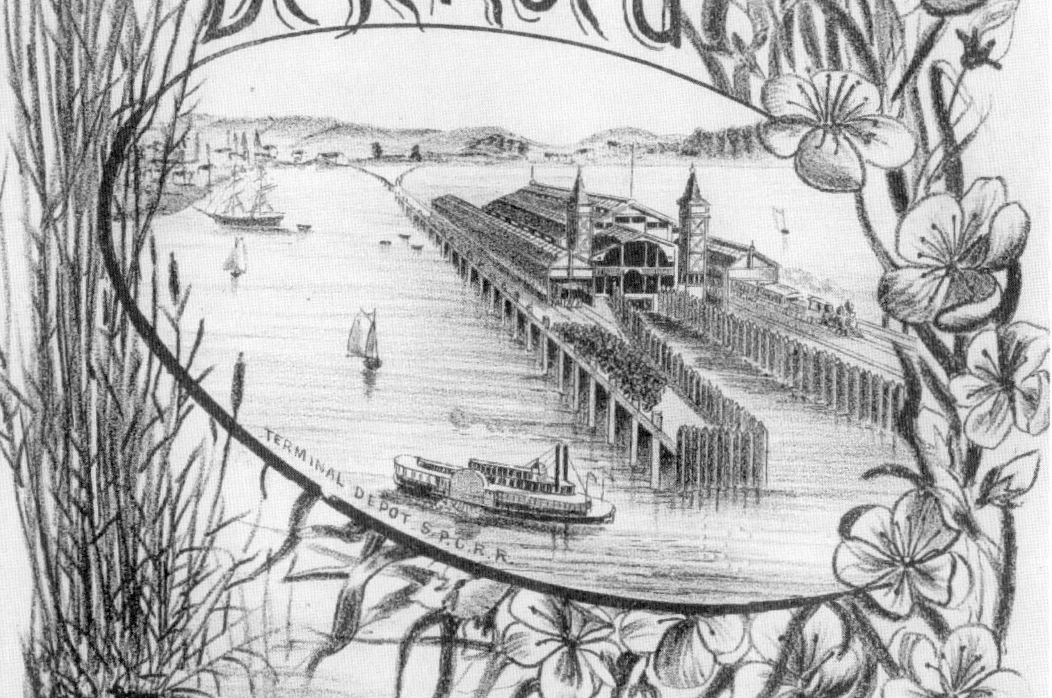

LITHOGRAPHED & PUBLISHED BY W. W. ELLIOTT, 921 BROADWAY, OAKLAND, CAL.

Marula

An imprint of Arcadia Publishing

Oakland and Surroundings
Illustrated and Described, Showing Its Advantages for Residence or Business
by W.W. Elliott

A Marula Historical Reprint
Originally published in 1885

Published by Arcadia Publishing
Charleston SC

ISBN 978-0-7385-9472-9

Printed in the United States of America

For all general information contact Arcadia Publishing at:
Telephone 843-853-2070
Fax 843-853-0044
E-mail sales@arcadiapublishing.com
For customer service and orders:
Toll-Free 1-888-313-2665

Visit us on the Internet at www.arcadiapublishing.com

OAKLAND

—AND—

SURROUNDINGS

ILLUSTRATED

AND

DESCRIBED,

SHOWING ITS

ADVANTAGES

—FOR—

Residence or Business.

W. W. ELLIOTT,
PUBLISHER,
921 BROADWAY, OAKLAND, CAL.
1885.

EXPLANATORY.

WE have aimed to furnish in convenient form for distribution a selection of some of the most impor tant features of Oakland and its surroundings, as represented in its scenery as well as public an private buildings, which of themselves are monuments to the taste and prosperity of our citizens To these have been added descriptive articles selected from a variety of sources.

Our object has not been to tell a glowing story, but simply to give facts in an interesting manner; t furnish residents with such a description of Oakland and surroundings as they can conscientiously send t friends; to put something in the hands of tourists, and especially to afford reliable and satisfactory informa tion to those who are longing to make a home where they can find health and comfort amid sunshine, frui and flowers.

In speaking of Oakland we almost involuntarily include the whole adjacent country of Temescal, Frui vale, Alameda, and Berkeley, and hence our work covers all these localities.

The lithograph illustrations are all made from nature, *not* from photographs. The views cover a gre variety of subjects and are of all grades and qualities of workmanship, and all were executed by the pul lisher at his lithographing establishment in Oakland. The views represent different kinds of artistic work the soft, fine lithograph, crayon etchings, zincographs, wood-cuts, photo-engraving, heliotype, and othe processes.

We expect criticism. It is the easiest thing in the world to find fault. Our work is not withou errors. Few persons without actual experience can comprehend the care and pains required to comple a work of this description.

We found many prominent citizens totally indifferent and unwilling to furnish the slightest informatio and much that we have gathered was under great difficulties.

We hope these imperfect pages and sketches will induce our citizens to further efforts to spread abroa the advantages of our city which we believe to be second to none on the continent.

There is little doubt but that Oakland stands to-day on the eve of great prosperity, if her citizens, wh have accumulated wealth here, would only act a little less selfish and strive for the general good and th aid in building up an active, vigorous, business city.

CONTENTS.

ILLUSTRATIONS.

List of Subjects.

OAKLAND.

OAKLAND has been little advertised. Its inhabitants, relying upon its superior advantages of situation, climate, and scenery, have settled down to a quiet life, trusting to these many excellencies for advancement. But it will not do to rely on this superiority. The world must be informed of our resources. Multitudes in the East would escape from the heat and cold, storms and floods. Thousands are longing for just such homes of health and comfort, amid sunshine and fruit and flowers, as Oakland offers.

That there are many wicked people in Oakland, and many unlawful things done, will not be denied; but it is undoubtedly true that the standard of public morals here is higher than that of any other city of its

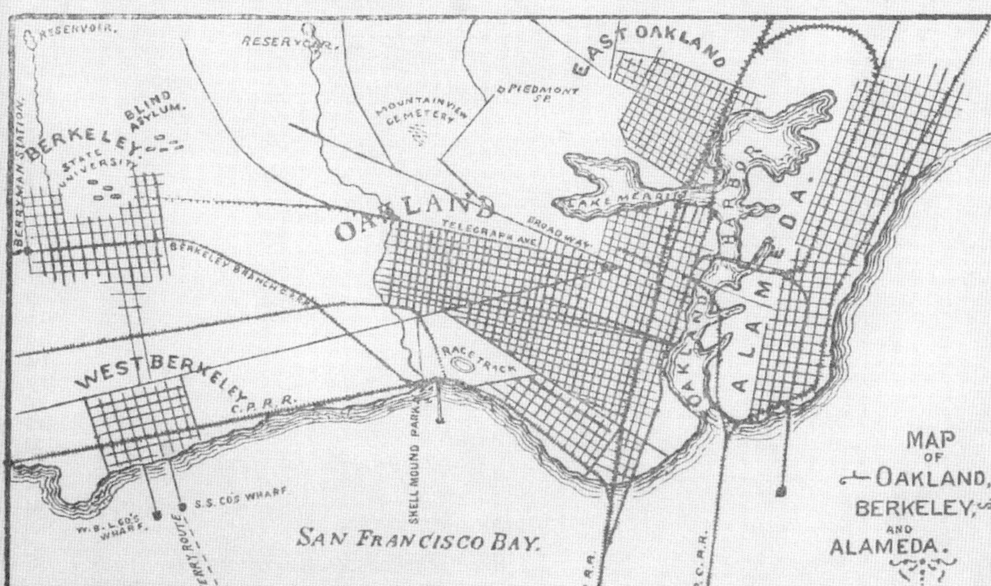

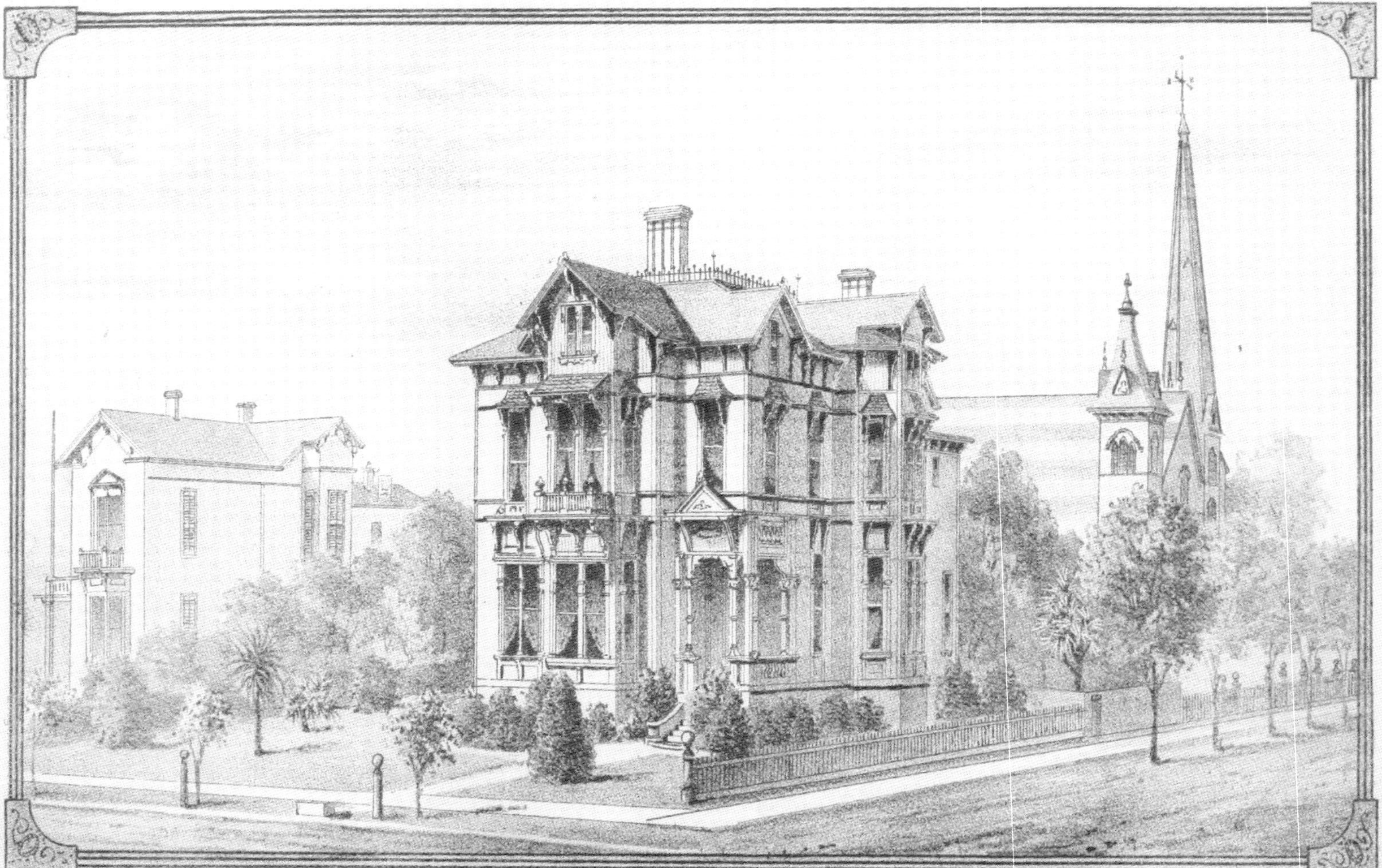

ELLIOTT, LITH. OAKLAND.

RESIDENCE OF E. W. PLAYTER. COR. 14th & CASTRO STS. OAKLAND, CAL.

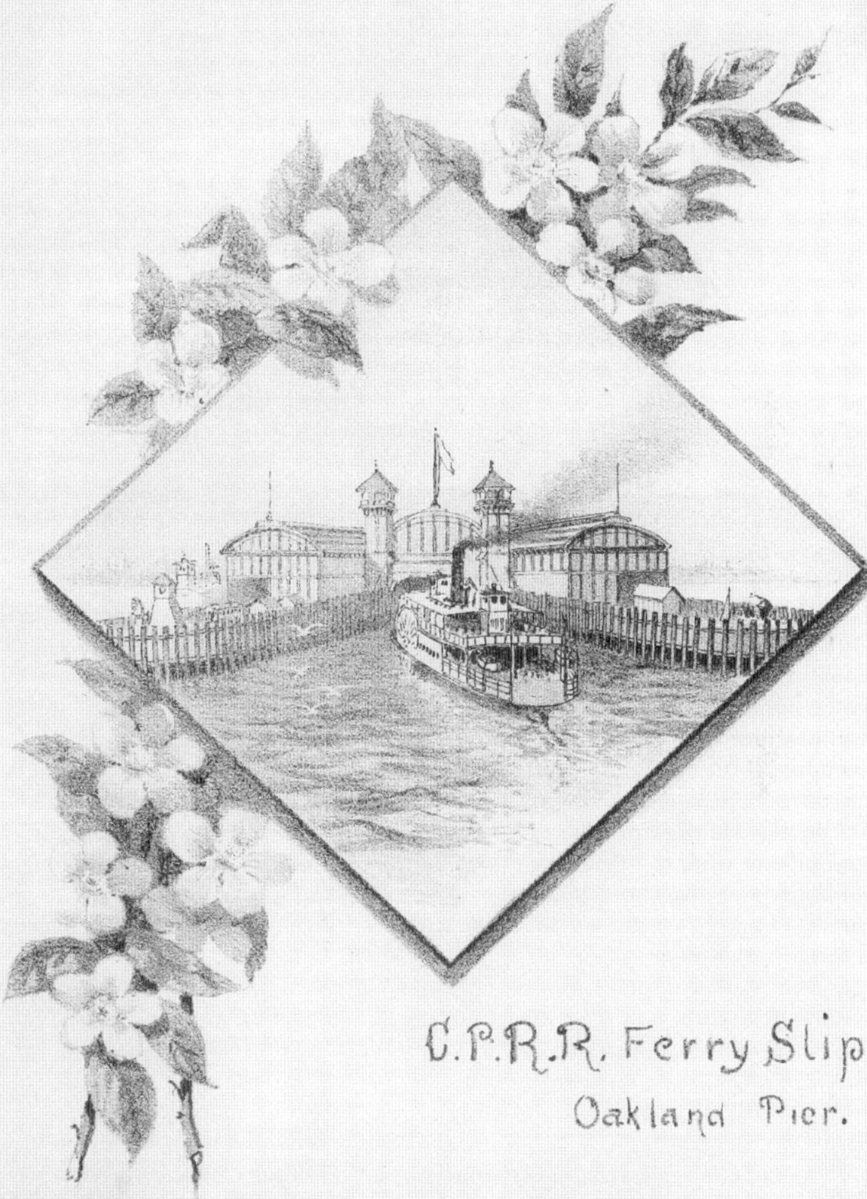

C.P.R.R. Ferry Slip
Oakland Pier.

size, and as high at least as that of most small towns. A very large proportion of the business and professional men are not only active, but they are also worthy members of some religious organization, and engaged, in one way or another, in some charitable work. Collect together any considerable number of representative merchants, manufacturers, financiers, lawyers, or physicians, and you will be sure to find among them representatives of leading churches and charities, and marked examples of high moral and social character.

The clergy have some able representatives of the profession, and interest in religious matters seems to be on the increase, judging from the number of new churches erected during the last year.

The Roman Catholic population is more numerous than that of any one branch of the family of Protestant churches, but much less than those branches united. Probably nowhere are the Catholic clergy more enterprising and intelligent than in this city; and in no city in the country is there less contention between the Protestant and Roman Catholic members of the great Christian religion.

The Young Men's Christian Association, comprising what the Romanists have not improperly styled the Jesuits of the Protestant church, has accomplished much towards the removal of the imaginary barriers that divide Christian people into denominations; while in the great works of benevolence, temperance reform, and the preservation of the Sabbath, Protestants and Romanists work harmoniously together.

The Medical College has a faculty composed of several of our most eminent physicians, skilled in the use of surgical appliances and the mysteries of disease.

The progress of manufacturing interests is also exceedingly gratifying; and there is abundant reason for the belief that in the course of a very few years this city will be an important manufacturing center.

Building of all kinds has been active during the past year. A large number of residences of all grades has been erected in all parts of the city.

The intelligent observer who spends a day in our public schools will be convinced that the teachers employed in instructing the pupils under their guidance are engaged in an earnest work. In some respects our schools stand prominently above all others in the State.

The University is at the head of all educational work and is the pride of Berkeley as well as of the State generally.

The free public library grows in popular esteem and is getting to be a noble institution. Its reading-room is also well patronized.

Of photographic and art establishments we have some that, for the production of excellent work, will yield the palm to none.

Our stores have largely increased their stocks of late years, and there is now little cause for trade leaving, as all varieties of goods are to be had at low rates.

Book and picture stores bright with chromos, and a variety of showy goods, arrest the eye, here and there, and give a cheerful variety to the aspect of the streets.

Theaters and places of amusement are generally well patronized, and most first-class artists and troupes visit Oakland.

Our home musical talent is various, and there are examples of proficiency in every branch of musical art. There is a widening circle here that is cultivated enough to enjoy classic music.

Private schools are well maintained and occupy a large field, ranging from the kindergarten to the seminary and academy.

The architects have had ample room

for their talent, and many fine blocks and residences are the result of their skill. All the new business blocks are massive, solid, and ornamental.

So far as the Bar is concerned, there is hardly a man of any prominence in the profession whose character for personal integrity, upright conduct, and good morals, is not equal to his reputation as a lawyer.

The press of Oakland is ably conducted and patronized. The people support four daily papers and numerous weekly publications of merit.

Of able physicians there seems to be no lack, and it is a mystery how so many obtain a living where so little sickness prevails.

The city is orderly, and, as a general thing, peace prevails, and person and property are reasonably safe, and all departments of city government move along quietly and smoothly.

Picturesque Situation of Oakland.

THE situation of Oakland is picturesque. Placed on the eastern shore of San Francisco Bay, on a plateau that rises gradually to the slopes of the Coast Range, it commands a wide and diversified prospect. To the west are the bay, the islands, San Francisco, and the ocean; to the east, the slopes of the Coast Range; to the north and south an expanse of water seen against a background of

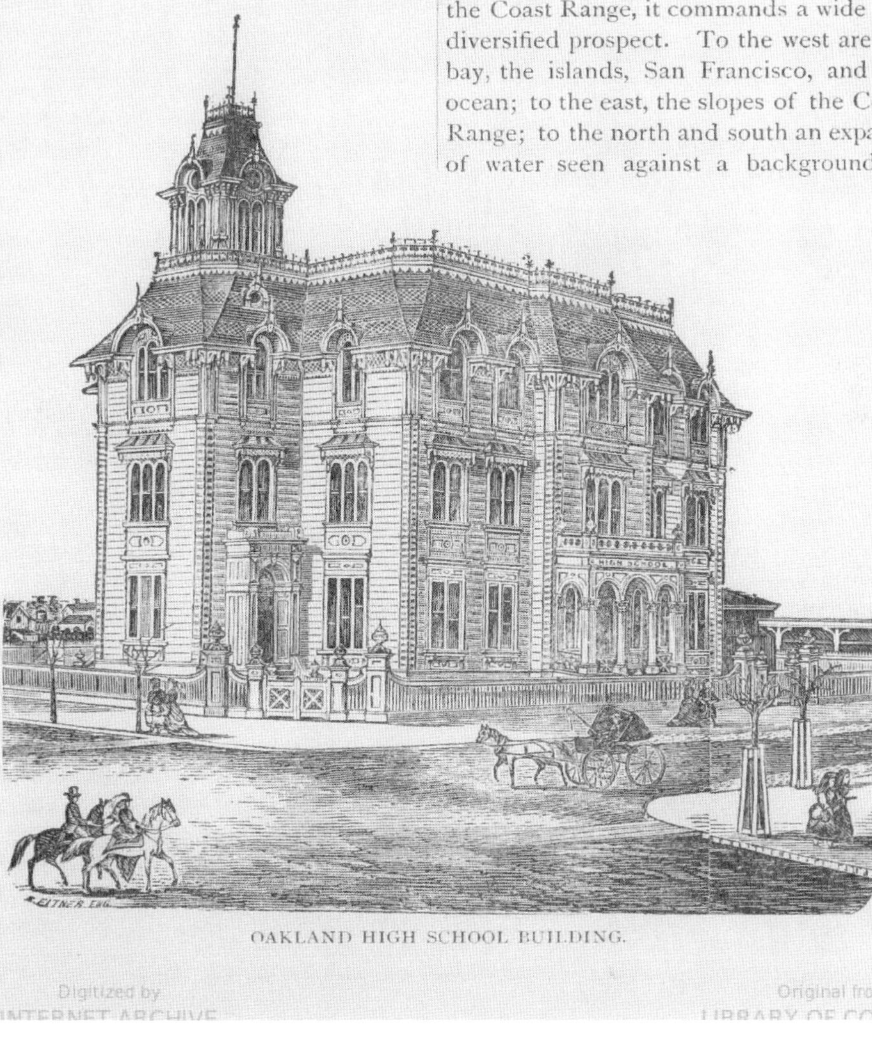

OAKLAND HIGH SCHOOL BUILDING.

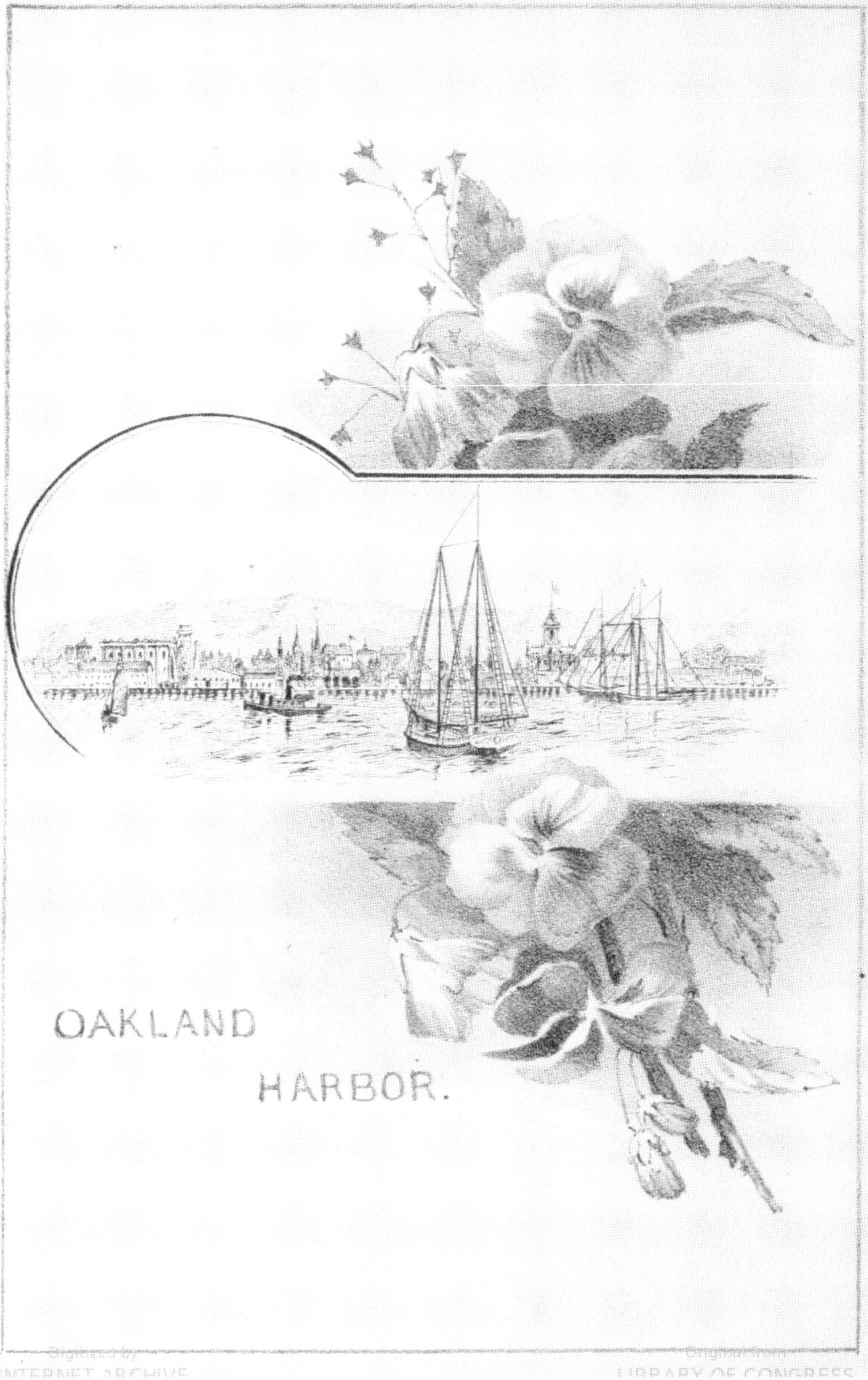
OAKLAND
HARBOR.

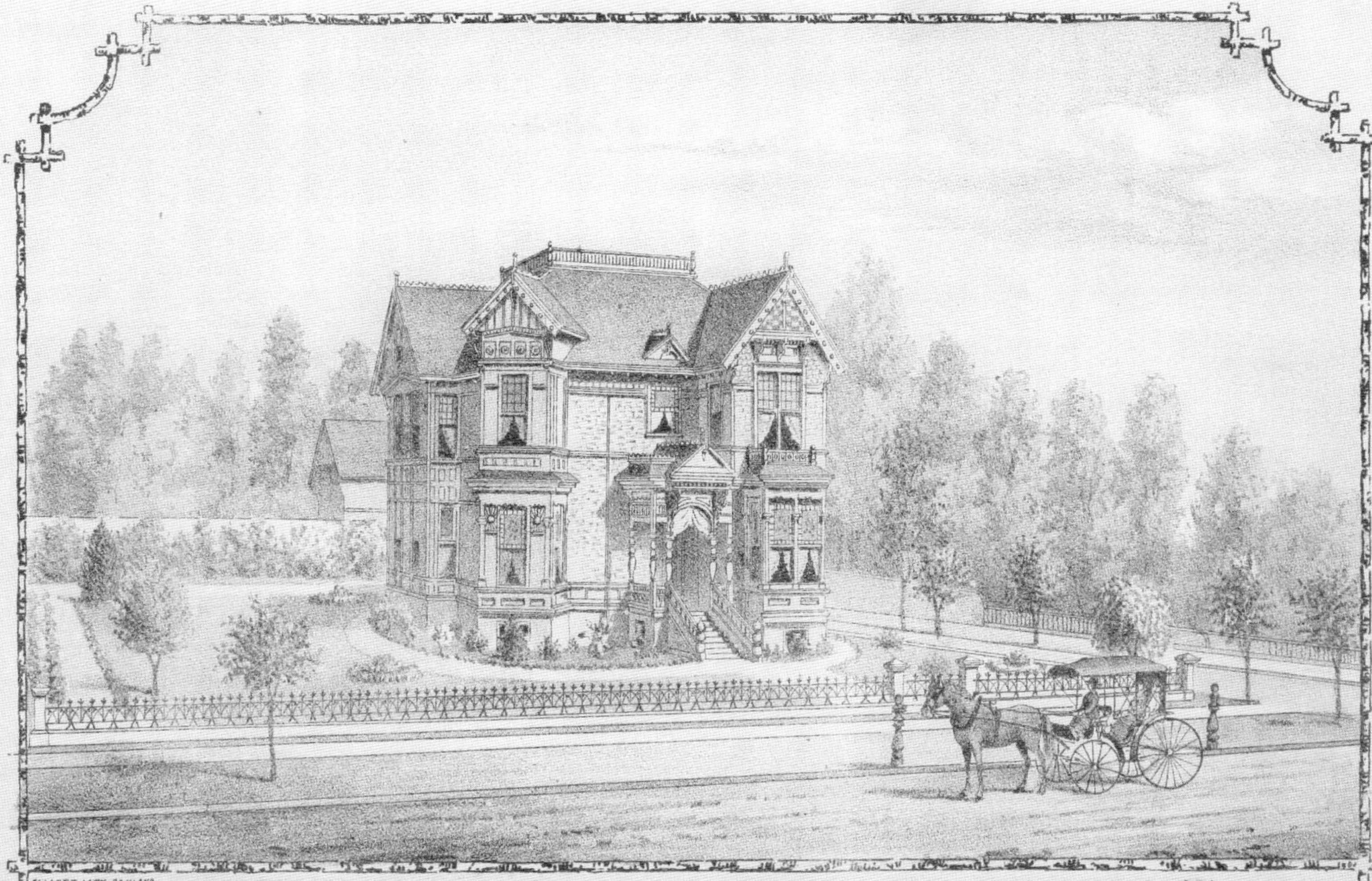

RESIDENCE OF J. M. BUFFINGTON COR OF OAK & TENTH STS OAKLAND CAL

hills, which rise into the heights of Tamalpais, 2,500 feet, Laguna Honda and San Bruno, and find their limit in the gray and faintly-seen ridges of Sonoma, Solano, and Santa Clara Counties.

The smooth hills of the Coast Range, worn into graceful outlines by the attrition of ages, do not at first please the stranger. He misses the wooded slopes to which he has been accustomed, and declares them to be plain and unattractive. But their physical peculiarities are the source of many beauties, which experience soon discovers.

From the absence of forests comes a wide range of brilliant and delicate color, having characteristic hues for every season of the year. In the long, clear days of summer or autumn, they are overspread with a dull brown, which would be monotonous except for the chocolate streaks and purple patches, which here and there mark the shadows, cañons, and depressions. As the day steals on, the prosaic aspect disappears; the colors become richer and deeper, and at sunset pass through many gradations of gold, yellow, amber, rose, pink, violet, and purple, and finally fade into the gray, ashen, and somber shadows of night. Sometimes all these hues can be seen at once, the brighter on the nearer peaks and hill-sides, the darker on the ridges that border the horizon. In the spring the fresh green covering of the hills assumes pearly tints, with purples in the distance. Flowers are in bloom everywhere, the yellow predominating, making the long ranges look at intervals as if draped with cloth of gold. In winter, while the valleys are green and beautiful, the higher elevations are often white with snow. So wide and various a landscape, including the picturesque peculiarities of all seasons, the quiet of landlocked waters, the blending of coast with nland scenery, the contrasting of ocean storm-effects and the serene skies which hang over sheltered valleys, can be seen nowhere else in the world.

A Handsome City.

OAKLAND is classed among the handsomest cities in the United States, and certainly has the right to claim it. Her beautiful streets and avenues are all, or nearly all, shaded by oaks, from which she derives the name. Orchards, parks, gardens, and vineyards are found on every side. Nestling amidst this forest of perpetual green or live-oak can be seen, peeping out here and there, the magnificent villa of the nabob, substantial residences of wealthy merchants, and the neat and tasteful cottages of the well-to-do mechanics, who have been attracted here by its grand scenery, mild climate, and quiet surroundings, being free from dust, noise, or the bustle of a large city.

As approached from San Francisco on a fine day in summer, Oakland presents all the illusions of a second Venice, which, by and by, will become a reality, as art aids nature to set off her charms. It is the home of many enlightened and wealthy citizens, and the number of those who plant their homes on its beautiful streets is rapidly increasing.

Oakland now covers an area of from 40 to 50 square miles. Its population is about 45,000. It has all the conveniences of a complete and perfect city—fine streets, gas, water, an excellent fire department, and a well-developed system of sewerage.

Elegant Homes of Oakland.

NO city on the coast has gained more relatively within the last ten years than Oakland. The wide extent and high cultivation of her ornamental gardens, and the elegance of her dwellings, contribute to make her one of the most beautiful cities in the United States.

The site of Oakland is part of one of the great Mexican ranches. Thirty years ago nothing existed here except groves of oak. There was scarcely a house. Later a small village appeared on the banks of the creek. It remained a village until

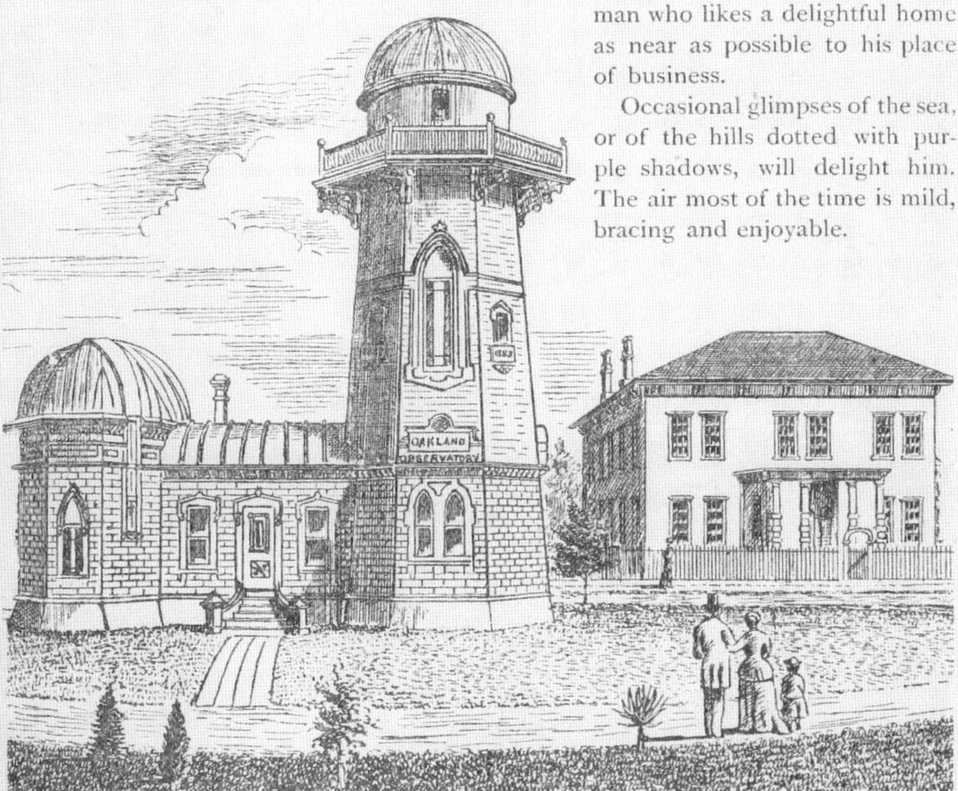

OAKLAND OBSERVATORY AND SCHOOL BUILDING.

about 1865, when boats and trains rendered it at all hours accessible. Population spread rapidly, until to-day it is the second city in the State. Oakland now covers an area of about fifty square miles. It has all the conveniences of a complete and perfect city.

Its streets are broad, smooth, and profusely set with trees. The finer residences have lawns filled with the variety of plants and shrubbery that can be seen only on the Pacific Coast, while even the most unpretentious cottage has its door-yard or terrace filled with flowers. The neighborhood is not, on account of its situation, shut out from a view of the hills, while its being within half an hour of San Francisco gives it an advantage to a busy man who likes a delightful home as near as possible to his place of business.

Occasional glimpses of the sea, or of the hills dotted with purple shadows, will delight him. The air most of the time is mild, bracing and enjoyable.

Oakland Harbor.

THE southern boundary of the city is the estuary of San Antonio, which was naturally inaccessible, at low tide, to boats drawing more than two feet; but stone walls have been extended out from the upland on each side of the estuary, across the mud flat in the bay, for a

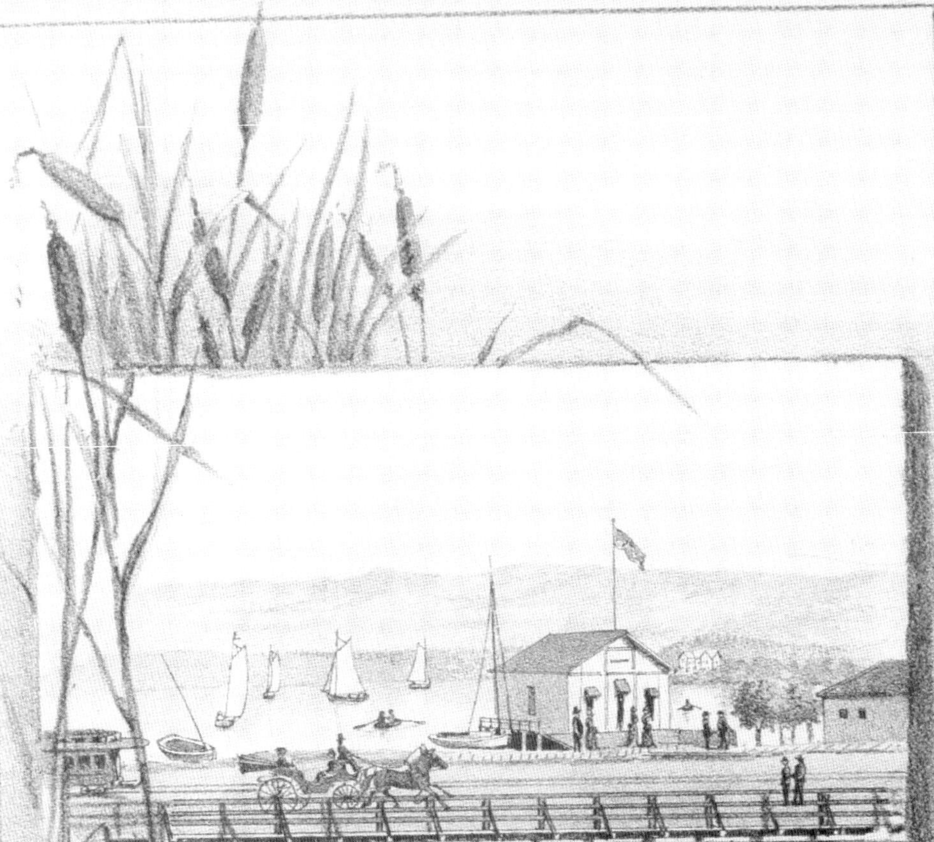

Scene on Lake Merritt.

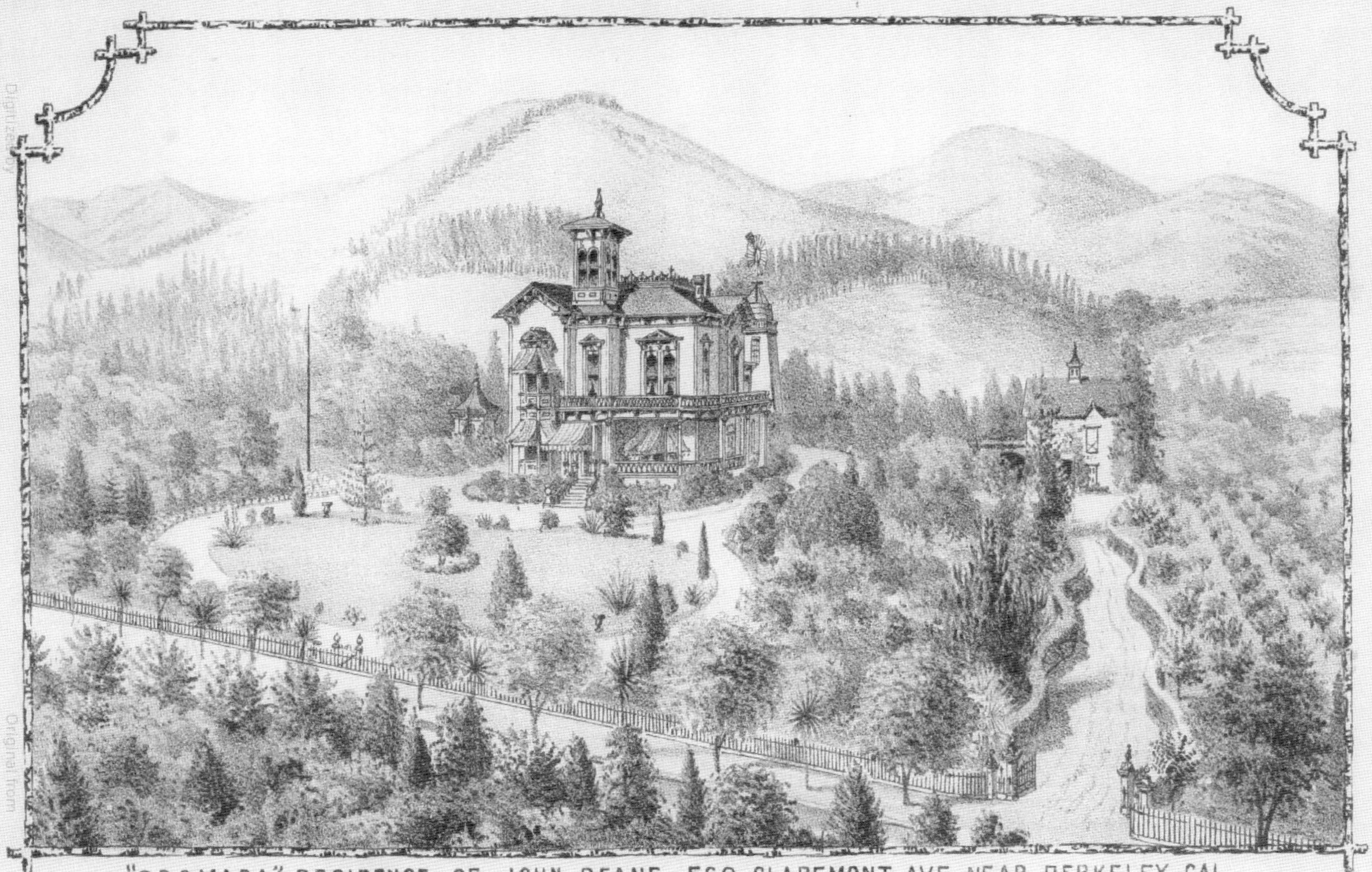

"DROMADA" RESIDENCE OF JOHN DEANE ESQ. CLAREMONT AVE, NEAR BERKELEY, CAL.

distance of nearly two miles, leaving space between them 300 yards wide. By dredging, and the natural wash of the tide, this channel has been so deepened that vessels drawing 10 feet can now enter the estuary at low water. The tide at neap adds 4 feet, and at spring 7 feet to the depth, so that vessels drawing 17 feet can reach Oakland wharf. The dredging contract requires that the depth of 10 feet, now limited to a width of 200 feet, shall be extended to 300 feet, and that for a width of 100 the depth shall be 14 feet, allowing vessels drawing 21 feet to load or discharge in the new harbor.

Much has been done, and seven years have elapsed since the first appropriation by Congress, and still the work is very far from completion. When the walls are properly completed, they are to rise to the level of high tide for more than a mile from the shore, and now they are for a considerable part of their length three or four feet below the requisite height.

A canal a mile long is to connect the San Antonio Estuary with San Leandro Bay, and the latter will be closed at its mouth by gates, so that the tide can pour in, but must flow out through the artificial harbor, thus scouring it, and saving expense in dredging. Congress has made seven appropriations in all; one in every year, except 1877, since 1874; and the total has been $535,000; the amount for each of the three years from 1879 to 1881 inclusive, being $60,000. The excavation of the basin at East Oakland is now going on, and when that has been done, Oakland's shipping interests will probably become important. The channel will be three miles long, with six miles of water frontage. The total cost, as estimated in advance, is to be $1,335,000, so that Congress has still $800,000 more to appropriate.

San Francisco Bay

THE bay of San Francisco occupies several long valleys and deep indentations, formed by the spurs and offshoots of the Coast Range. It is a magnificent sheet of water. Taken with the series of tideways of which it forms a part, it is nearly one hundred miles in length. It poorly suggests its splendid proportions to say of it that it would float the navies of the world, for it would not only bear on its bosom the vast war marine of all powers, but permit them to maneuver and decide the world's destinies in fair battle within an amphitheater of hills on which the nations themselves could gather and witness the result.

Its beauties have never been duly appreciated by those who paint in phrases or delineate in oils. Yet they are rare and diverse, with rich hues and shifting tones that run a chromatic scale of color through every season of the year. It responds sympathetically to all changes of the sky and hills. To the cold, gray cloudless heaven it shows a steel blue. When roughened by the north wind, it is black, scarcely relieved by the white fringes of its short waves. Scattered cloud-masses dapple its surface with many tints, and lines of rifted cloud throw upon its waters bars of blue, green, olive, chocolate, brown, and purple, with shades for which an artist can find no equivalent either in word or in color.

In winter the showers chase one another across its surface, and when the sun breaks through, it illuminates the slanted lances of the rain, which glisten like the bayonets of a retreating army. The ocean fogs touch it with their white and fleecy masses, sweep across its broad plains in solid phalanx, or lie gloomily upon its breast, lifting now and then to show the black waters below.

The tides rush in through the Golden Gate, spread to the north, south, and east, ripple along the wharves, break in foam about the islands, lap up against the bases of the hills, and run far up the deep estuaries twice each day, carrying life and motion to the brown and silent heart of the Coast Range.

Center for Railroads.

OAKLAND is the natural center of the railroad system of the Pacific Coast, while it is the terminus of all the roads running north and east, including the great overland road; it is also the terminus of roads penetrating the southern portion of the State. This city is reached by an easy grade, following the broad and level valleys which stretch along the eastern side of the bay of San Francisco. It is also the terminus of the Southern Pacific, and the South Pacific Coast. Over two hundred trains pass through the city daily, including the local and freight trains to Alameda, and the clanging of bells and the shriek of the locomotive whistle may be heard at almost any hour of the day or night.

The Central Pacific, with its vast traffic, gathered from the distant Orient and the far-away Atlantic, and including tributary trade flowing in from tributaries in the South, Southwest, and along the northern borders of the country, necessarily controls the bulk of the carrying trade that enters Oakland.

The South Pacific Coast Railroad is now about extending its lines through the city, which will greatly increase the travel by this route, which is destined to be a favorite one with Oakland people, as its time from the center of the city to San Francisco is much reduced—no small matter with business men.

Ample Water Supply.

OAKLAND is mainly supplied with water from Lake Chabot, which is situated in the hills east of San Leandro.

It was first constructed about 1874, and has since been largely increased and large mains have recently been laid to Oakland. The water is clear, but of a deep greenish tint; the banks are clear, and no animals are allowed to pasture in its immediate vicinity. The lake now contains 5,000,000,000 gallons, and when the dam is completed will have a capacity of 15,000,000,000 gallons. It is now four miles in length and will eventually have a length of eight miles.

From the lake near Temescal, which is 425 feet above the level of the city, pipes are laid to Piedmont, Oakland Heights, and other high elevations in the vicinity. Highland Park and Fruitvale draw their supplies from a reservoir on Sausal Creek.

Before 1875, when the water from Lake Chabot at San Leandro was first introduced, Oakland was abundantly supplied from the other two systems. The three could easily furnish water to a million people, not only for domestic use, but for irrigation. The present daily consumption of water is 8,000,000 gallons. The San Leandro reservoir can alone supply 13,000,000 daily without increasing its capacity.

A very large amount of water is used in keeping lawns and gardens green during the summer, for which reason the consumption *per capita* exceeds that of any other city in the world. The table on next page is compiled to show the gallons furnished per day per individual in several American and European cities, which are thought to be well supplied with water.

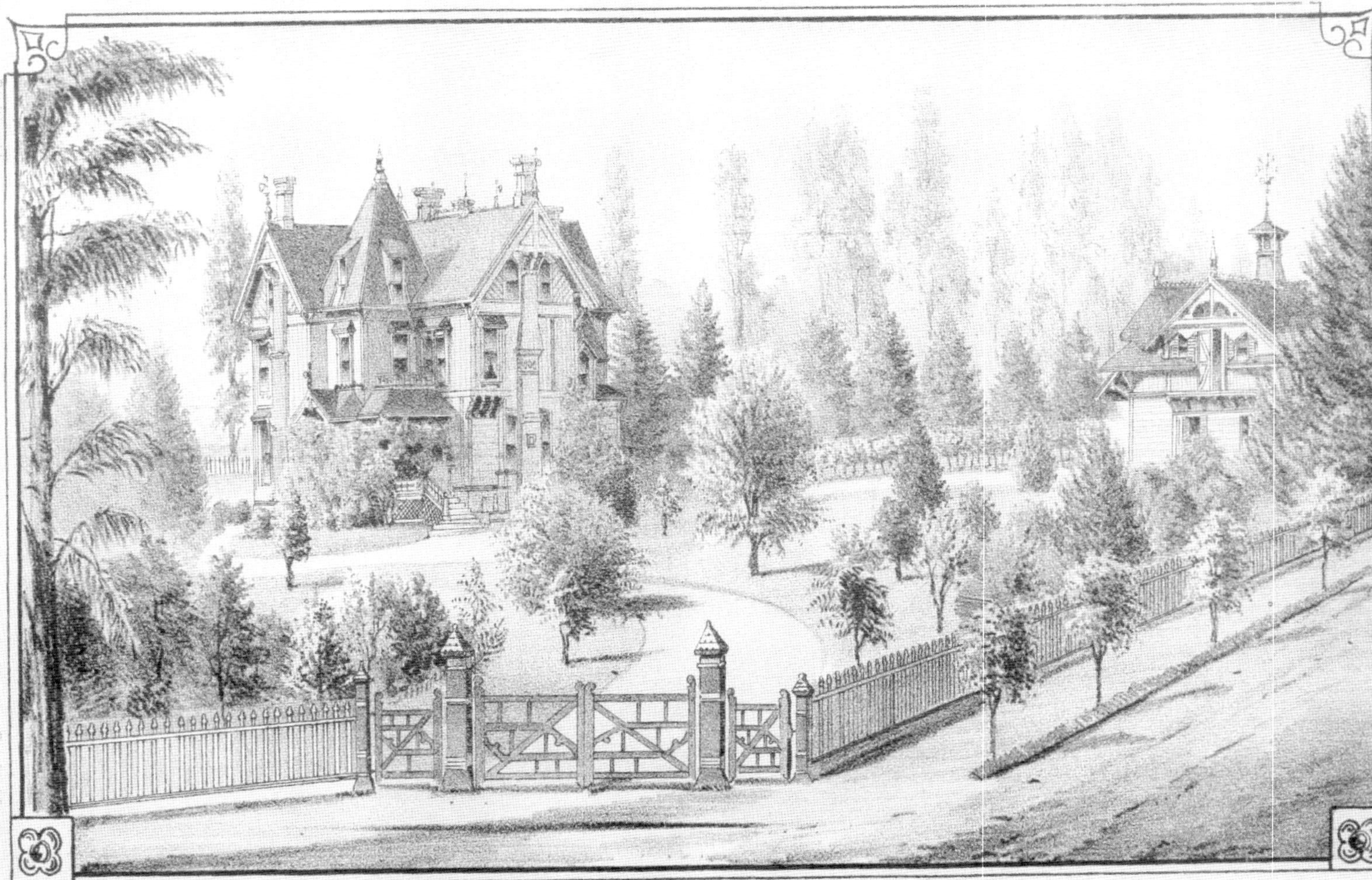

ELLIOTT, LITH. OAKLAND, CAL.

RESIDENCE OF JAMES GAMBLE, PIEDMONT & BONITA AVENUES, PIEDMONT, CAL.

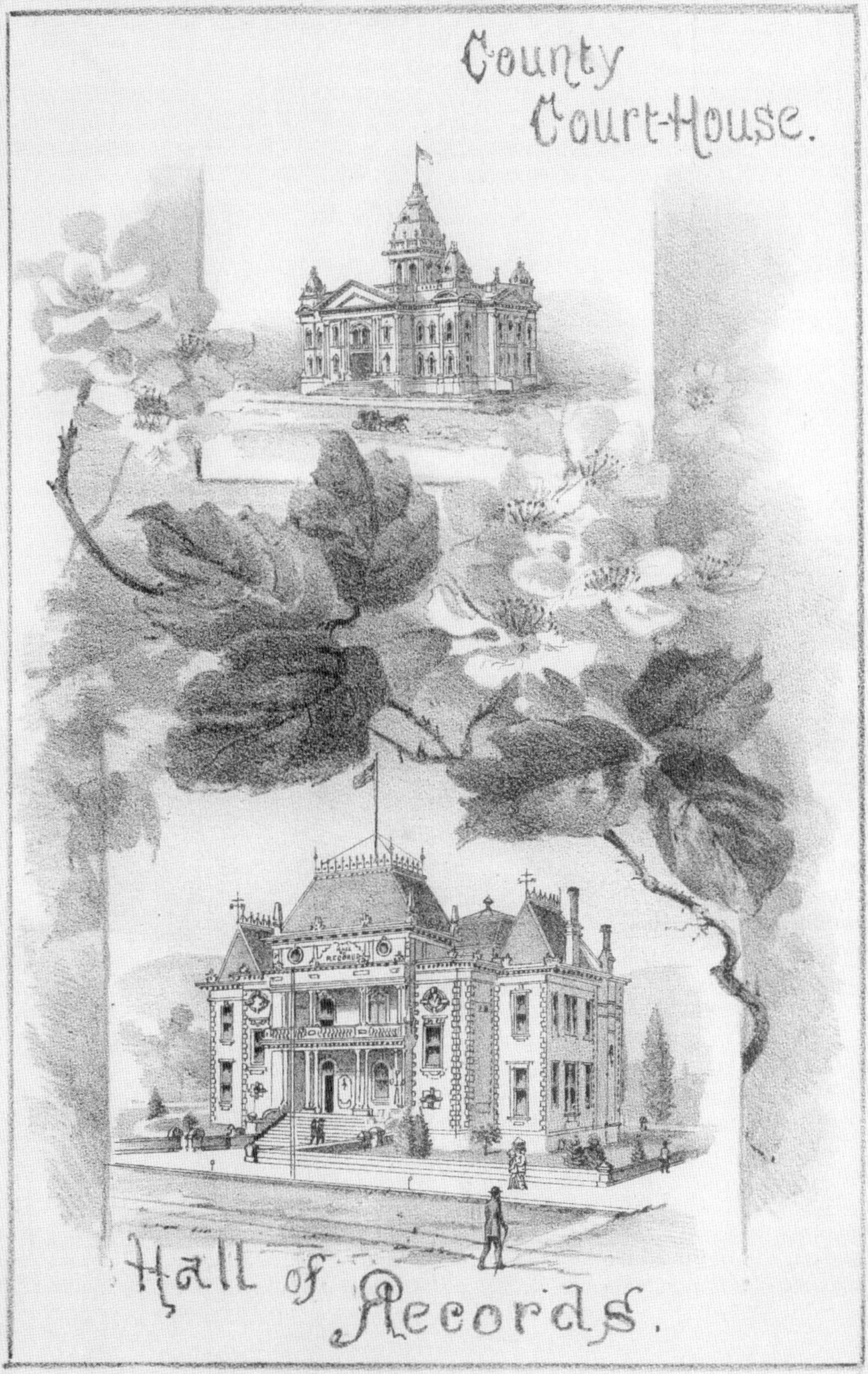
County
Court-House.
Hall of Records.

	GAL.		GAL.
London	33	Cincinnati	80
New York	95	Chicago	114
Glasgow	52	Buffalo	122
Paris	68	Detroit	127
Philadelphia	67	Washington	176
Pittsburg	102	San Francisco	75
Brooklyn	54	Oakland	230
St. Louis	71		

The water has been at different times analyzed by the City Board of Health, the chemical department of the University of California, and the State Board of Health, and classified among "the good water which may be used for all domestic purposes."

Beautiful and Delightful.

OAKLAND is held by many travelers and writers to be the most beautiful and most delightful suburb in the United States. It certainly has the right to claim unsurpassed ferry and railway facilities, a genial climate, perfect accessibility, and magnificent surroundings. It is flanked by Alameda and Berkeley, each a large and flourishing suburban town. The population of Oakland comes close on to 45,000.

The homes of the rich are very beautiful, and the drives within and outside the city are numerous and delightful. No place in the world can show so much shrubbery and so many flowers the year round. Like Brooklyn, Oakland is a city of churches, while her public and private educational institutions are numerous and take high rank. There are several good hotels, where rates are moderate.

The trains of the Central Pacific and South Pacific Coast Railroads carry passengers to every portion of the city, while the street railroads run almost to every man's door. Most branches of manufacture, nearly every line of mercantile pursuit, and nearly all the kinds of industry necessary to personal convenience, are found in Oakland.

Business and Commercial Center.

[From the *Express*.]

OAKLAND is no longer a mere suburb of San Francisco, but has laid deep and broad the foundation of a separate business and commercial center that will at no distant day be a formidable rival for a share of the expanding commerce of the Pacific; still it is true that a very large portion of our population are attracted here from sanitary, social, and economical reasons. They are charmed by the healthy and exhilarating climate and the picturesque surroundings. They find the educational privileges, from the kindergarten to our magnificently endowed university, unsurpassed.

Cheap ferriage is no small consideration. The broad gauge officials are careful and obliging, the boats elegant and commodious, and the depot at the end of the Oakland pier a model of architectural beauty and convenience. The narrow-gauge people are sparing no pains to make their transit to San Francisco all that could be desired. Their cars and boats are of the best, the officials polite and watchful, and if these two companies could be induced to run their boats at alternate intervals of fifteen minutes, and recognize each other's tickets, travel would be as near perfection as could be wished.

A Well-Lighted City.

THE Oakland Gas Light Company was incorporated in 1866, and its street lamps were first lighted on New Year's night of 1867. At first the works of the company were located on the block bounded by Broadway, First, Second, and Washington Streets, upon which were both their retort house and coal yard. During the year 1877 the company built upon the block bounded by First, Grove, Second, and Jefferson Streets, additional works, consisting of a double lift holder of 500,000 cubic feet capacity, a purifying house 154 feet long by 36 feet wide, a meter house of proportionate size, and a tower scrubber with independent water-works. These additions were planned upon the latest improvements known to the science of gas-making.

On the first day of September, 1884, the name of the company was changed to the Oakland Gas, Light and Heat Company. On January 1, 1885, it originated a system of electric lighting, and has now in daily operation seventy-five arc lamps of the Thomson-Houston Company. A large building was erected for that special purpose on its property, corner Second and Washington Streets, and some seven miles of wire have so far been used to supply customers.

The fact that the city of Oakland covers such an extent of territory necessitates a very large outlay in the way of street mains in proportion to the amount of gas consumed. The mains of the company extend from Alameda to Berkeley, and from Fruitvale to the water's edge. The number of miles of mains laid is sufficient to supply a city of three times the inhabitants of Oakland. The company started with twenty-five street lamps, but the number has now been increased to about eight hundred and twenty. The coal used in the manufacture of gas is English and Australian, no first-class gas coal having been discovered, up to this time, on this coast.

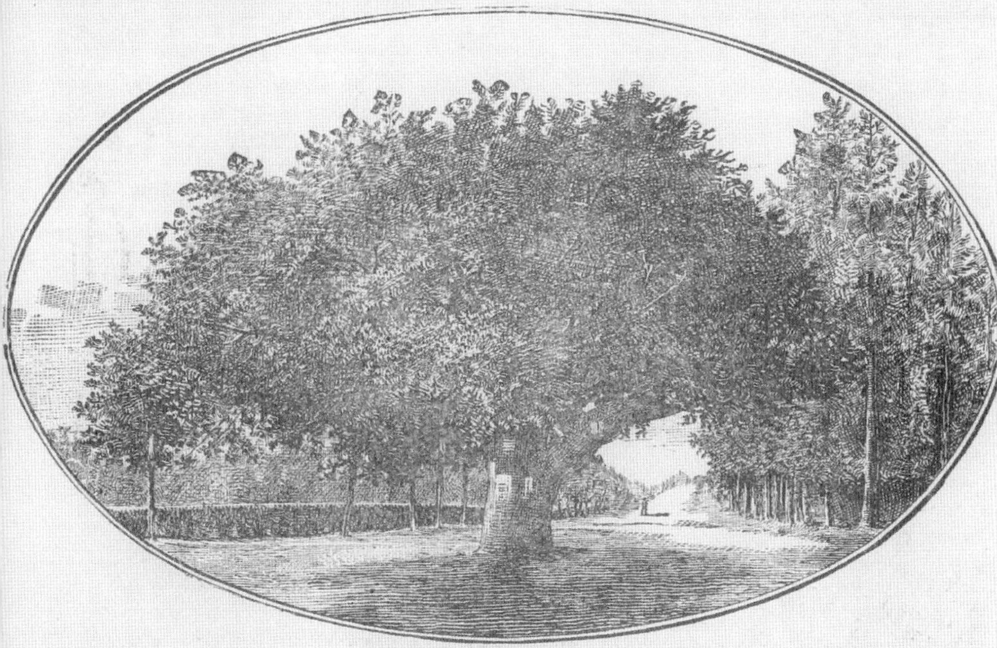

AN OAKLAND LIVE-OAK.

No Finer Spot than Oakland.

THE evening *Express* publishes a letter taken from the Hubbardston (Mich.) *Advertiser*, in which the writer says:—

I freely venture the assertion that no finer spot than the city of Oakland and

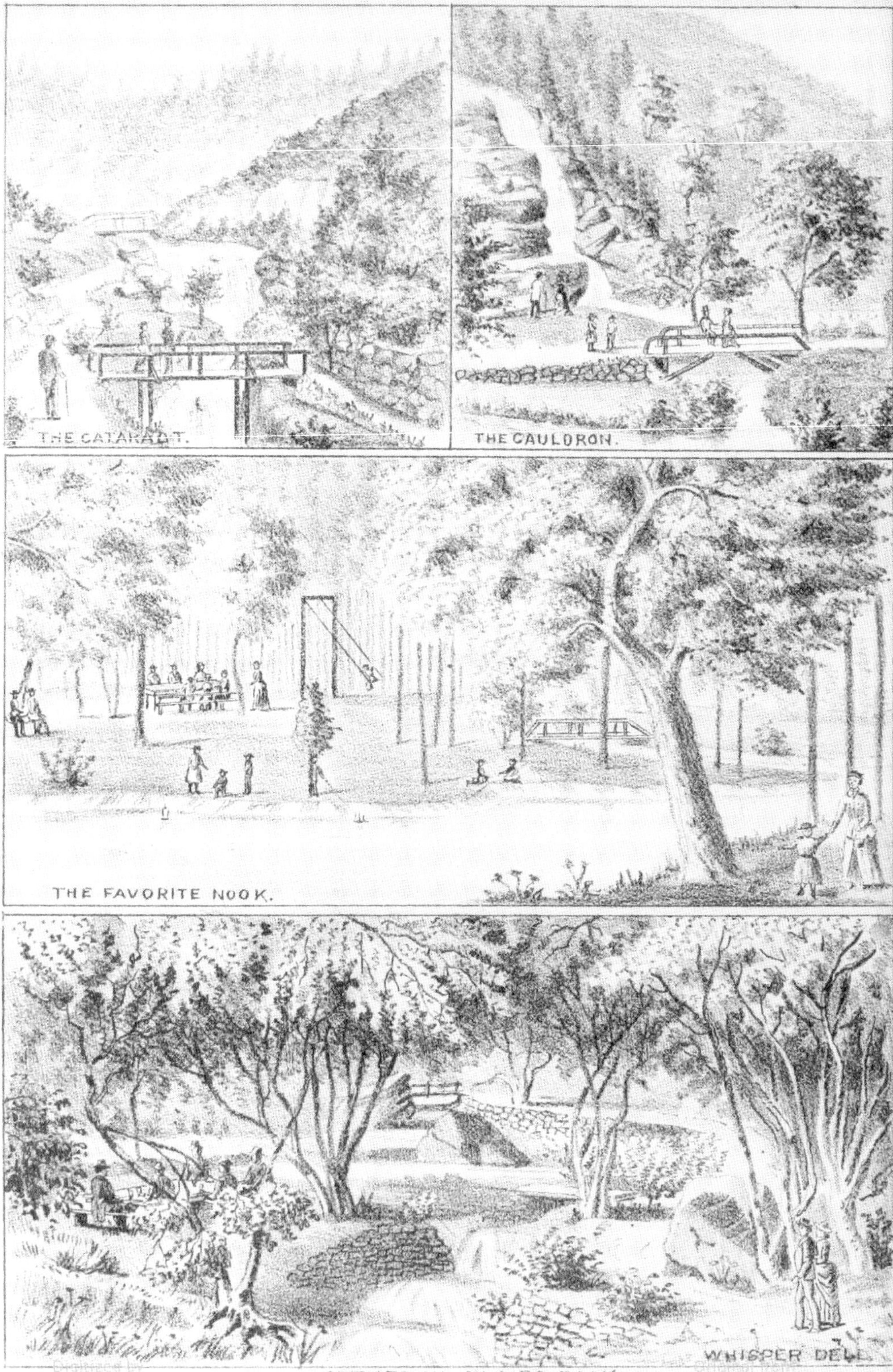

SCENES IN BLAIRS PARK.

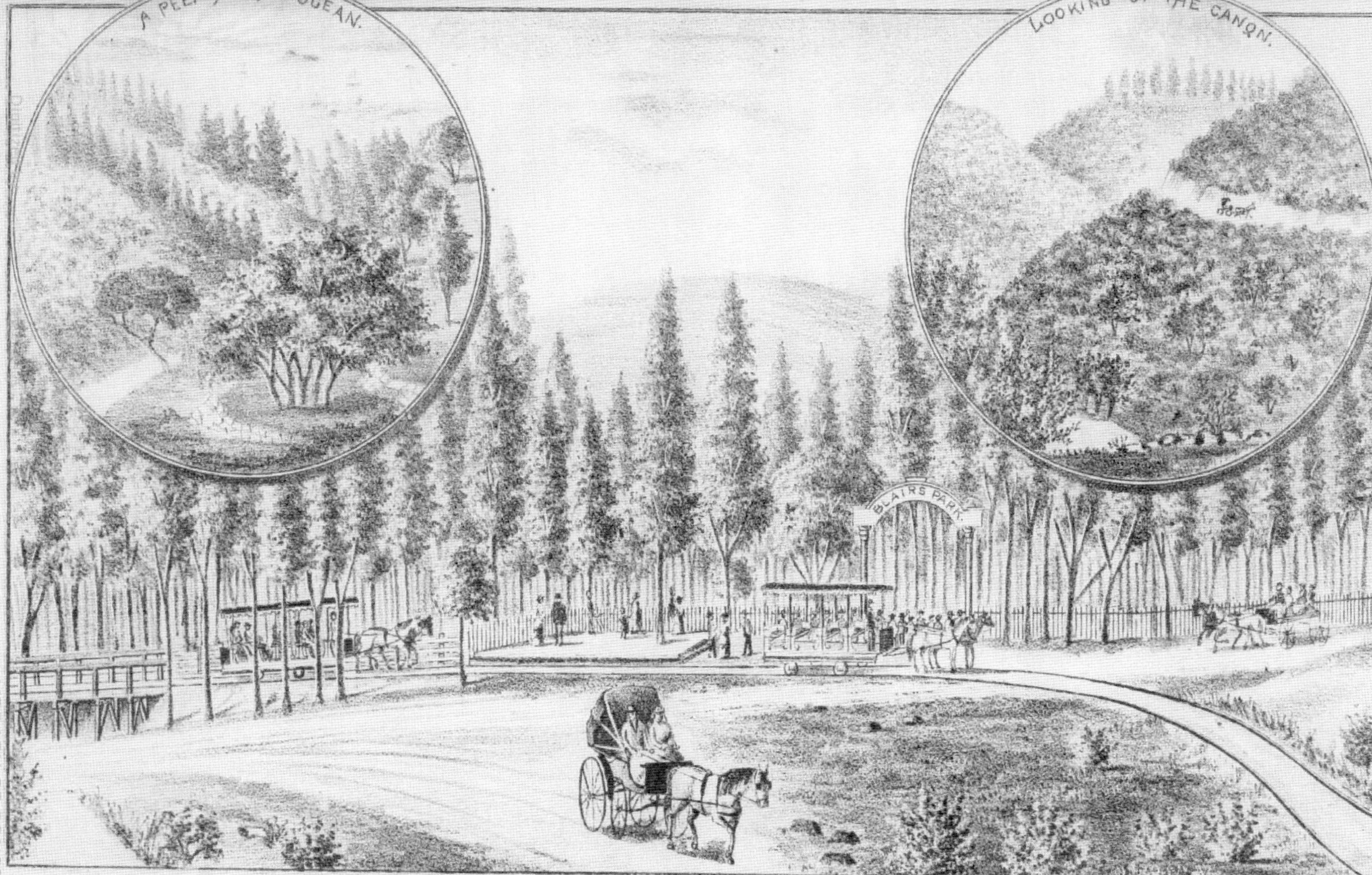

ENTRANCE TO BLAIR'S PARK. NEAR PIEDMONT. CAL.

ELLIOTT. OAK. CAL.

its surroundings can be found on American soil, Los Angeles or Hubbardston not excepted. My first impression was good, and it improves the longer I stay. I do not wish to be considered an enthusiast, and I think that my expressed disapproval of some of the places I have visited will go to prove that I am not.

Oakland is clean, and "cleanliness is next to—" etc. It is quite level, making access to any part of its limits an easy task. It is quiet, making it a home-like place to live. It is cool in summer, the thermometer rarely getting above 70° in the shade, and mild and pleasant in winter. It never rains except in winter, but a splendid water system furnishes all that is needed for any purpose. It is never smoky. There are a number of good schools, with an average attendance of about 6,000 scholars. There are also a goodly number of grand church edifices, and their pulpits contain a corps of most efficient clergymen. There are several lively first-class newspapers, both daily and weekly.

As a fruit market no city on the face of the globe can excel this; fruit of all kinds, fine, fresh, and cheap, twelve months in the year. Free local passenger trains are run each way every half hour within the city limits. There are eight cars in each train, and it is surprising to what an extent they are patronized. There are a goodly number of manufacturing establishments.

Oakland is to San Francisco what Brooklyn is to New York. Ferry boats cross the bay every half hour; fare, fifteen cents. A great many wealthy business men of San Francisco have their residences and fine yards here, which necessarily adds much to the beauty of Oakland.

Just between Oakland proper and East Oakland, formerly Brooklyn, lies the beautiful Lake Merritt well supplied with sail and row-boats, and a more lovely sheet of water for an evening sail could not be asked for. I speak from experience; for a few nights ago I formed one of a party that took a ride over the placid waters. We started at 8 P. M., the sky was perfectly clear; the stars were fast appearing in the east while in the west the last faint rays of the sun yet lingered over the blue Pacific just outside the Golden Gate. Soon after 9 o'clock the moon came creeping above the rugged peaks of the Contra Costa Range. A large house with an observatory on top happened to stand upon the mountain-side between us and the moon, and the bright rays of the queen of night shining through its windows produced a sight that needed little stretch of the imagination in addition to make one think one's self on the beautiful lakes on the other side of the Atlantic, with the grand old castles along the shores. To the north, was a continuation of the range in the distance, with a rolling farming country nearer at hand; to the south, the masts of the vessels in Oakland harbor, with glimmering beacons of Alameda nearly back of them; and to the west, the bright gas and electric light of Oakland.

Sewerage and Streets.

ALL the principal streets are already supplied with substantial sewers. A large part of the city north of Twelfth Street is drained into a large main sewer, which is flushed twice a day from the tidal overflow of Lake Merritt.

The report of the city engineer shows that there are thirty-eight miles of sewers in the streets of Oakland, excepting main lake sewer, which is two and one-half miles long, and that there are fifty-one and one-half miles of macadamized streets.

In one year the property-owners paid for sewers and grading and macadamizing $254,140, which, itemized, shows that 24,000 feet of sewer-pipe was laid, or about four and one-half miles, costing $24,140.

The length of streets macadamized, 36,000 feet or seven miles, costing $180,000; length of streets graded, 40,447 feet, or about eight miles, which cost $50,000; all of which speaks well for property-owners, who are so liberal to improve our city. There is a resolution of the council against macadamizing streets until sewer, gas, and water-pipes are laid. This rule ought to be adhered to most rigidly; the damage caused by tearing up improved streets is very great; and it is a burden which should not be imposed upon property-holders.

Landscape Views.

WHILE strangers are prone to bewail the short-lived green of our landscapes, they should not forget that it is from the death of our natural verdure that comes the life and prosperity of the greater portion of our people. The drought which covers the midsummer traveler with dust, is the secret of the successful harvesting of our immense grain crops. With an Eastern summer, grain growing on the scale now practiced would be impossible. And if the earlier drought is thus salutary, the continuance of it is not less so, for it gives the fruit-grower his opportunity.

Cloudless skies from September to November are the secret of full success in our vineyards. Without them the ten ton yield of wine grapes would be partly sacrificed, and our vigorous raisin industry would be impossible. Therefore mourn not the death of the green, as one mourns without hope; for as we have said, it is the key to the prosperity of a number of our agricultural industries.

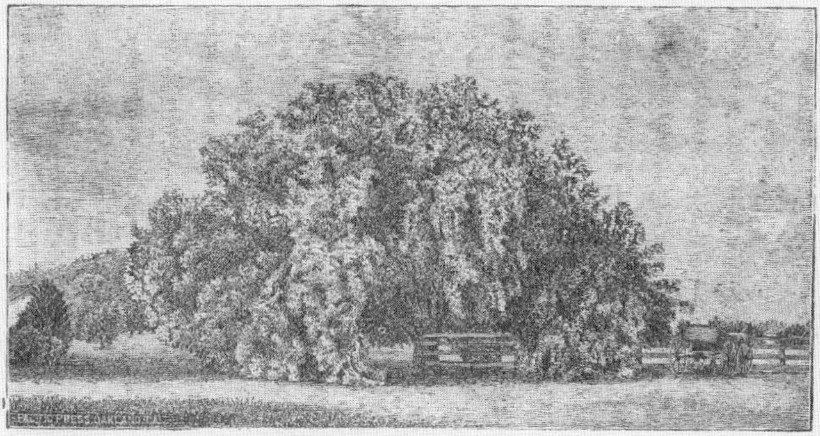

SPECIMEN OF PEPPER TREE, OAKLAND.

In May the visitor now turns his eyes upon the California landscape and sees the height of its loveliness. It is true that in some parts the yellow of summer ripeness is stealing in upon the scene; but taking the State as a whole it is in its loveliest dress. Fortunate are those who now look upon it. It is the peerless time when earth and air and sky play their sweetest parts, until house-walls become

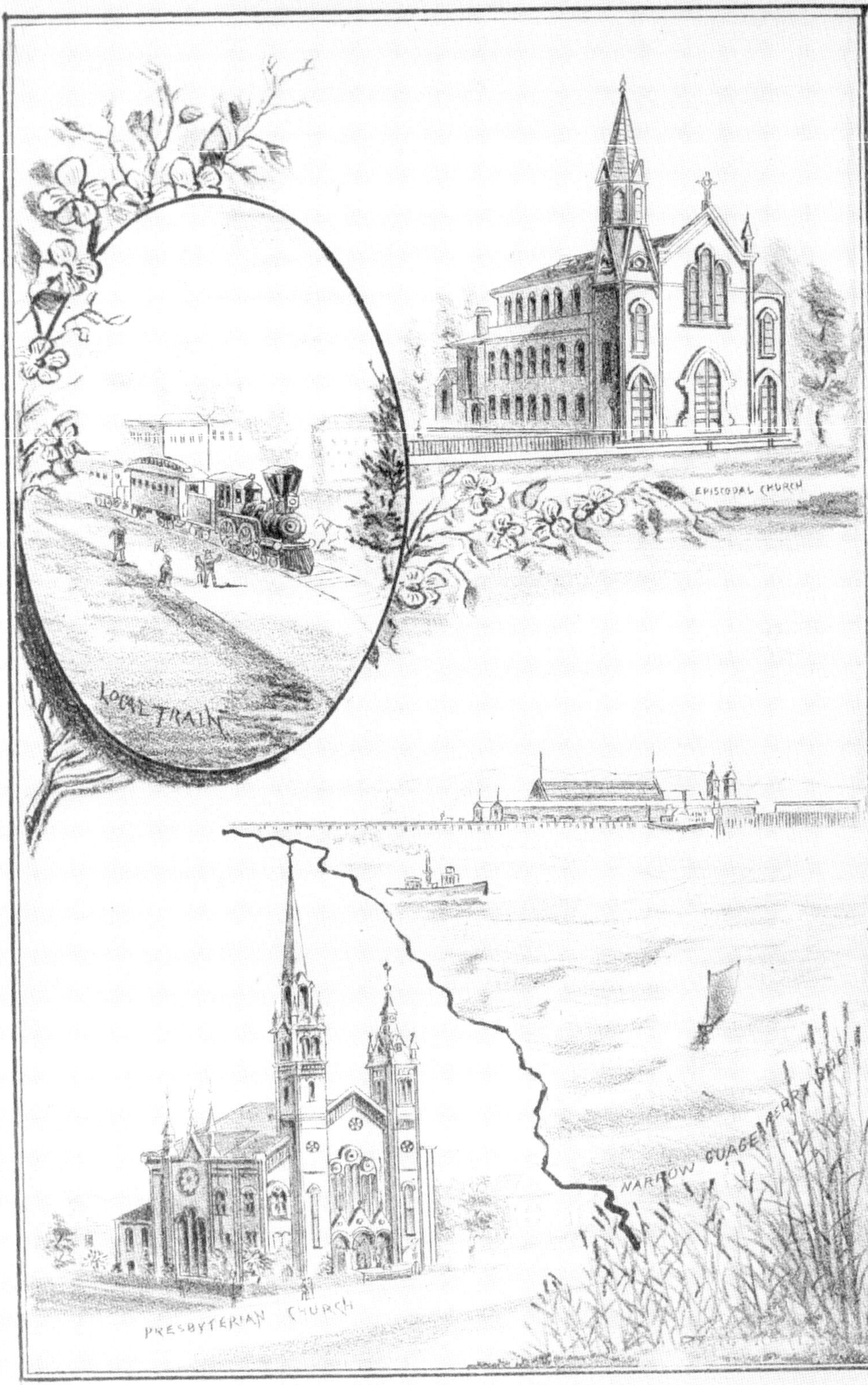
EPISCOPAL CHURCH
LOCAL TRAIN
NARROW GUAGE FERRY DEP.
PRESBYTERIAN CHURCH

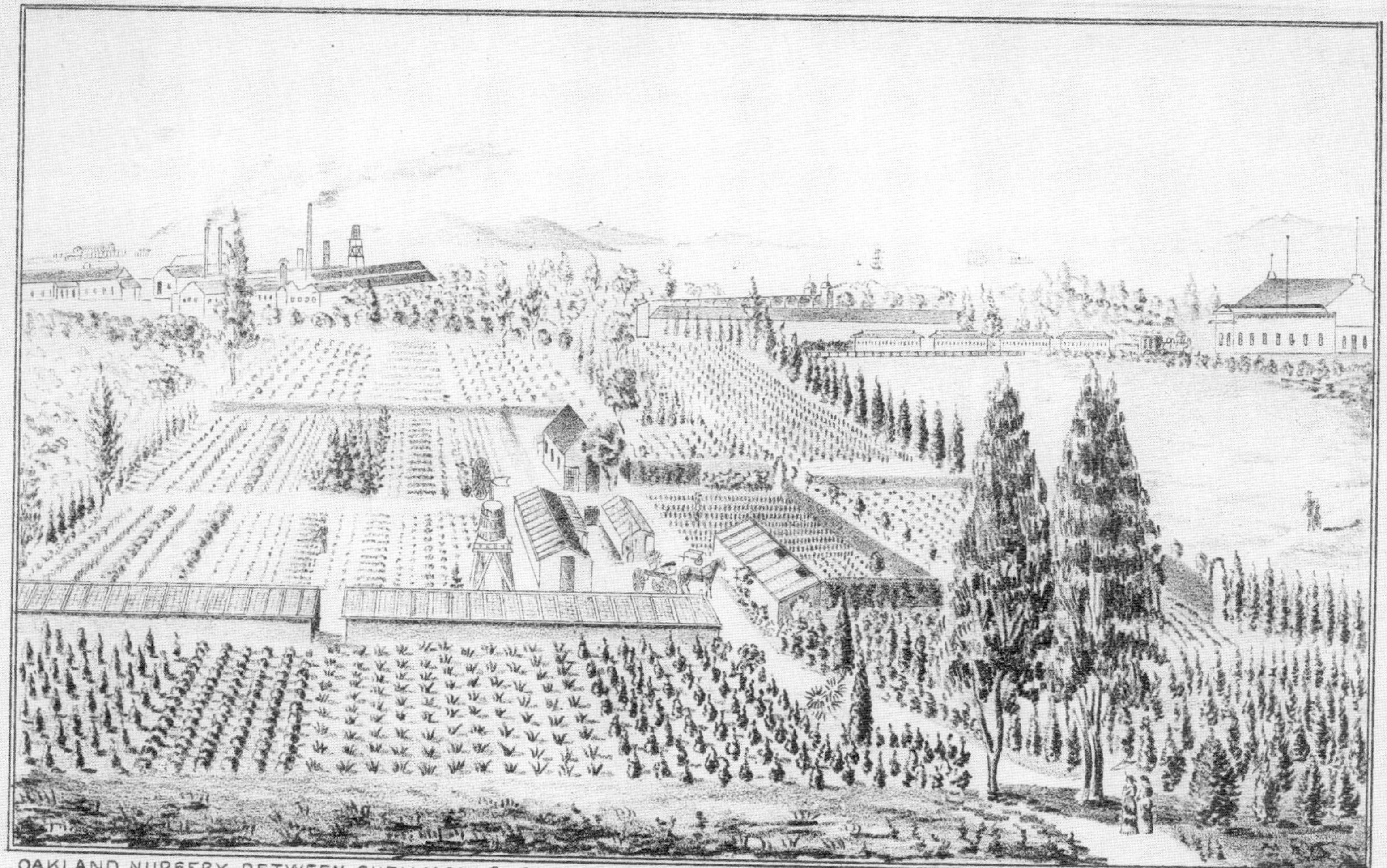

OAKLAND NURSERY BETWEEN SHELLMOUND PARK AND OAKLAND RACE TRACK OAKLAND CAL. REUBEN GROVES PROP.

prisons and roofs a burden. It is the time when California goes out-of-doors.

Diversified Views.

IN the distance, Oakland is seen, the numerous church steeples of the goodly city rising as plenteous as the Moslem minarets of Bagdad, while on the low lands between, the eye has glimpses of a succession of charming villas which wed town and country without usurping the prerogatives of the one or deforming the beauties of the other.

Before it are the placid waters of the bay, shimmering in the sunshine, or lashing themselves into a white passion in the wake of some passing steamer; girdled with mountains to the east, the north, and the west, and rocking upon their bosom a fleet of stately ships thickly clustered about the base of the San Francisco hills. A bank of fog is usually drifting past the rugged heights of Saucelito, but above the misty barrier rise the mountain tops, calm and restful, and distinctly defined against a sky that on three hundred days of the year is a deep azure blue. Several miles to the west, directly before the town—for Berkeley, unlike most cities inhabited by men, has a face, and turns it resolutely and forever toward the Golden Gate—lies the rocky fortress of Alcatraz, standing in the center of the channel, grim and invulnerable warder of all approaches from the sea. Far off to the west, seen through rocky walls which near each other and almost clasp hands, only to widen away as if awed by the majesty of the presence they would fain shut out, flooded with light, resistlessly throbbing against its rocky barriers, stretching calmly away into an infinite perspective, which is finally lost in the low arching sky, appears the mighty, surging, unresting, matchless ocean.—*Alta California.*

Many Beautiful Drives.

INTERESTING localities are not wanting in the neighborhood of the University town. The roads in all directions are good in the season, and all command a fine prospect. It is a charming drive from Berkeley to Oakland by way of Telegraph Avenue, and thence to Alameda or toward San Leandro. The roads leading up the many cañons into the Coast Range, and even to its summit, are all pleasant and romantic.

The soil is easily trodden into hard, compact road beds which make excellent drives unexcelled for ease and smoothness. These lead in every direction along the plateau near the bay, along the base of the Coast Range, or follow up one of the many small streams that wind through beautiful gorges of the mountain sides.

To the tourist, the scene is peculiar and fascinating, as he passes mile after mile between rows of villas, in whose lawns the flowers, shrubs, and trees of the tropics mingle their beauty and brightness with the soberest hues of the pines, firs, larches, cypresses, and hardier vegetation of the north.

On either side the visitor will see, except in the six months of midsummer, wild flowers in countless numbers, far handsomer and more delicate than the common garden flowers of the Eastern States.

Occasional glimpses of the sea, or of the hills dotted with purple shadows, will delight him, also the air, which most of the time is mild and bracing.

Good roads lead into the cañons and up the sides of the Coast Range, from whose summit a vast range of picturesque scenery is visible. The ascent is easy, and the drive will disclose constant changes of view.

Climate and Healthfulness.

Charming Winter Resort.

IN Oakland the cloudy days are comparatively few, and the wet days, even in the rainiest season, still fewer. The climate throughout the year is equable, healthy, comfortable, agreeable, stimulating, soothing, and invigorating to the invalid, and rendering life more keenly enjoyable to those in perfect health. Could any resort be imagined more desirable for persons in delicate health, or those who dread the rigors of an Eastern winter?

The afternoon winds that prevail in San Francisco during the summer months reach Oakland with diminished force. The close proximity of the hills in the rear of the city, and the many large and stately trees, serve as a protection. There are other reasons, perhaps, difficult of comprehension; but the fact is well known that when the winds prevail in San Francisco with great violence, only a moderate breeze is felt in Oakland. The sea fogs of summer, which roll in from the ocean, vanish from Oakland several hours before they cease to overshadow San Francisco. Perfect immunity from wind and fog can be found only in the interior, but intensely hot and scorching weather is an annoyance that more than counterbalances the pleasure to be derived from a sky that is always clear, and freedom from the ocean mists.

The city lies sloping to the west and north, fully exposed to the sea breezes, which lose their chill as they approach the Oakland shore. Its atmosphere is, therefore, pure, and at the same time mild; bracing, yet with an Italian softness. The death-rate is about one-half that of San Francisco, a fact that is of itself sufficient proof of the remarkable healthfulness of the city.

Health Statistics.

THE following carefully compiled table of health statistics, comparing the health of Oakland with that of the following cities, has been prepared by Dr. E. W. Buck, health officer of this city.

CITIES.	POPULATION.		DEATH RATE.
Cleveland, Ohio	200,429	IN JULY	40.04
New Haven, Conn.	75,000		30.03
Baltimore, Md.	408,520		19.57
New Orleans, La.	234,000		24.00
Cincinnati, Ohio	325,000		24.62
Nashville, Tenn.	60,000		26.46
Chicago, Ill.	630,000		28.44
Norfolk, Va.	26,188		38.30
St. Louis, Mo.	400,000		25.68
Milwaukee, Wis.	160,000		18.67
Wilmington, Del.	54,000		30.66
Detroit, Mich.	165,000		28.40
Oakland	43,000		13.95

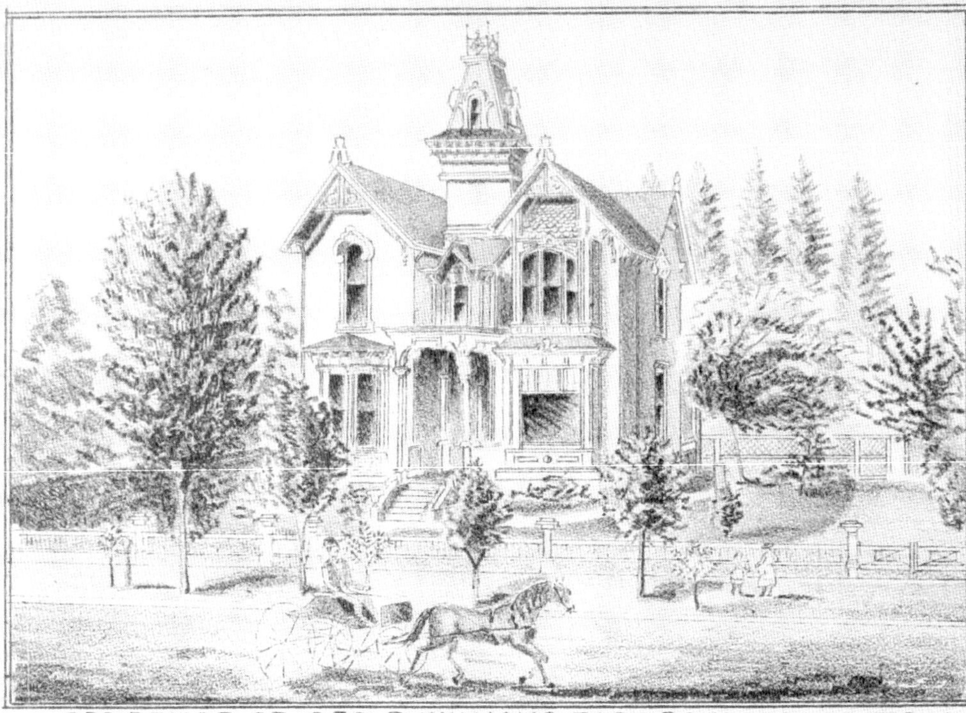

RESIDENCE OF GEO. R. WILLIAMS EAST OAKLAND, CALIFORNIA.

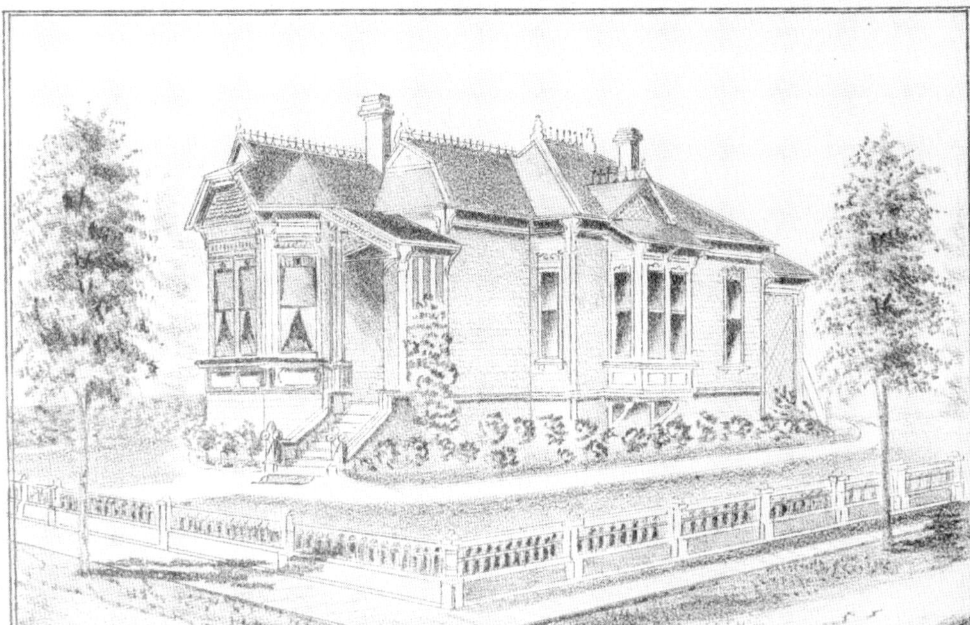

RESIDENCE OF G.E. YATES. COR. 17TH ST. AND 10TH AVENUE EAST OAKLAND CAL.

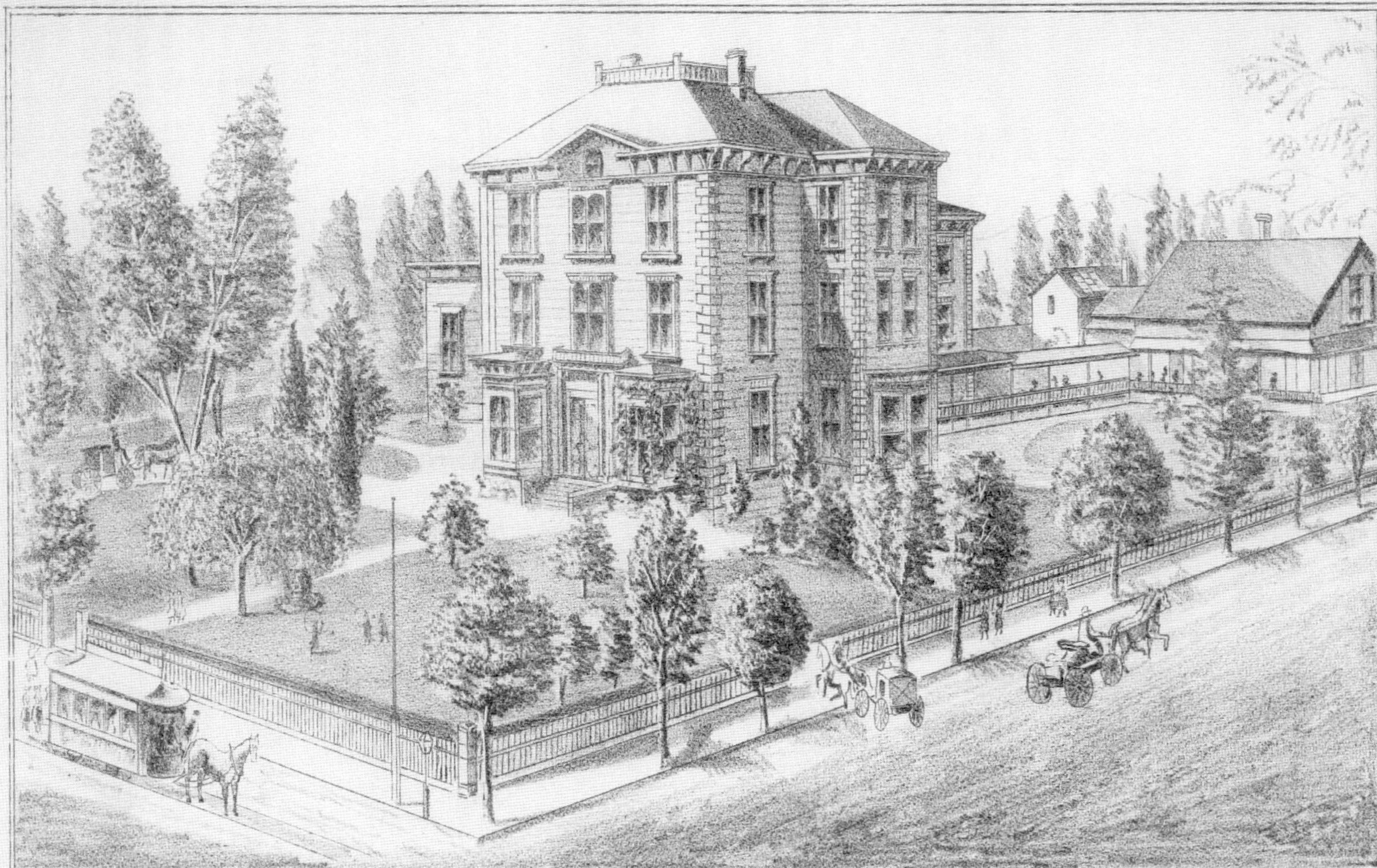

FIELD SEMINARY OR HOME SCHOOL FOR YOUNG LADIES, 1825 TELEGRAPH. AVE. OAKLAND ALAMEDA CO. CALIFORNIA.

Rainfall Table.

THE annual averages of San Francisco and Oakland show less than half an inch difference, that of San Francisco being 24 inches, Oakland's 24.45. One cause of this excess, small as it is, is found in the absence of fog in Oakland as compared with San Francisco. In many other respects, notably the temperature of the prevailing winds, Oakland has a long ways the more enjoyable climate, and is therefore free from disease.

The rainfall record at top of next column was taken by Mr. J. Hutchison, of this city.

SEASON.	INCHES.
1873-74	26.03
1874-75	21.67
1875-76	28.46
1876-77	11.71
1877-78	32.15
1878-79	23.57
1879-80	26.04
1880-81	30.84
1881-82	18.13
1883-84	31.10
1884-85	17.95

The following table will prove an interesting study to those in less favored climates who suffer from extremes of heat and cold. It will be observed that the thermometer rarely passes below the freezing point. In only one of the years mentioned does it indicate an uncomfortable degree of summer heat:—

COMPARATIVE ANNUAL METEOROLOGY.

	1876.	1877.	1878.	1879.	1880.	1881.
Mean temperature of the year	5[illegible].09	56.29	55.28	55.11	53.69	55.62
Mean temperature of the warmest day	4.	76.	69.33	75.33	70.66	70.
Mean temperature of the coldest day	3[illegible].	41.63	37.	33.66	41.	42.
Maximum temperature for the year	97.	95.	84.	93.	89.	87.
Minimum temperature for the year	30.	30.	27.	27.	29.	31.
Rainfall in inches during the year	21.56	11.09	31.71	28.91	28.07	26.07
No. clear and fair days during year	2[illegible]8	301	255	26[illegible]	258	276
No. cloudy days during year	98	64	110	99	108	89
No. days in which rain fell	63	58	78	89	53	67
No. foggy mornings	23	8	17	19	27	28
No. mornings overcast	51	44	64	63	86	52
No. mornings frost was seen	35	35	36	46	62	47
Wind, direction from SW. and W	342	364	311	3[illegible]5	346	402
Wind, direction from NW. and W	210	150	173	150	136	136
Wind, direction from NE. and N	34	63	45	50	59	58
Wind, direction from SE. and S	163	150	164	126	172	138
Calms	340	368	402	372	385	331

On December 3, 1873, Oakland was treated to quite a respectable fall of snow—not so heavy, however, as that which occurred on December 31, 1882—and as such meteorological luxuries do not come around very often, Oakland made the most of it. The ground on the lee side of buildings, and clear, open spaces, was covered with the flaky visitant of sufficient depth to enable an industrious person to scrape enough together to form snow-balls, and snow-balling was indulged in by all so long as the material lasted. Youngsters who had never seen so much snow in all their lives, took to the sport as naturally as though they had been born and reared in a snow-bank, and men who remembered the sleigh-rides they used to take "back in the States," became quite gleeful over the old familiar sight, while its presence developed a number of jokes and much pleasantry.

Such occurrences, as may be seen, are very rare, and for this reason, no doubt, they are heralded with all the more joy when they do come. Our candid belief is, should a *real* Eastern storm sweep down upon us, it would be an unwelcome visitor.

Climate and Healthfulness.

EVEN the lightest frosts are almost unknown in the portion of the town used for residence, which lies in or near the stratum of air called the "warm belt," that extends like a girdle about the valleys embraced by the Coast Range and its hilly offshoots.

The sanitary conditions of the town depend severally on excellent drainage, neighborhood of the sea, absence of malarial vapors, evenness of temperature, superior quality of water used for drinking, and general freedom from the class of winds regarded as unhealthy. The north winds are the most troublesome, but they are the exceptional air currents of the year. The southeast gales strike the town with some force, but they are moist, healthful, and desirable.

The trade winds impinge upon the shore of the bay with greatest violence near Shellmound. They are diminished in strength as they approach the hills, and in keenness by the layers of still air along the foot and in the cañons of the Coast Range, which are warmed by the sun during the long pleasant afternoons. Often when San Francisco and other towns about the bay are enshrouded in fogs, Oakland has its milder airs and its unclouded skies and starlight.

The district for which the following table has been prepared includes the University buildings and grounds, the populous neighborhoods for a mile north and south of them, and has for its western limit a north and south line about half way between East and West Berkeley. The population within this area is about 1,300. The list covers a period of two years. It may be considered approximately accurate as regards cases, and almost absolutely correct in respect of the number of deaths.

	No. Cases.	No. Deaths.
Small-pox	0	0
Scarlet Fever	9	0
Malignant Scarlet Fever	0	0
Typhoid Fever	8	0
Typhus Fever	6	0
Malarial Fever	2	0
Typho-malarial Fever	3	0
Bilious Fever	(not known)	0
Cholera Infantum	1	1
Erysipelas	4	0
Kidney Disease	5	0
Croup	5	0
Bronchitis	10	0
Diphtheria	5	0
Tonsilitic and Throat Diseases	18	0
Pneumonia	5	0
Whooping Cough	25	0
Consumption	2	2
Pleuro-pneumonia	1	1
Convulsions	1	1
Diarrhea	10	0
Measles	0	0
Inflammation of Liver	1	1
Heart Disease	2	1
General Debility	2	1
Spinal Disease	2	1

DEATHS BY ACCIDENT.

Upon the Rail	1
Strangulation	1
Suicide	1
Poison	1
Gunshot Wound	1
No. of deaths in two years	14

The death-rate shown by these figures is phenomenal. Including deaths by accident, it is but 7 per annum in 1,300, or a little over 5 in 1,000.

Of the cases of consumption, it is only necessary to say that both were recent arrivals. One of the patients came to Berkeley a week before his death. The scarlet fever is invariably of mild type, and yields quickly to treatment.

A Winter Scene.

IN January, or February at the latest, comes out the glory of the hyacinths, tulips, and their queenly allies, the early varieties of lily and gladiolus.

At this season the beautiful family of acacias, most graceful of tropic shade trees, in almost countless varieties, are yellow with the profusion of their flowers, every-

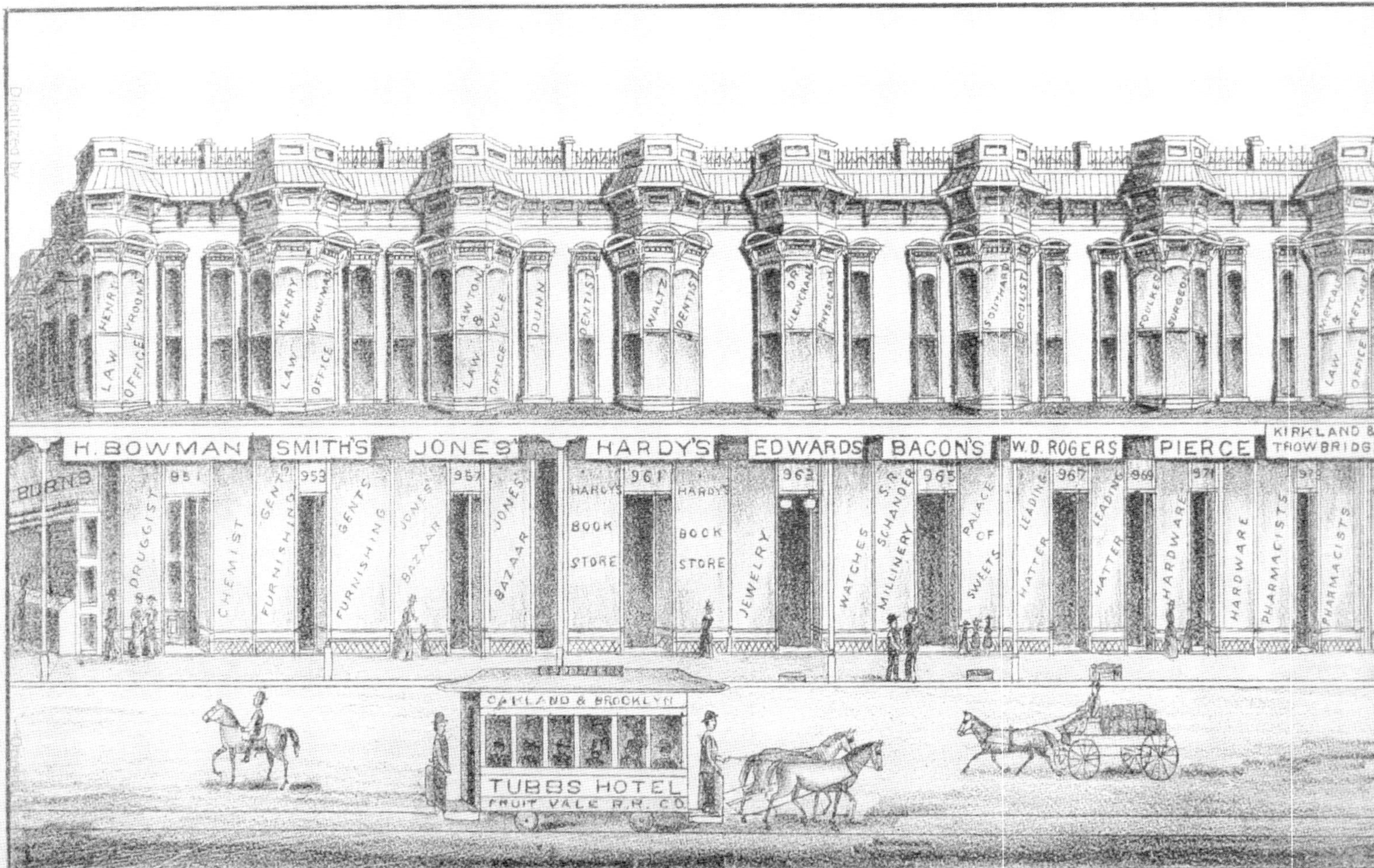

BUSINESS BLOCK BROADWAY BETWEEN 9TH & 10TH STS.

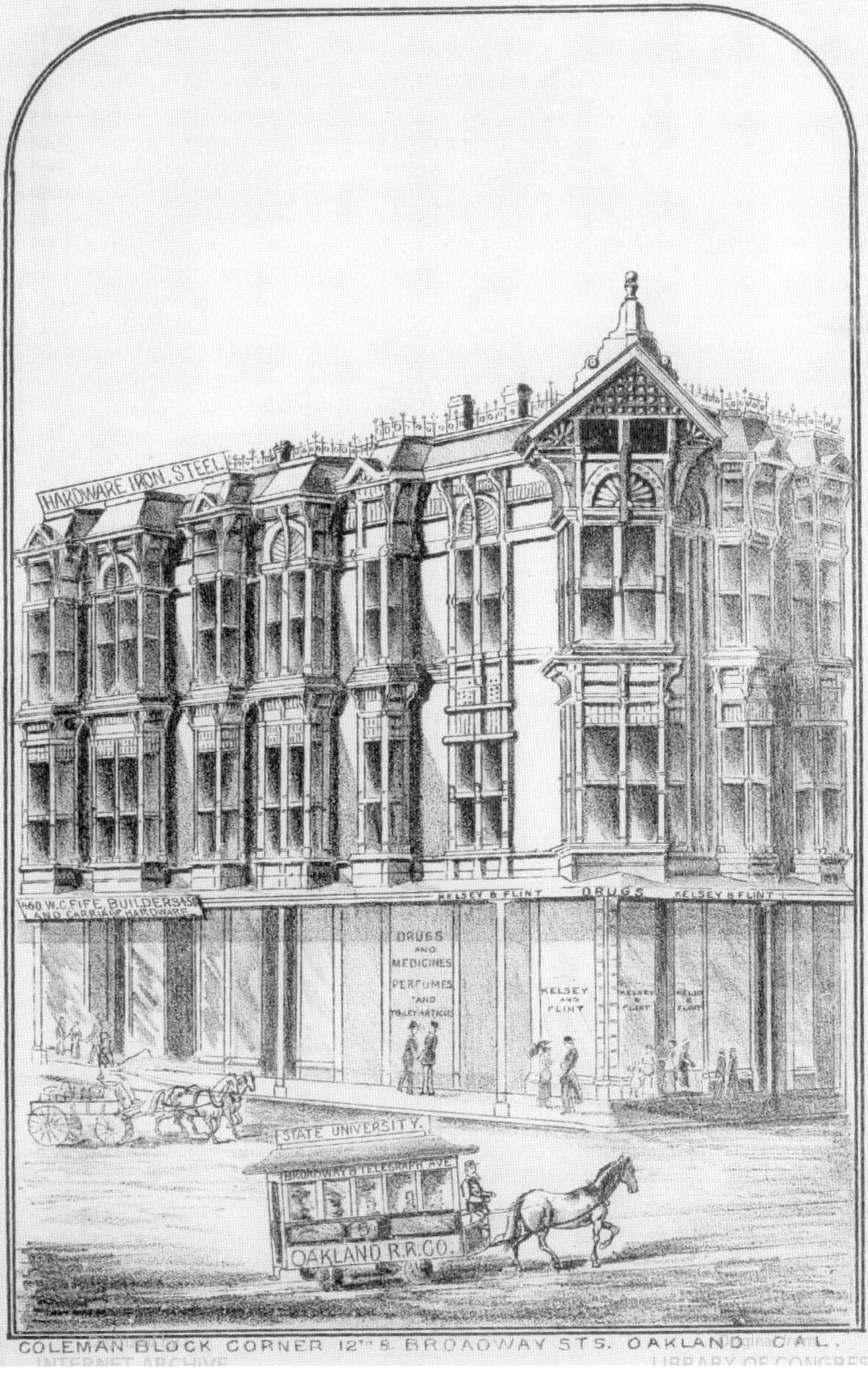

COLEMAN BLOCK CORNER 12TH & BROADWAY STS. OAKLAND CAL.

where presenting a most pleasing contrast to the dark green of those rugged and venerable native live-oaks which good taste has left standing at random along all streets, in every public park and private lawn, their massive trunks now often mantled with English ivy.

Such is the peculiar geniality of the climate that hardly any quarter of the globe has failed to contribute its rare and beautiful trees and shrubs to the adornment of our homes. Lilac and snow-ball, laburnum and spirœa from northern Europe; elegant ericas and brilliant tecomas from southern Africa; magnolias and rhododendrons from the Carolinas; camellias and azaleas from Japan; cacti, yuccas, and agaves (century plants) from Central America; stately dracænas from the Sandwich Islands; palms and cistus from the East Indies; all these and unnumbered other species which at this latitude on other northern coasts require the shelter and heat of the conservatory, grow here uncovered, at all seasons.

Even the giant cactus and graceful dasylirion from Arizona deserts do not refuse to become acclimated; while side by side with them there flourish, as if equally at home, the firs and larches of northern Europe, and young specimens of the majestic sugar-pines and sequoias of the snowy Sierra.

Of the rose, the queen of the floral kingdom, all possible varieties, the tenderest as well as the most hardy, reward the cultivator's care with an almost perpetual harvest of bloom. The graceful fuchsias in all their forms are, in this region, strong, woody climbers, overhanging arbors, or mantling the walls of buildings and hanging forth their drooping, flower-laden branches, in almost equal perfection of beauty, at every season of the year.

The vast wealth of arboreal and floral beauty which the landscape gardener has here at his command, is shown delightfully on many a lawn, where, on one side, back of the compactly-rounded heads of the ancient live-oaks, the tall and slender eucalyptus hangs its lithe and leafy branches, while intermediately are ranged the dark, stalwart ranks of vigorous pine and cypress. Set off by such a background, various palms, in groups perhaps overshadowing a moist rockery, planted with delicate and graceful ferns, present a scene altogether tropical in its richness. Or one sees stretches of velvet lawn enclosed by hedges of scarlet-geranium, and dotted either with beds of verbena, petunia, pansy, or brilliant foliage plants, or with clumps of bronze-leaved canna, or silver-plumed pampas grass; trellises covered with jassamine and honeysuckle; rustic alcoves shaded deeply by giant fuchsias and fragrant heliotrope—such are a few mere hints at the luxury here easily attainable in the beautifying of the surroundings of home.

TEMPERATURE TABLE.

County.	Town.	Temperature.			Av. Fall.
		Max.	Min.	Mean.	
Alameda	Oakland	95	28	60	20
Butte	Chico	114	22	64	21
Colusa	Williams	112	22	63	12
Fresno	Fresno	115	18	67	7
Kern	Sumner	112	18	66	4
Los Angeles	Los Angeles	112	28	65	12
Merced	Merced	112	20	63	10
Napa	Napa	104	19	59	25
Sacramento	Sacramento	103	22	61	19
San Diego	San Diego	100	32	61	10
San Francisco	....	94	25	59	23
San Joaquin	Stockton	110	20	59	14
Santa Cruz	Pajaro	99	22	55	18
Santa Clara	San Jose	108	24	57	12
San Mateo	San Mateo	104	25	56	19
Shasta	Redding	110	24	63	39
Stanislaus	Modesto	113	21	63	9
Sonoma	Petaluma	95	18	56	23
Solano	Suisun	106	25	61	20
Tehama	Red Bluff	119	24	64	27
Tulare	Goshen	116	14	64	7
Yolo	Woodland	112	20	62	18
Yuba	Marysville	107	24	64	17

Churches of Oakland.

City of Spires.

THERE are nearly forty churches in the city of Oakland, of all denominations, but our space will only admit a notice of a few of the oldest of these. From the days when "two or three were gathered together" under the shade of one of Oakland's spreading oaks, up to the present, the city has been the home of churches that have grown in beauty of design and magnificence of architecture, as the years flew by. She is sometimes called the "City of Spires," as she deserves to be, for more graceful outlines are not to be found anywhere. Her number of devotees is large, and, in truth, Oakland is a city of families, boasting in her churches and her schools.

We give in this work illustrations of a few of the most prominent churches, as well as brief descriptions of such as cared to furnish the items. All the churches are good buildings and have large congregations.

First Religious Services.

IN November, 1854, the Right Reverend Bishop Kip made arrangements to have Dr. Carter's large and commodious hall fitted up as a temporary Episcopal church, and to perform the duties of pastor himself. The building was located on Broadway. Saint John's Episcopal Church, however, was organized in June, 1852, and is the oldest church foundation in the city, except the Roman Catholic. In 1852, when Oakland was less than a village, having but half a dozen houses in it, two Episcopalian families met and worshiped unitedly, and thus continued till a member of one of the families fell dangerously ill, when the little *coterie* ceased to meet.

About a year later, the Rev. Dr. Ver Mehr, who was then rector of Grace Church, San Francisco, visited Oakland, and a meeting of twelve persons was with difficulty convened. Towards the close of the year 1853, an Episcopal clergyman, Rev. Mr. Morgan, appeared on a bright Sunday morning and read the prayers and preached under the branches of one of Oakland's shady trees. The next Sabbath-day the little flock in Oakland determined to have a covered church of some kind ready for the preacher ere the following Sunday. A large tent, 25x70 feet, was accordingly erected, a communion-rail put up, a temporary pulpit contrived, and a few benches arranged in the body of the tent. A cross outside designated the object of the building. But when all things were ready, through some accident the clergyman came not. "Is there no minister present?" was the question asked by all. The Rev. Mr. Walsworth, afterwards

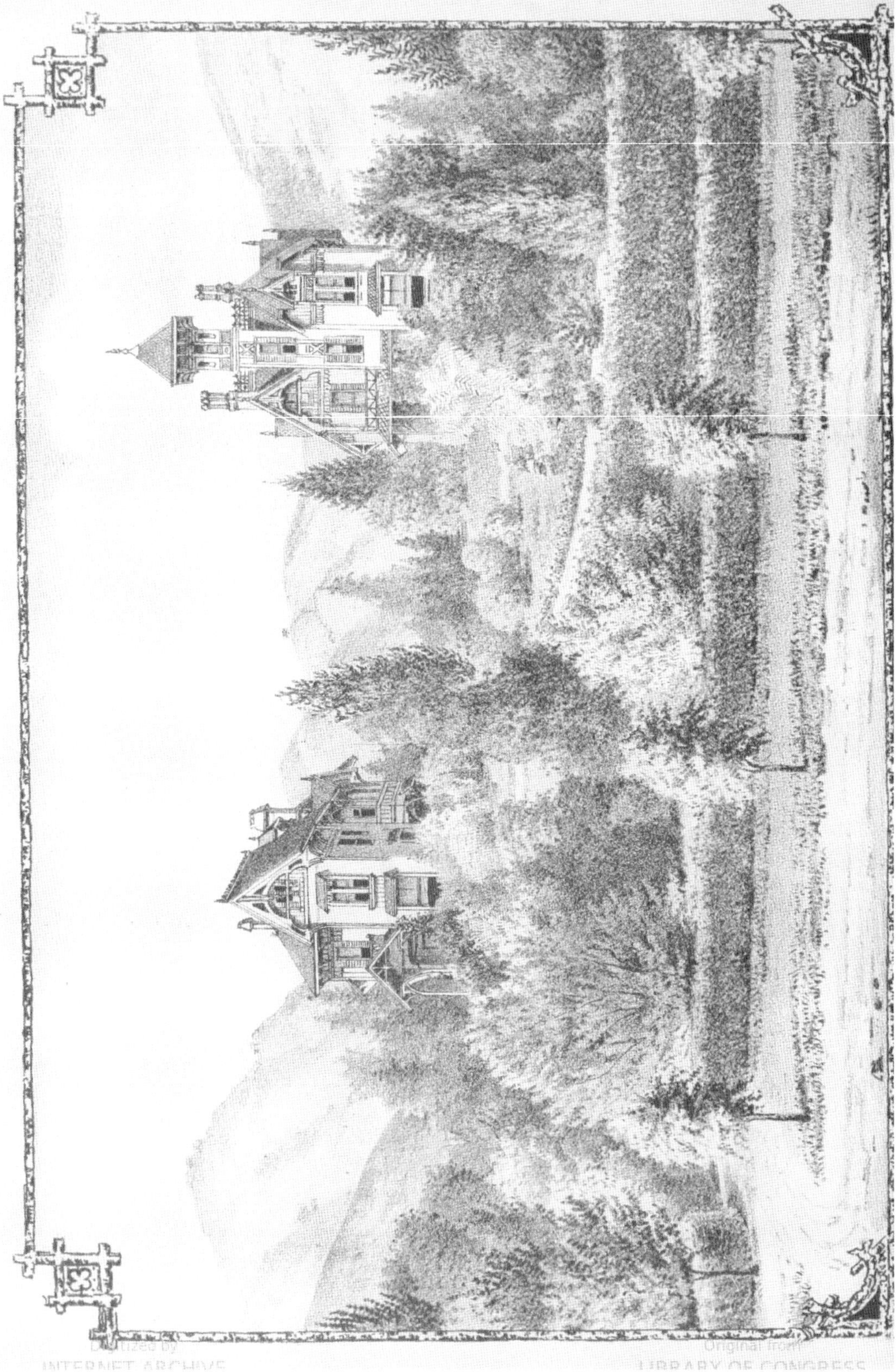

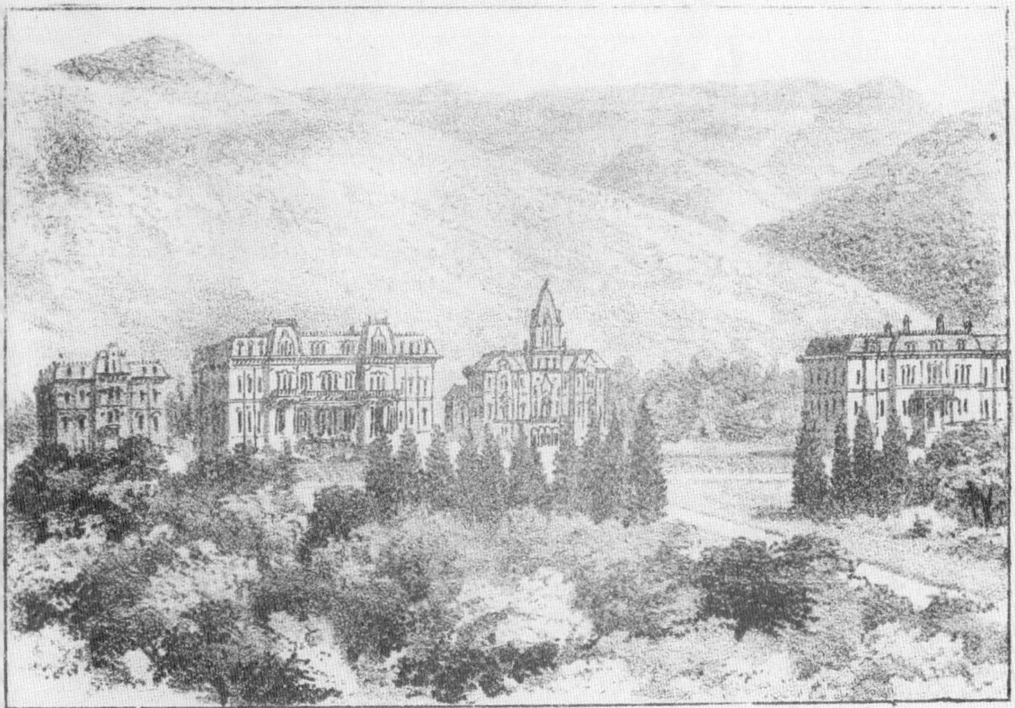

UNIVERSITY BUILDINGS. BERKELEY. CAL.

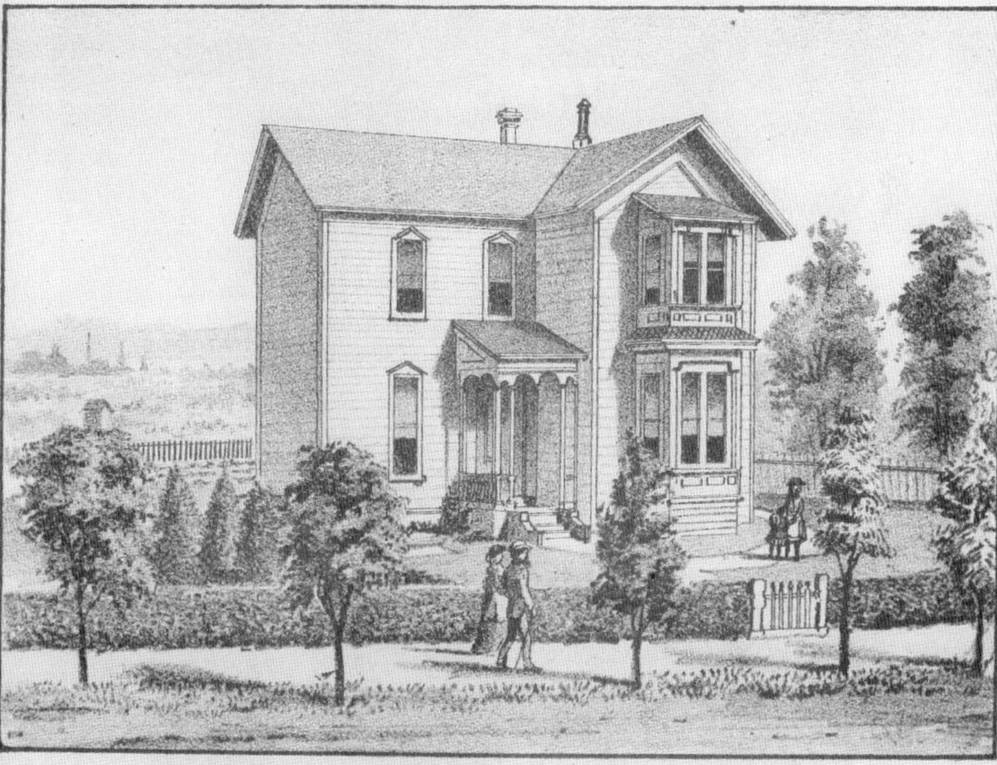

RESIDENCE OF J. K STEWART. BLAKE ST. BERKELEY CAL.

head of the Pacific Female College, then stood up, and said, "I am a minister but not an Episcopalian. I am a Presbyterian, and will preach to you if you desire me to do so." His offer was joyfully accepted and a collection of nineteen dollars taken up. Next day the tent and all the seats were bought by the Presbyterians, which was the origin of that branch in Oakland, who called, as their first pastor, Rev. Samuel B. Bell.

FIRST PRESBYTERIAN CHURCH.—This church was organized in April, 1853, being one of the oldest of any denomination in Oakland. The first services were held in a cloth tent, and afterwards in the public school-house, under the pastoral charge of Rev. S. B Bell. The original church building occupied by this society was erected about 1856, at the corner of Webster and Sixth Streets, at a cost of about six thousand dollars.

The present church edifice, situated on the northeast corner of Fourteenth and Franklin Streets, was built in the year 1875, at a cost of about fifty-two thousand dollars, and was dedicated for public worship January 16, 1876. It is one of the handsomest structures in the city. The present pastor, Rev. Francis A. Horton, assumed the pastorate April 8, 1883.

FIRST CONGREGATIONAL CHURCH OF OAKLAND is the largest church edifice, occupying one-half block on Clay between Twelfth and Thirteenth Streets. This church was dedicated January 21, 1879. Rev. J. K. McLean is pastor.

The cost of the present structure, with ground and furnishing, was in the neighborhood of one hundred thousand dollars. It contains sittings for fourteen hundred persons. Its auditorium is undoubtedly the most complete on the Pacific Coast.

Four other Congregational Churches have, since the organization of this church, been formed within the territory it originally held, to all of which it has made liberal contributions, both of members and of funds.

At the twenty-fifth annual meeting of the First Congregational Church of Oakland, report was made that 161 members had been received during the year and 44 dismissed (including deaths) making a gain of 117. The total membership is at present 930.

The amount raised for current expenses, including repairs and improvements, was $12.582 94; the amount for benevolence, $6,728.35; making a total of $19.311.29. The total enrollment of the Sunday-school is 1,074, with an average attendance of 628. The average attendance at church of members of the Sunday-school was 381; and 111 members of the school united with the church during the year.

The annual report of the Sunday-school gives the following interesting items:—

Total disbursements		$1,302.11
Number of officers		16
" " teachers		74
" " scholars (seniors)	574	
" " " (juniors)	152	
" " " (primary)	242—968	
" " helpers not otherwise enrolled		24
Total enrolled membership		1,671
Largest attendance during the year		788
Smallest " " " "		274
Average " " " "		621

The number of deaths reported for the year (only three) speaks volumes for the health of Oakland, *three deaths out of 1,671 children*.

ST. PAUL'S (EPISCOPAL) CHURCH is located on Harrison Street, near Thirteenth. This church has drawn within its doors a congregation comprising large influence and wealth from a field comparatively unoccupied before, and is solidly established on a broad temporal and spiritual basis as a great and growing Christian power. Rev. Hobart Chetwood, rector.

ST. JOHN'S (EPISCOPAL) CHURCH.—This church had an humble origin when Oakland numbered but a few houses, and not over one thousand inhabitants. During the summer of 1852, two families met and worshiped unitedly. A lot was purchased on Eighth Street, in 1860, and an edifice erected, which has been twice enlarged. Rev. Benj. Akerley has been pastor for about twenty-five years.

SEVENTH-DAY ADVENTIST CHURCH — In January, 1876, a movement was started by the State Conference to secure a suitable location for a house of worship. After careful canvassing, the very desirable northeast corner of Clay and Thirteenth Streets was selected, and purchased at a cost of $4,000. Here a neat and commodious building was erected, costing about twelve thousand dollars.

As the name indicates, the distinctive features of this body of Christians are the keeping of the seventh-day Sabbath, "according to the commandment," as also the doctrine of the near advent of the Lord to execute judgment—although no time is fixed for that event. They acknowledge no creed but the Bible, and inscribe upon their banner, "The commandments of God, and the faith of Jesus." They totally abstain from every form of intoxicating beverage, and disfellowship the use of tobacco. They teach abstinence from tea and coffee as a doctrine of health reform, but do not make it compulsory upon members. Eld. J. H. Waggoner is pastor.

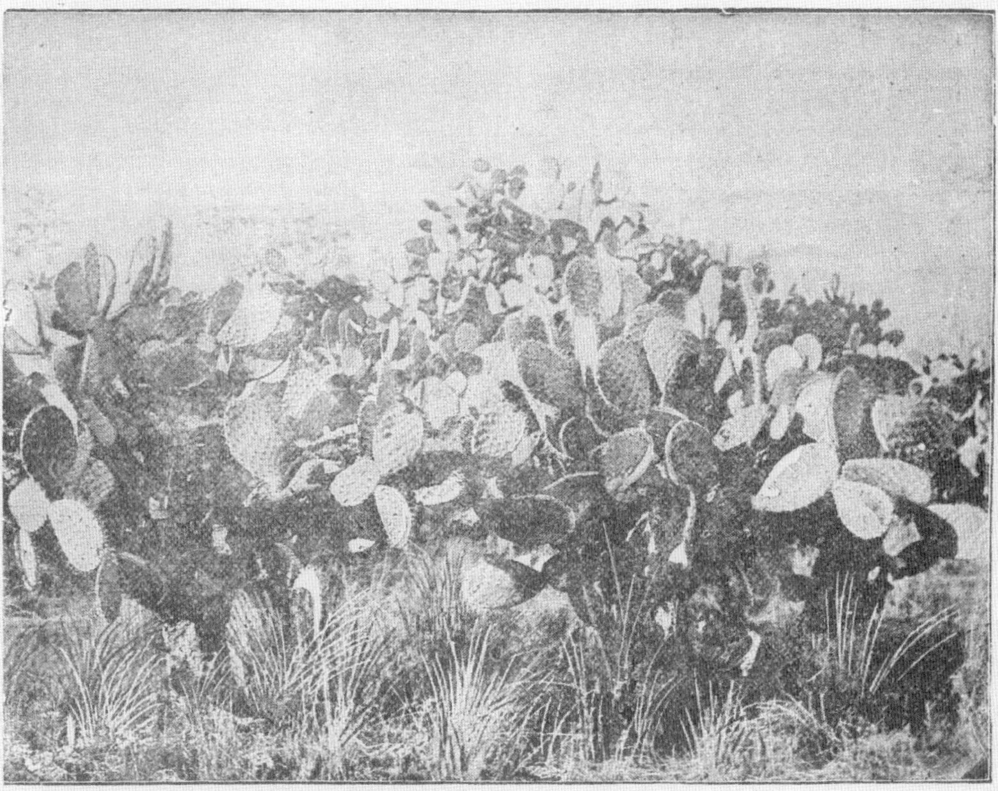

PRICKLY PEAR CACTUS. *(Opuntia Vulgaris.)* IN OAKLAND GARDEN.

CHURCH OF THE IMMACULATE CONCEPTION is situated on Jefferson Street

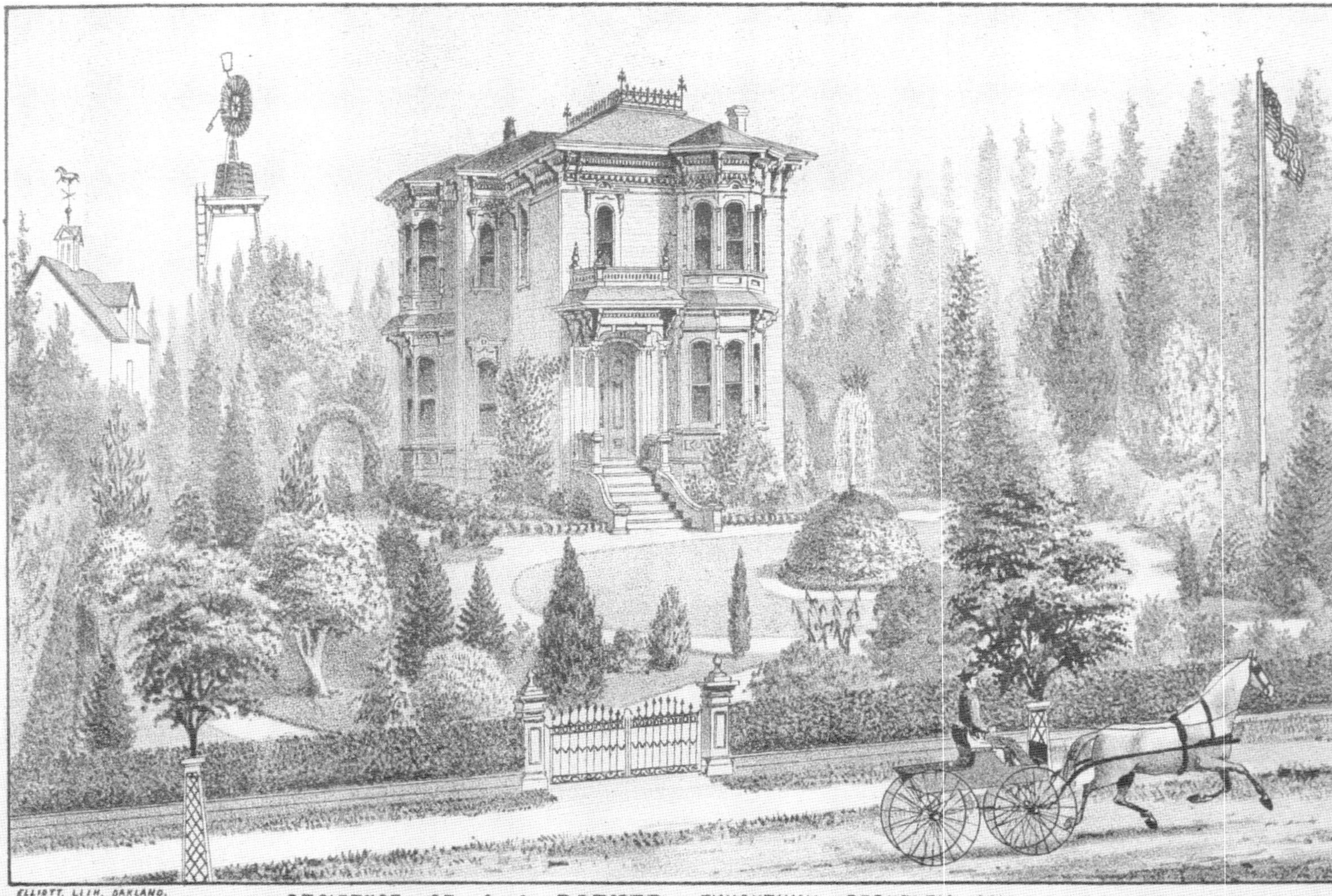

ELLIOTT, LITH. OAKLAND.

RESIDENCE OF J. L. BARKER, DWIGHTWAY, BERKELEY, CAL.

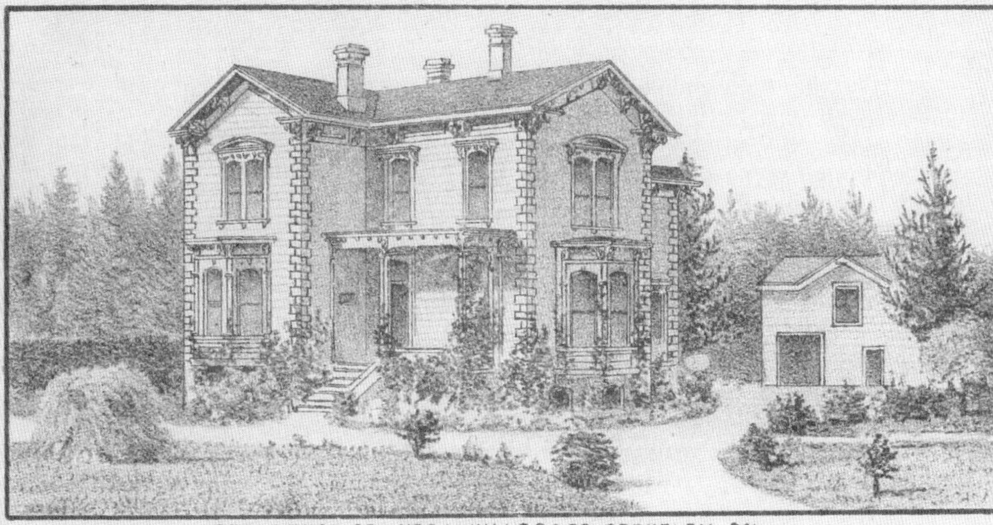

RESIDENCE OF MRS. M. HILLEGASS. BERKELEY, CAL.

Oakland offers to Berkeley its stores, churches, and all its numerous places of resort, which will be brought within a fifteen minutes' ride on the completion of the South Pacific Coast local line. Alameda, with its pleasant streets and sea-bathing, is scarcely more distant. Piedmont Springs are within an easy drive, and the fair and fertile district of which San Pablo is the center lies just beyond the point where the Coast Range descends to the shore of the bay. The new drive around Lake Merritt is expected to be one of the loveliest of its kind.

Floral Scene in Winter.

THE freshness and beauty of lawns and gardens in winter are delightful. The light frosts of the midwinter season only brighten the verdure of the hardy lawn grasses, and hardly check the bloom of geraniums, pelargoniums, heliotrope, tender and choice roses, and other green-house plants which here thrive

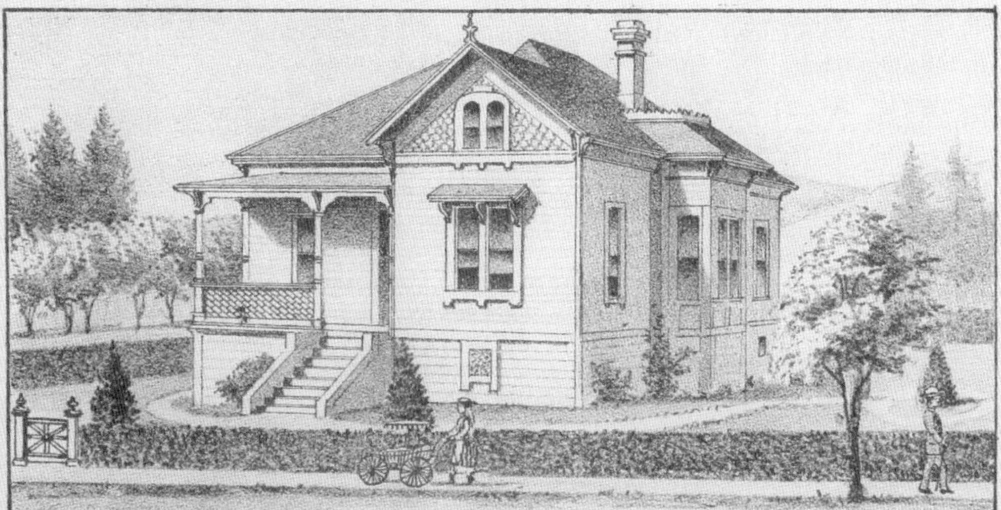

RESIDENCE OF F. H. LAWTON. CHANNING WAY. BERKELEY CAL.

between Seventh and Eighth. The style of the building is early Gothic, and it consists of a nave, side aisles, chancel, and two front towers. The latter are to be surmounted by spires at a future period, but even in their present state their height (104 feet to the top of the pinnacles) and size give a highly imposing appearance to the front. The roof is open; on the inside the spaces between the principals and tie-beams, and the latter and the arch braces, in both nave and aisle roofs, being filled in with light and elegant open-work tracery. The ceiling is paneled and painted blue, with stars; the wood-work being painted white, with flower patterns with tertiary colors. At the sides the arch braces under the roof-timbers are terminated in carved niches, intended to receive statues of the twelve apostles. The cornices are also of wood, the arches between the naves and aisles and the chancel arch being, with the walls and ceiling under the organ gallery, the only plaster-work in the building. The windows are filled with rich stained glass, the heads being ornamented with emblematic figures, and the large front window being quite a fine specimen of artistic design. It is not the least satisfactory matter in connection with this building, that it is entirely the product of California design and workmanship.

FIRST METHODIST CHURCH is a large building on the corner of Fourteenth and Clay Streets. It has a large and flourishing congregation and Sunday-school. Rev. John Coyle is pastor.

FIRST BAPTIST CHURCH is a handsome edifice at the southeast corner of Fourteenth and Brush Streets, and was erected at a cost of thirty thousand dollars, the lot whereon it stands having cost twenty-five hundred dollars. It was formally dedicated in March, 1869, the chapel in the rear having been occupied three months before, and used while the main building was being completed. The Sunday-school was organized in 1854. It has an attendance of thirty teachers and about three hundred children. The library has some eight hundred volumes, which are well calculated to advance the reader in higher spiritual attainments. Rev. E. H. Gray, pastor.

SECOND CONGREGATIONAL CHURCH.—This church was organized on the 31st of May, 1868, in the West Oakland school-house. Previous to this organization a Sabbath-school had been held for some time in the school-house, and a "Religious Society" had been formed, and preaching services had been conducted by Prof. Martin Kellogg, of the College of California. On the 10th of May, 1868, this society was dissolved, and in its place the "Second Congregational Religious Society of Oakland" was formed, of which the same persons were elected trustees. In 1874 measures were taken for purchasing a lot and building a church on Chase Street, the one now occupied by the church. The following year the old building was removed to the rear of this lot, and fitted up for a lecture room; and a neat and commodious church edifice was erected at a cost for building and furniture of eleven thousand dollars. It was dedicated December 26, 1875.

THE SALVATION ARMY has just completed a new building on Eighth Street. The "castle," the first building erected by the Army on the Pacific Coast, is ninety feet long, forty-four feet wide, and two stories high. The main room, on the first floor, will accommodate six hundred or seven hundred people. In the upper story will be the office of Major Wells, Division Commander, and of Captain Cozens, of the First California Corps. These officers will also live in the building.

The Public Schools.

Public Schools of Oakland.

THE education of youth is amply provided for by the city. There are seventeen roomy, well-lighted, and well-ventilated school buildings with a seating capacity of 6,000, which is 600 more than the average daily attendance. These are conveniently placed in the different wards according to the concentration of population. At the head of the list stands the High School, with classical, scientific, and literary courses, well supplied with school apparatus, accomplished teachers, and thoroughly competent to fit pupils for the colleges and universities of the country, or for any sphere in life. It has been for the last fifteen years in charge of Prof. J. B. McChesney. The teachers of the public schools are selected from the most experienced members of the profession to be found on the Pacific Coast. Many of the buildings have grounds ornamented with trees, shrubs, and flowers. Surroundings and appliances are agreeable, and in the mild, healthy, and stimulating air, pupils find every incentive to study. There is probably no other city in the world where nature supplies so many aids. The aggregate value of the school property is over $400.000. which in convenience, comfort, and educational advantages represents twice the amount in any Eastern city, where, owing to a vigorous climate, school buildings are necessarily of a more substantial kind.

The following figures are taken from the annual report of City Superintendent of Public Instruction, J. C. Gilson, to the State Superintendent. The figures relate to the public schools within the city.

Number of classes, employing one teacher each, 133; made up of 46 grammar classes, 8 High School classes, one commercial class, two evening classes, and 76 primary classes.

Number of boys enrolled on register, 3,964; girls, 3,951; total, 7,915. Average number belonging, 5,830.65; average daily attendance, 5,608.83. Percentage of attendance, 96.20.

The pupils are distributed as follows: In High School, 379; grammar grades, 2,398; primary grades, 5,138.

Number of teachers, 142—male, 13; female, 129. There are 115 teachers with first-grade certificates and 23 with second-grade certificates.

The number of teachers who are graduates of the State Normal School is 18; graduates of other State Normal schools,

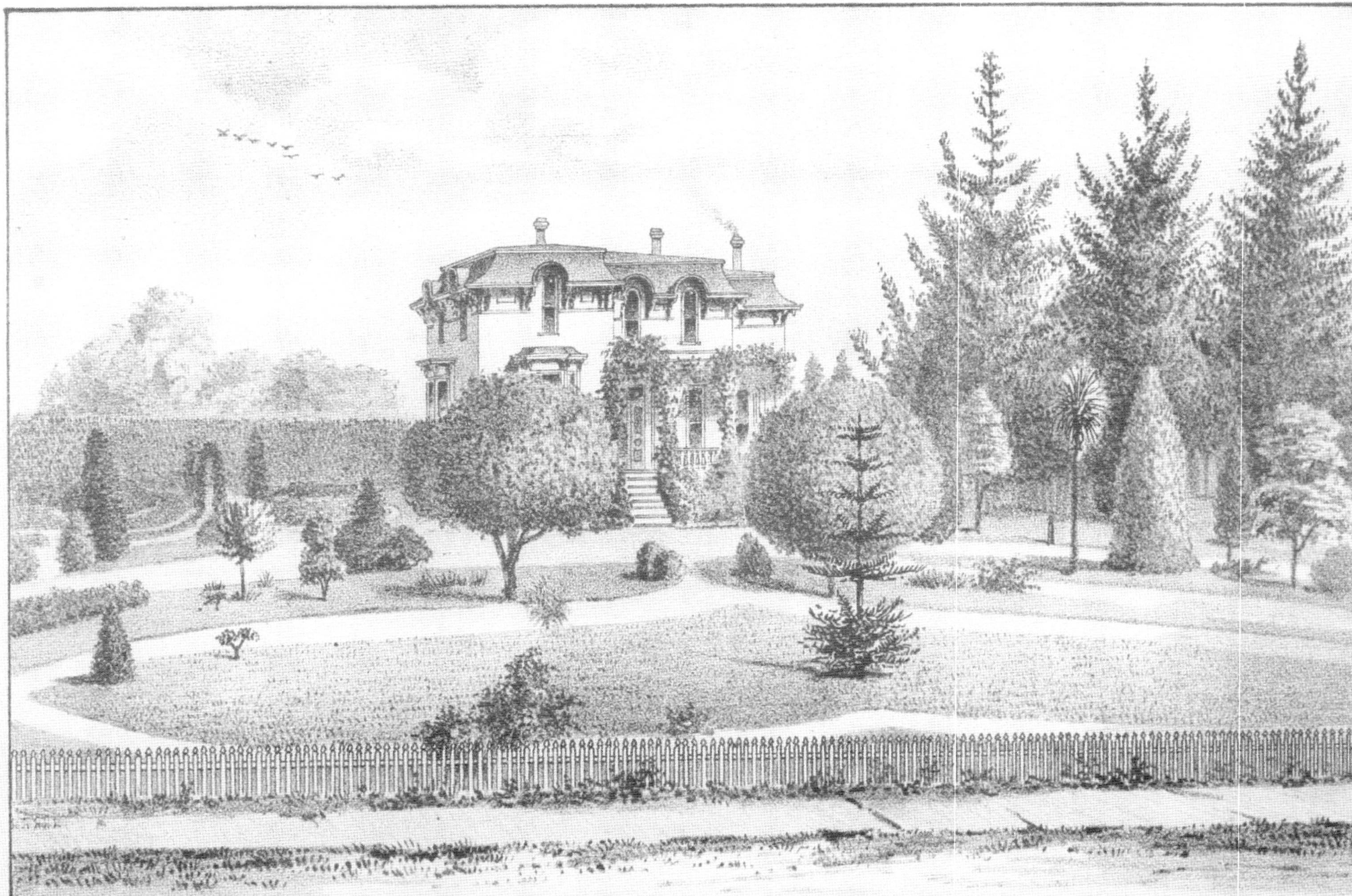

ELLIOTT. LITH.

RESIDENCE OF **F. K. SHATTUCK.** SHATTUCK AVENUE, BERKELEY.

Organization of University.

IN accordance with the organic act, the Board of Regents was composed of twenty-two members, of whom the following were *ex officio:* The Governor and Lieutenant-Governor of California, the Speaker of the Assembly, the State Superintendent of Public Instruction, the President of the State Agricultural Society, and the President of the Mechanics' Institute of San Francisco. Of the remaining sixteen, eight were to be appointed by the Governor, with the approval of the State Senate, and eight were to be honorary members, chosen from the body of the State by the official and appointed members.

Prof. LeConte in conjunction with the Committee on Instruction prepared a synopsis of a course of study appropriate to the colleges of the University. They are now as follows:—

1. College of Letters; 2. College of Agriculture; 3. College of Mechanics; 4. College of Mining; 5. College of Engineering; 6. College of Chemistry; 7. Literary Course; 8. Course in Letters and Political Science.

The University began its labors in the buildings at Oakland on the 23d of September, and the first graduating exercises were held in June, 1873, in a church in Oakland. The new buildings were occupied the next September. Prof. LeConte had the active co-operation of J. W. Dwinelle during the arduous work of organization. He acted as president for more than a year, presided at the first commencement exercises, and conferred the first degrees on a graduating class of three, who had been advanced students in the College of California. During his incumbency several measures of vital importance were taken, among which were the selection of suitable building-plans, making tuition free, the adoption of the Rules of Order and General Regulations.

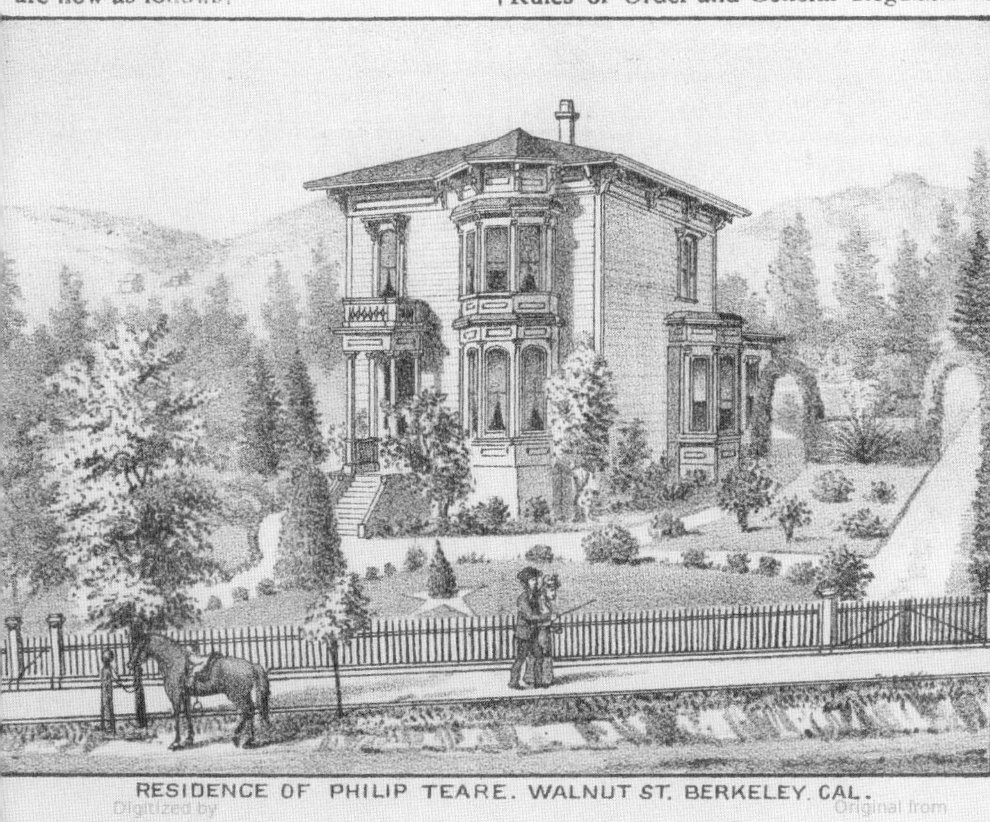

RESIDENCE OF PHILIP TEARE. WALNUT ST. BERKELEY. CAL.

15; teachers who hold life diplomas, 64; State educational diplomas, 21; first-grade city certificates, 119; second-grade city certificates, 23.

EXPENDITURES.

Teachers, salaries	$135,122 85
Rents, repairs, fuel, etc	27,333 11
School library	738 65
School apparatus	210 00
Sites, buildings, and furniture	19,559 32
Total expenditures	$182,963 93

RECEIPTS.

Balance on hand July 1, 1884	$ 17,066 96
From non-resident pupils	1,547 40
From city taxation	57,701 75
From county taxation	30,957 01
From State taxation	75,093 24
Total receipts	$182,366 36

SCHOOL PROPERTY VALUATION.

Lots, school-houses, and furniture	$411,500 00
School libraries	2,700 00
School apparatus	5,250 00
Total value of school property	$419,450 00

Oakland High School.

THE High School, which is the head of the Public School Department of this city, has long been the pride of the citizens of Oakland. Its rank among the foremost educational institutions on this coast entitles it to the high esteem of the public, and the liberal support it has always received. It needs no praise from us, but is able to stand upon its own merits and sustain the enviable reputation it has achieved.

The Oakland High School was organized July 12, 1869, with twenty-nine pupils. The curriculum adopted provided a liberal course in natural science, mathematics, literature, and language, requiring three years for its completion. For the first two years the classes were accommodated in connection with a grammar school, but at the commencement of the third year they were moved to the commodious building situated at the corner of Central Avenue and Market Street. At first but one teacher was employed; now there are nine. J. B. McChesney is principal.

Public and Private Schools.

THE University buildings are large and commodious. The public schools of Berkeley also occupy handsome buildings, and are supplied with competent instructors. The Kellogg School at East Berkeley stands near Strawberry Creek, and almost in the shadow of the old oaks of the University. The merits of the Kellogg School have been recognized by the State University in admitting its graduates on certificate of Principal. Since the adoption of this policy by the University it has been among the first to secure this privilege. To non-resident pupils the Kellogg School offers advantages which cannot be enjoyed elsewhere in the State. The central location of the school makes it equally accessible to residents from all quarters of Berkeley; the tuition fees of non-resident pupils contribute materially to its support; while its intimate connection with the grades below, render it the common ambition of graduates of the San Pablo and Kellogg schools.

The West Berkeley public school, as will be seen by our illustration, is also a fine structure.

Bowens Academy was opened January 2, 1884, under the name of the HOME SCHOOL FOR BOYS. By request of many of the patrons and well-wishers of the Institution, the name of the School was changed into that of BOWENS ACADEMY. The success of the school has been marked from the beginning, each term bringing its increase, and the prospects for the future are most encouraging.

The Principal of the School is a graduate of one of the oldest and highest Universities of Europe. He has had an experience in teaching of over twenty years, six of which were spent teaching in this State.

The Libraries.

Free Public Library.

OAKLAND takes pride in the free public library which is located in the library building on the corner of Fourteenth and Washington Streets. First opened November 7, 1878; contained, June 1, 1883, 9,229 volumes. There are about 7,000 members; the average monthly circulation is about 12,000 volumes. Of the total books drawn out about 60 per cent is classed as fiction, and the remaining is classed as history, geography, travels, poetry, and fiction in proportion as named. The library is open from 9 A. M. to 8 P. M., daily except Sundays.

The reading-room in this building occupies the first floor and is well furnished with news and periodical literature of the day. It receives over 100 papers and 25 magazines. The rooms are open daily from 7 to 9 o'clock. There are also free reading-rooms at East and West Oakland. All are managed by a Board of Trustees elected by the people, who also manage the library. The following comprise the Board of Trustees: C. W. Kellogg, R. G. Graham, J. B. McChesney, J. H. Boalt, S. H. Melvin.

Odd Fellows' Library.

AUGUST 12, 1867, there was a meeting of Odd Fellows for the purpose of founding a library, and it was determined to establish an association, to be composed of such members of the Order as might choose to unite with it The first event of any importance was the transfer of 295 volumes from the "Oakland Philomathean Ljbrary Association," immediately followed by a large donation from W. W. Crane, Jr, and in quick succession by smaller donations from many individuals. There is at present in the library or in circulation 4,300 well-selected volumes.

The Odd Fellows Society and their families are the only persons entitled to draw books from the library, but others are always welcome to examine the books in the library for reference, and many are daily availing themselves of the privilege. It is in the Odd Fellows' Hall on northwest corner of Eleventh and Franklin Streets. There are about 700 members, and the average monthly circulation is about 1,500 volumes. The library is opened from 9 A. M. to 9 P. M., daily,

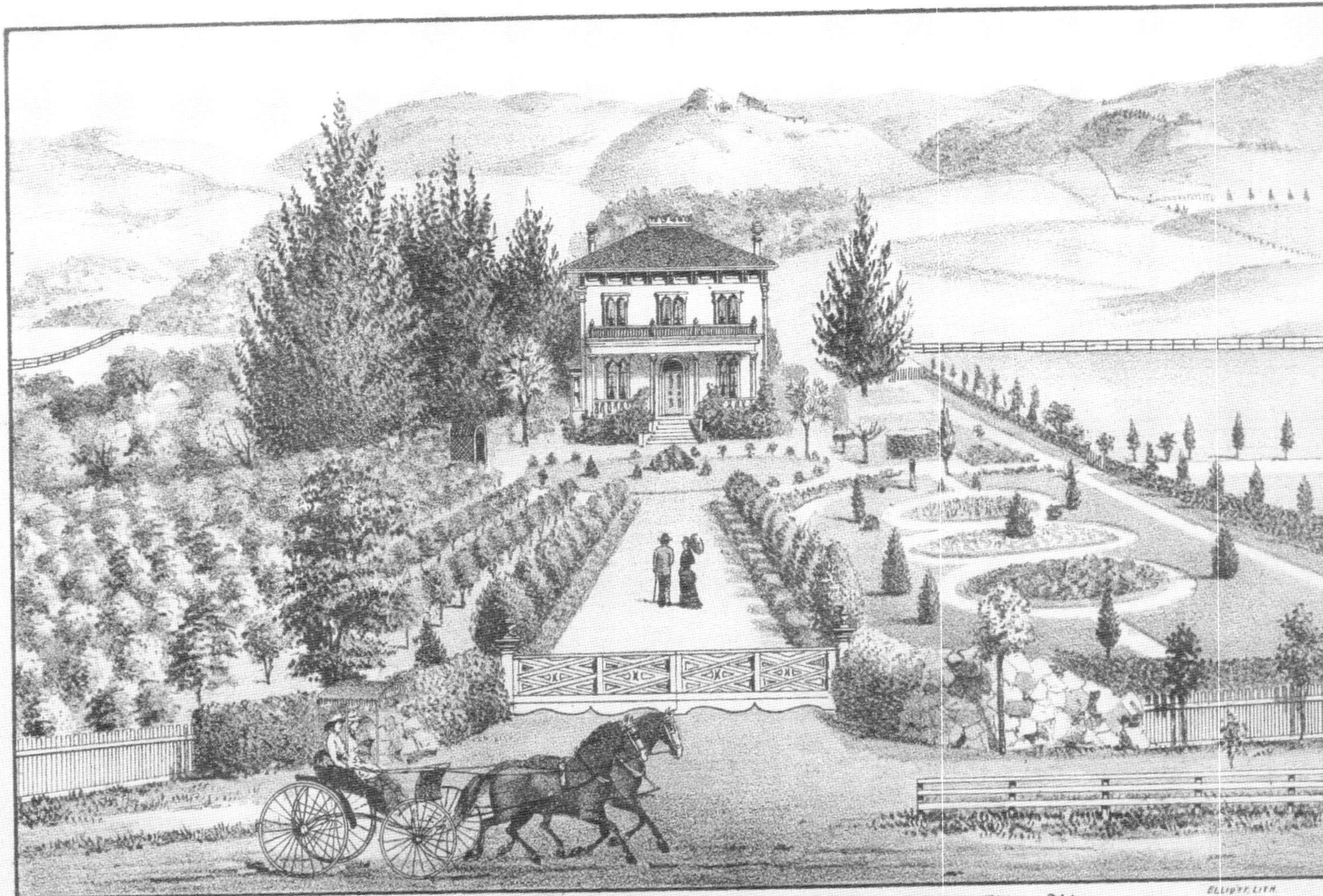

RESIDENCE OF **H. B. BERRYMAN**, BERRYMAN STATION, BERKELEY, CAL.

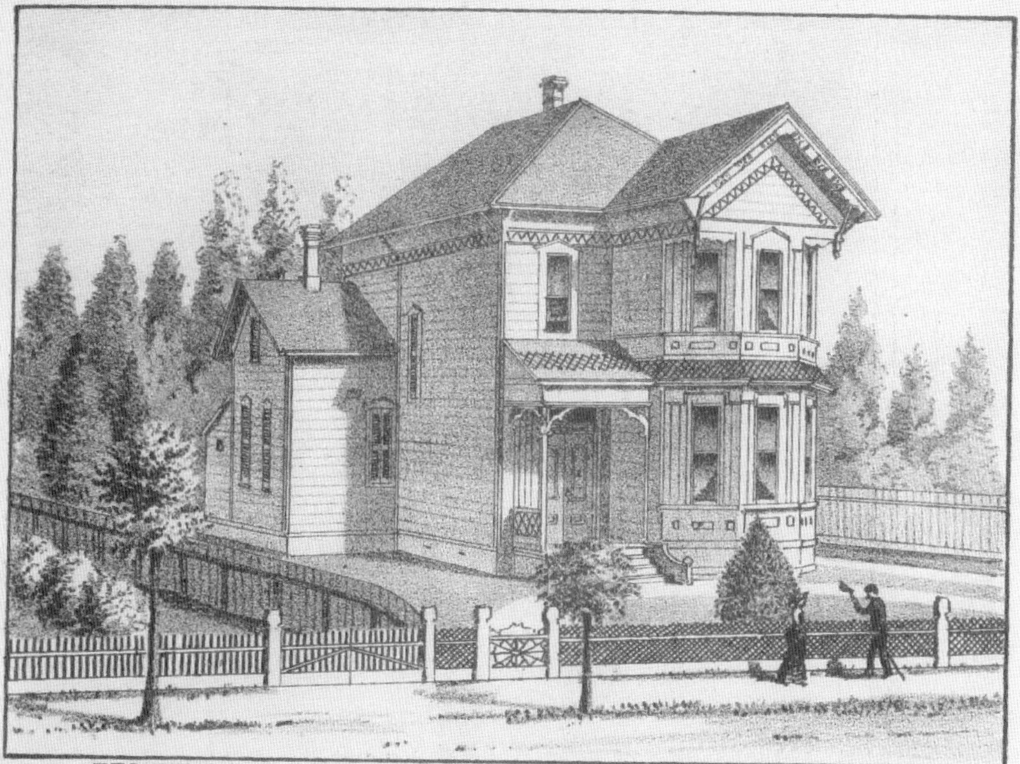

RESIDENCE OF ROBERT STEWART. DWIGHT WAY. BERKELEY CAL.

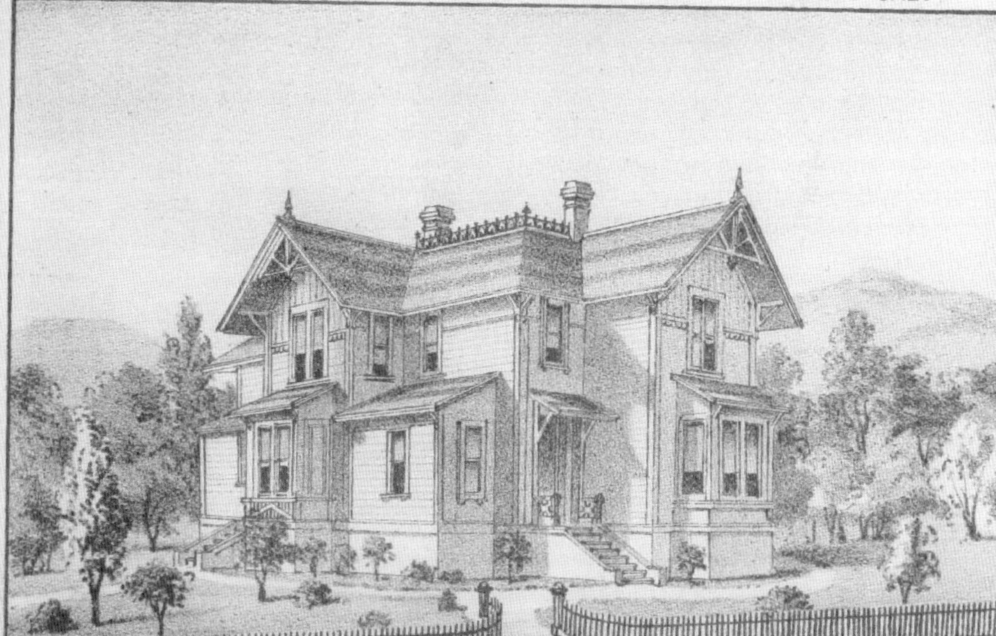

COTTAGE OF CHAS. K. CLARK. ESQ. BERKELEY. CAL.

except Sundays. The librarian is P. J. Ipsen.

Oakland contains a great many Sunday-school libraries. Among the largest are the First Presbyterian, First Congregational, First Methodist, St. John's, St. Paul's, and the Y. M. C. A. The State University library is also a large and valuable collection, described in another place.

Library of the University.

THE General Library, containing now over twenty-two thousand volumes, has been arranged with a view to making it especially valuable as a reference library. It receives a large number of periodical publications, literary, scientific, and general. Furnished with author and subject catalogues and full indexes, the library is preëminently a working collection. It is being constantly augmented by gift and purchase, especially from the income of the Reese Fund of $50,000. The beautiful and commodious Bacon Building affords abundant space for further growth.

The library began with one thousand volumes transferred with the property of the College of California. It has since rapidly increased. The present yearly income of about $4,000 is from a bequest of $50,000, made by Michael Reese. The library must grow from similar accretions, large and small. Its future magnificence will depend, therefore, largely on the liberality of wealthy citizens and the grateful gifts of those who have experienced the benefits of the University. As the library is a department of the University, the property of the State, and accessible to all citizens, it will be specially interesting and valuable to residents of Berkeley.

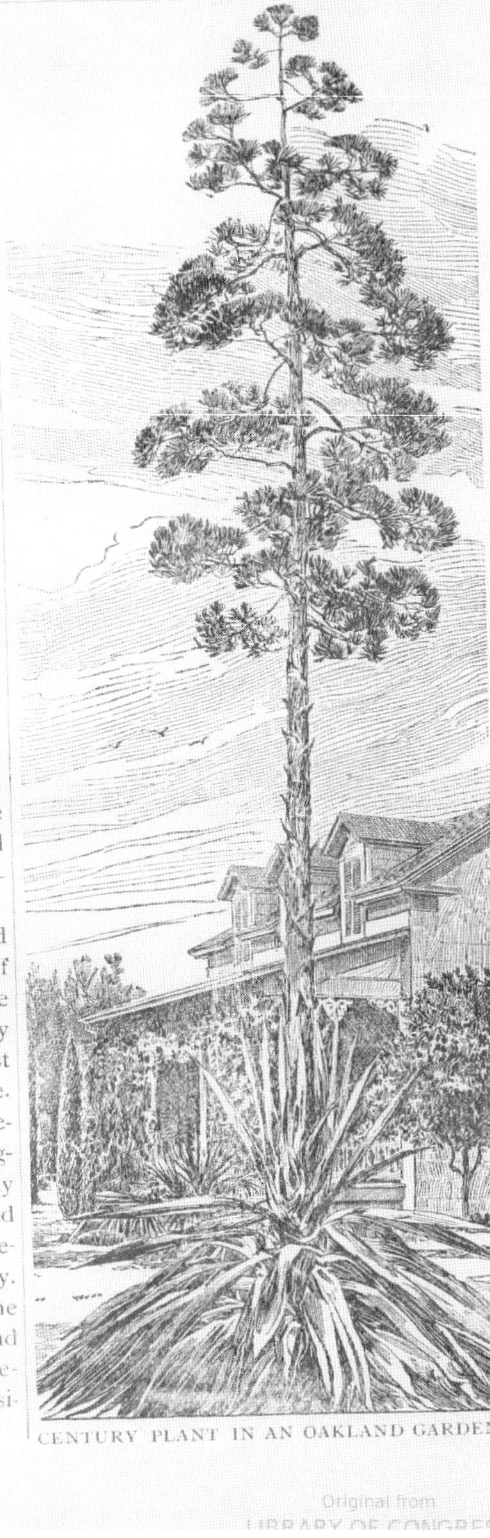

CENTURY PLANT IN AN OAKLAND GARDEN.

Parks and Places of Resort.

Blair's Park.

BLAIR'S PARK is a secluded and shady nook in a ravine or cañon of the foot-hills, and reached by the Piedmont cars. It has peculiar charms for picnic parties from the city and Oakland. With characteristic public spirit and good taste Mr. Blair has taken advantage of the natural surroundings of the gorge and of its native trees, and, by constructing walks and creating dams and bridges, has added to the natural charms of the locality. The walks are constructed without regard to the points of the compass, and the happy consequence is that, instead of uniform monotonous straight lines, there is a variety with natural curves and grades.

There is one quite large lake surrounded with oaks, laurel, and other trees, making it a delightful resort. In another place the creek has been dammed up by a substantial stone wall, thus forming a perfect little gem of a lake, from which the water falls by a beautiful cascade as shown in our sketch. The gentle undulations, the graceful slopes, the abrupt acclivities of the hills, all carpeted with the soft greensward, which, bedecked and bespangled with an endless variety of brilliant wild flowers intermingled with those of more modest hue, but not, therefore, less beautiful; the surface dotted here and there with copses of native shrubbery, the flowering madrona, the evergreen oak, the lofty and wide-spreading laurel,—all these constitute an extended and lovely parterre, which gratifies the eye, and constantly appeals with an irresistible charm to the innate sense of the beautiful.

On one side of the gorge is the narrow road, or highway, clinging to the hill-side, while at the bottom of the short, deep declivity the merry brooklet dances among the rocks. Tall brakes wave over its mossy banks, and here may be found their more delicate sisters,—

"The witching tangle of the maiden-hair,
The sweet grace of the gold and silver ferns,
The nodding coffee-fern with beauty rare,"—

Intermingled with a profusion of trailing vines and softly-tinted woodland denizens.

The sprightly little stream is spanned by a rustic foot-bridge, as shown in our illustration.

He who climbs the hill is enchanted with the landscape spread before him,—a view of the Golden Gate, and on out, till the eye catches the dim outlines of the Farallone Islands, some thirty miles away. One of the most magnificent views to be seen anywhere can be obtained by following up the pathway leading to the top of the mountain.

On either side the visitor will see, except in the six months of midsummer, wild flowers in countless numbers, far handsomer and more delicate than the common garden flowers of the Eastern States.

Occasional glimpses of the sea, or of the hills dotted with purple shadows, will delight him, also the air, which most of the time is mild and bracing.

To reach Blair's Park take the Piedmont cars at Washington Street on the arrival of the local train.

Mountain View Cemetery.

THIS beautiful cemetery is located in a northeasterly part of Oakland and easily reached by the Piedmont street-car line. It is two and one-half miles from the city hall, and is a beautiful place and well worth a visit. Its avenues are lined by choice flowers and supplied by beautiful fountains. There are handsome and costly monuments scattered through the grounds.

The plan of the Mountain View Cemetery was laid out by Mr. Frederick Law Olmstead, one of the most distinguished experts in landscape gardening, and his recommendations for its improvement and ornamentation are being carried out as nearly as possible.

It is recommended that each family lot contain one monument, with space for the several inscriptions likely to be required. Greater beauty will thus be secured than by separate head and foot stones. It is also more appropriate that the deceased members of a family be laid to rest around one monument, and that their names be grouped upon one tablet.

It is a part of the duty of the Superintendent to explain the plans to persons wanting lots, to give information concerning the choice of trees, their adaptation to the soil, and their arrangement with reference to the landscape. The laying out and platting of the extensive grounds of this association was the work of Frederick Law Olmstead, and the plans throughout bear the mark of a master hand.

Improvements are constantly being made, and the grounds, naturally picturesque, are receiving all the embellishments that art can suggest.

Entering this broad gateway, which is flanked by lodges and an inclosing wall, the road diverges into three separate avenues, the one on the left leading to the Catholic, the central one to the Hebrew, and the right hand to the Protestant quarter.

To the present time about six thousand interments have been made. The cemetery grounds are easy of access, the Piedmont street-cars running to the gateway.

Piedmont Springs and Surroundings.

FROM San Francisco and the bay a cluster of houses can be seen far up in the foot-hills, where they merge in the steeper ascents of the Coast Range. This is Piedmont, a place of retired elegance and unlimited prospect. It has an altitude of from three to six hundred feet, and is therefore above the frost-line. It enjoys comparative freedom from the fogs that cover the plains below. The trade-winds lose much of their severity before they reach it.

From no point can the peculiarities of the scenery of the region be better observed. The hills rise above into peaks crowned with farms and wooded lands. Below, they fall away in graceful undulations. Here the eucalyptus shows masses

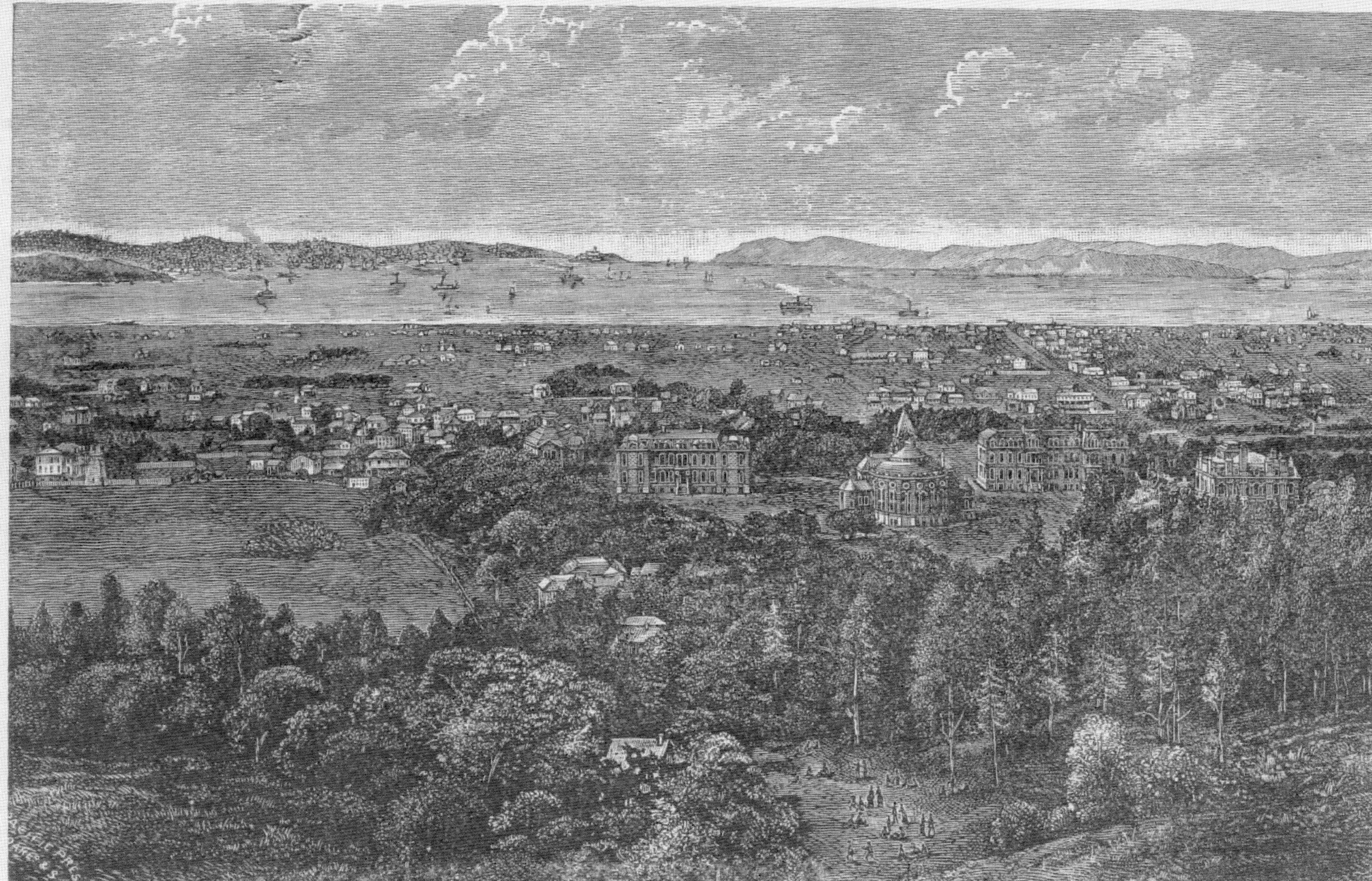

VIEW OF BERKELEY FROM HILL IN REAR OF UNIVERSITY GROUNDS SHOWING THE BAY, SAN FRANCISCO, ALCATRAZ, AND THE GOLDEN GATE.

of forest. There it clusters in groves, stretches out in martial lines, or expands in squares of military exactness. The chaparral covers with its mantle of dark green the great wrinkles of the hill-sides. The view combines the boldness of mountain scenery with the soft and pleasing qualities of English landscape. From every point, hill, plain, city, and ocean is visible and present an enchanted view to the beholder.

Many eligible sites are already occupied with dwellings that fit into their handsome surroundings as into a natural framework. On one sightly knoll stands the home of James Gamble, formerly Superintendent of the Western Union Telegraph Company. An artist has made a sketch of this fine place, and it appears in our illustrations of fine residences. The grounds are on a location commanding the entire country from the Napa and Solano Hills to Mount Bache in the Santa Cruz Range. Its sloping lawns are filled with trees and shrubbery artistically arranged. Many well-known men have purchased lots in Piedmont, on which they intend building. A. N. Towne, General Manager of the Central Pacific Railroad, has chosen one of the most desirable locations.

A line of street-cars, which winds up through fields, groves, orchards, and avenues set with cedar and red-stemmed eucalyptus, affords easy and pleasant access to Piedmont. Water is supplied abundantly from living springs, and from pipes connecting with the city water works. Gas is also plentifully supplied and can be had at a moment's notice.

Springs containing sulphur, magnesia, and iron flow from the hill-sides, and possess such rare medicinal virtues that the place would quickly become a fashionable health resort, were hotel accommodations furnished, and were the presence of fashion desired.

Neptune Gardens.

THE Neptune Gardens and Long Branch Baths were constructed by the South Pacific Coast Railroad. The big pavilion combines the features of an immense roller skating rink, dancing pavilion, refreshment saloon, cafe chantant, or military drill-room, as necessity required. The site chosen was on the beach line just under a small bluff that bounds the Neptune Garden on its water front. Here a foundation was laid by pile driving in the sand, no less than 710 piles being driven ten feet apart down to hard bottom, and a structure reared that now, in a nearly completed state, measures 413x150 feet. The floor, which is about this area, is laid with asphalt cement over timbers, and the space from it to the bridge of the roof is fifty feet in the center, sloping to twenty-eight feet at the sides. A line of twelve heavy columns in the center helps to support the twenty-one trusses that form the roof cap, the trusses being braced by iron rods and the roof shingled. Two hundred and fifty thousand feet of lumber have been used in the construction of the pavilion. These places of resort are reached by the cars of the Southern Pacific Railroad from either San Francisco or Oakland every half hour.

THERE are three theaters generally in successful operation. The oldest is Dietz Opera House, situated on the corner of Twelfth and Webster Streets.

Oakland Theater is the largest building used for theatrical plays and will seat a very large number of people. It is located on Twelfth Street near Webster and is only one story high and very convenient of entrance and exit.

The Park Theater is, as its name indicates, situated opposite the City Hall Park and under new management has improved.

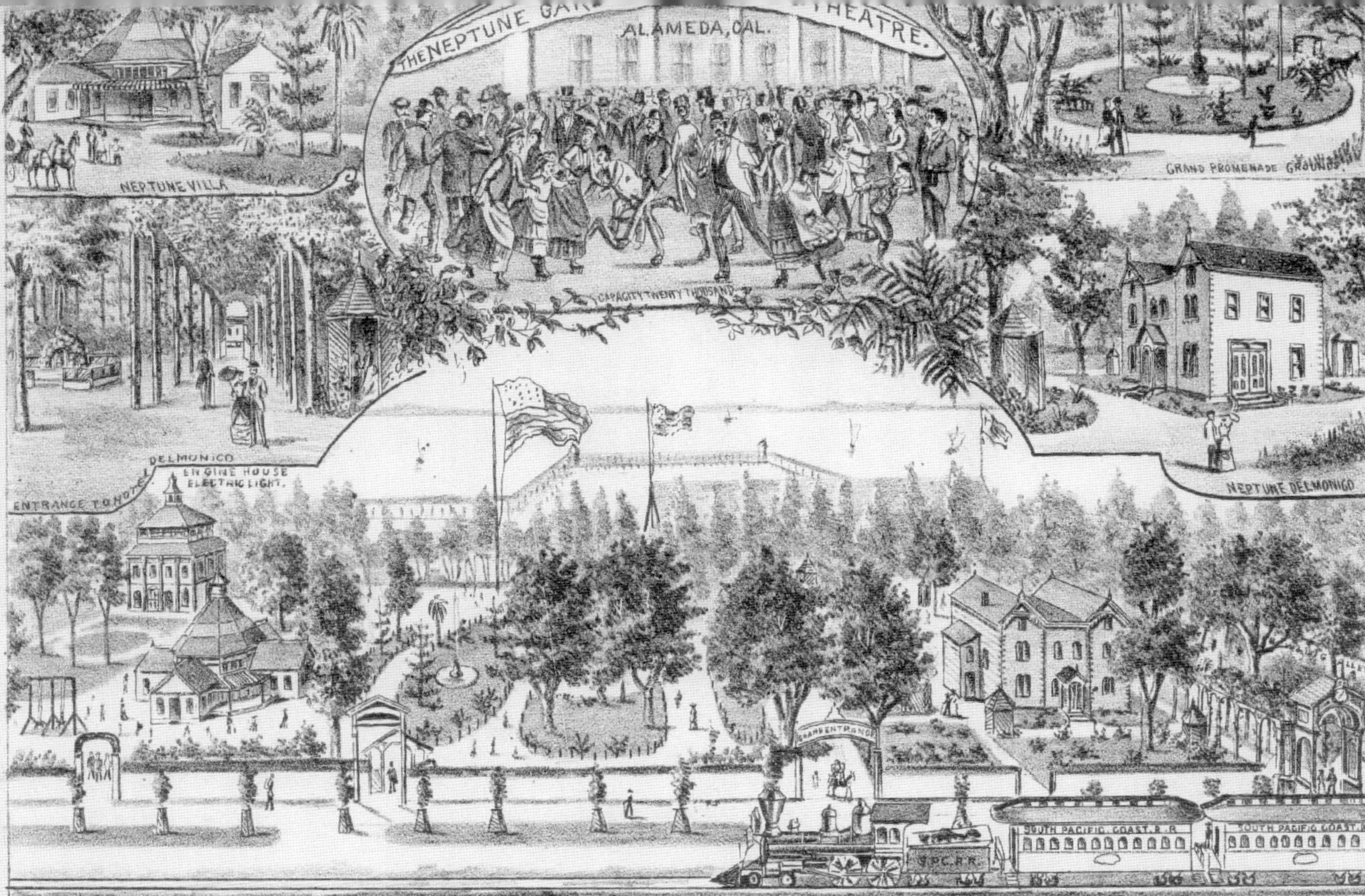

ELLIOTT LITHO.

NEPTUNE GARDENS A DELIGHTFUL FAMILY RESORT MUST BE SEEN TO BE APPRECIATED.
☞ LOCAL TRAINS OF NARROW GAUGE R. R. STOP AT DEPOT IN FRONT EVERY HALF HOUR.

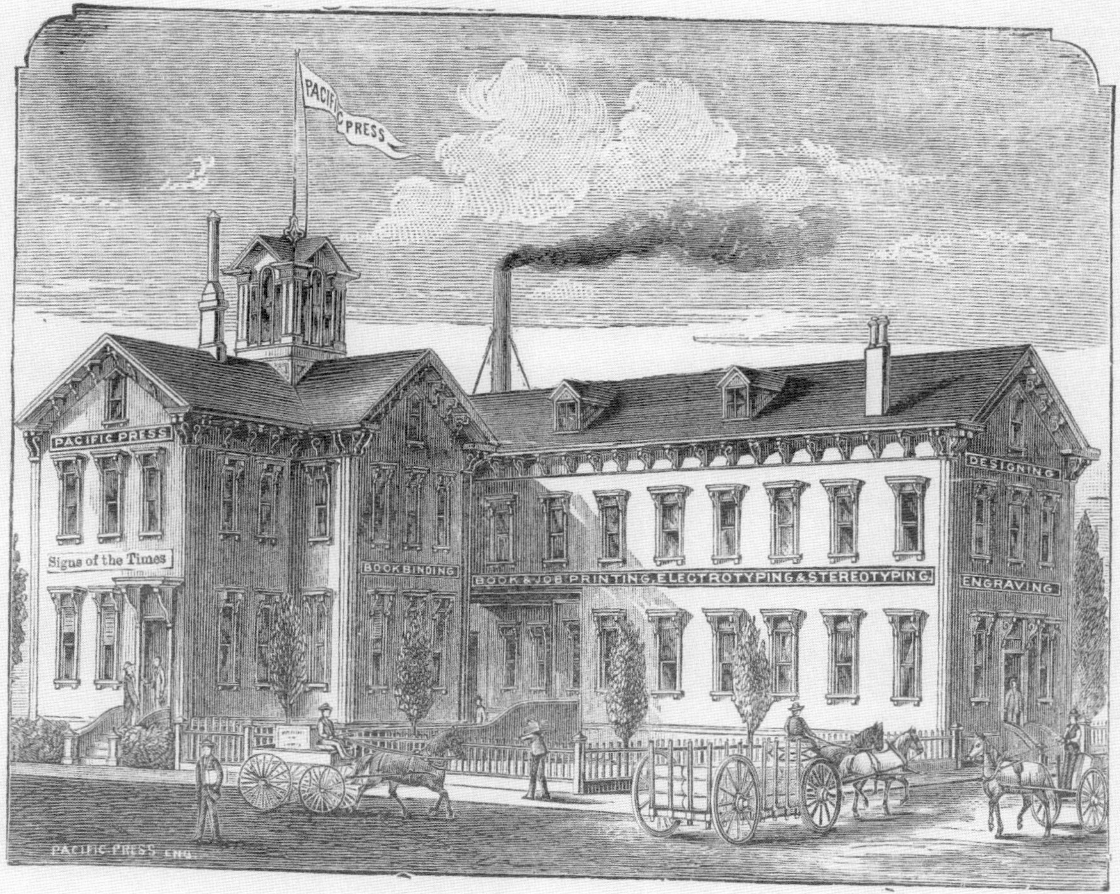

PACIFIC PRESS PUBLISHING HOUSE, CORNER TWELFTH AND CASTRO STREETS.

University Museums.

THE museums of the University at Berkeley are made up from materials obtained mainly from the following sources: The *State Geological Collection*, which has been placed at the disposal of the University; the *Voy Collection*, consisting of a large number of fossils, minerals, rocks, etc., collected by Mr. C. D. Voy, and presented to the University by D. O. Mills, Esq.; the *Pioche Collection*, an extensive miscellaneous collection of oil paintings, minerals, rocks, ores, shells, etc., from all parts of the world, and especially from South America, presented to the University by the late F. L. A. Pioche; the *Hanks Collection*, consisting of miscellaneous minerals and rocks, presented by James R. Keene, Esq., of San Francisco; oil paintings and statuary, presented by Henry D. Bacon; purchase by the University, and current donations.

The MUSEUM OF FINE ARTS, first opened on May 29, 1882, is located in the Bacon Art and Library Building. It contains sixty-six paintings and three pieces of statuary, presented by Henry D. Bacon, and several paintings.

The MUSEUM OF CLASSICAL ARCHÆOLOGY contains a small cabinet of coins and medals, including over four hundred ancient coins, mostly Roman, about three hundred and fifty medals, and a like number of modern coins.

The MUSEUM OF ETHNOLOGY contains many remarkable stone implements and skulls from the Pacific Coast.

The MUSEUM OF ZOOLOGY contains a small collection of mammals, birds, reptiles, fishes, and recent mollusks and radiates.

The MUSEUM OF ENTOMOLOGY contains the collection of beetles made by Mr. E. Ricksecker. It contains over two thousand species, well determined, and fully accessible for purposes of instruction.

The MUSEUM OF BOTANY contains a valuable herbarium of Australian plants, a collection of native woods, cones, and photographs of the characteristic trees of California. The private collection of Professor Hilgard, containing some twelve thousand specimens of American and foreign plants, is deposited in the agricultural lecture room for the use of the students.

The MUSEUM OF HISTORICAL GEOLOGY is in process of formation.

The MUSEUM OF PALÆONTOLOGY contains a full suite of the fossils of California, both animal and vegetable.

The MUSEUM OF PETROGRAPHY contains many foreign rocks, but is especially rich in California material, collected by the corps of the State Geological Survey, and by Mr. C. D. Voy.

The MUSEUM OF ECONOMIC GEOLOGY, although so recently founded, is already large, and is in frequent receipt of valuable acquisitions from all parts of the Pacific Coast.

The MUSEUM OF MINERALOGY is very large and fully arranged, and is supplied with ample case room.

The MUSEUM OF METALLURGY is designed to illustrate the metallurgical processes pursued at all the mills and reduction works on the coast, by means of sets of specimens from each establishment, showing ores, fluxes, fuels, roasted products, slags, chlorination products, etc.

The MUSEUM OF MODELS contains a small but valuable collection of machine and furnace models.

The MUSEUM OF AGRICULTURE contains a collection of about eight hundred specimens of the soils of this State, to which frequent additions are made. The interest is good in this department.

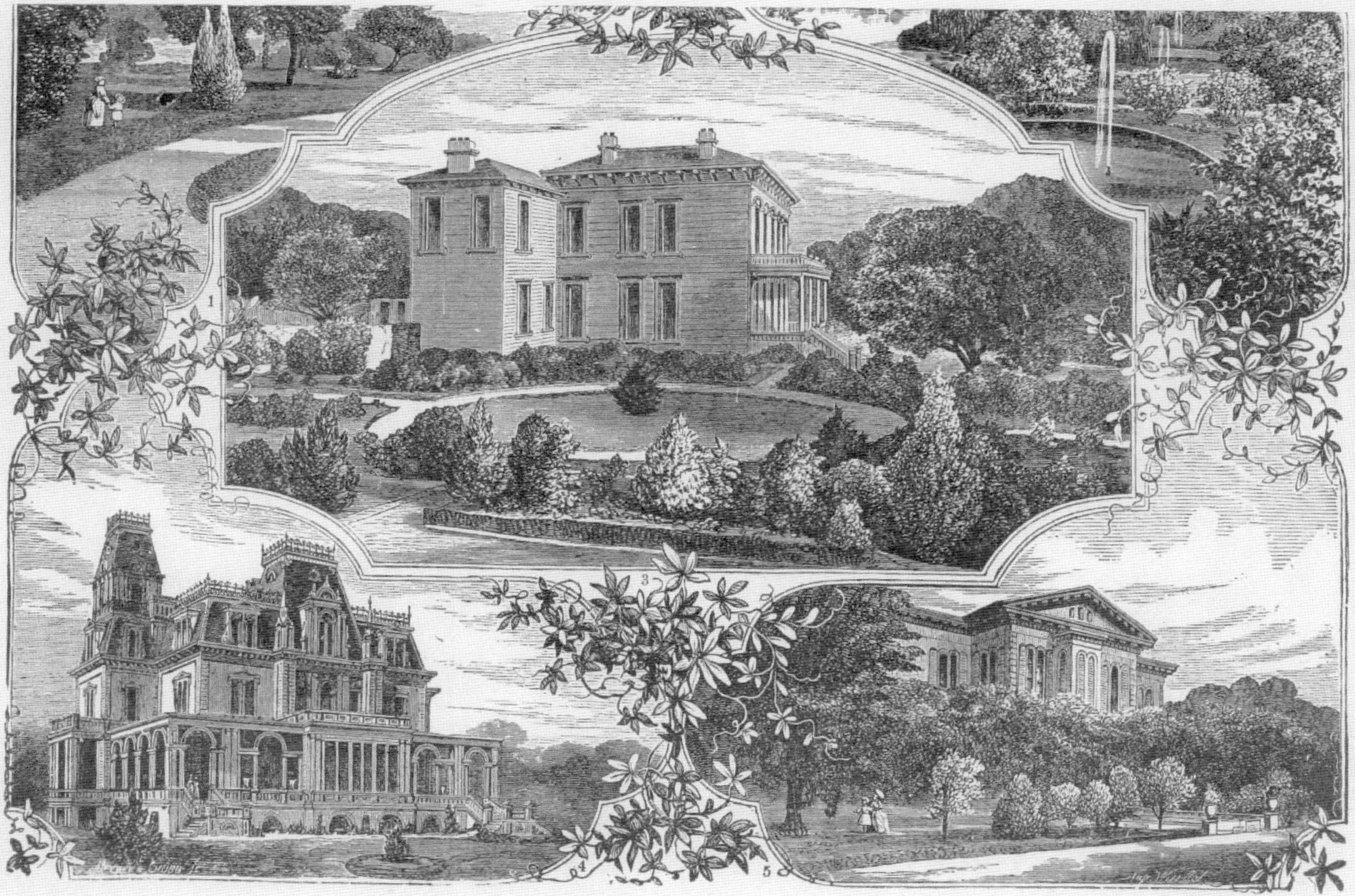

RESIDENCES, GARDENS AND SCENERY IN OAKLAND.

Shell Mound Park.

THIS park is situated between Emery Station and the Oakland Trotting Park, on the Berkeley Railroad, and is reached every thirty minutes, *via* Oakland Ferry, from San Francisco. It derives its name from one of the ancient Indian shell-mounds, which is still in a fine state of preservation, and rises to a height of sixty feet, its summit being crowned with a dancing pavilion. The park was first opened as a holiday resort in 1876, by E. Wiard, but in 1880 it was leased for ten years to Capt. Ludwig Siebe, who has made various and extensive improvements within the domain. The park contains two of the largest dancing pavilions on the Pacific Coast, a race track for games, with covered seats accommodating 2,000 people; turning apparatus, swings, flying-horses, bowling-alley, a shooting-range, containing four thirty-yard targets, one one hundred-yard target, twelve two hundred-yard targets, and four five hundred-yard targets; fruit and ice-cream stand, and shooting-gallery, and a dining-room, where meals are served in good order to the satisfaction of the public in general.

Oakland Trotting Park.

THIS tract was originally laid out in 1871, by E. Wiard, the present proprietor, and is justly considered among the finest on the Pacific Coast. It is one mile in circumference, being also fitted with all modern and necessary improvements. It contains 200 box-stalls for horses, and 200 cattle-stalls, and is situated opposite Shell Mound Park, on the line of the Central Pacific Railroad, trains passing it every half hour. In 1879 it was here that the famous St. Julian lowered the record of the world, and trotted a mile in two minutes twelve and a quarter seconds.

Schutzen Park.

THESE excursion grounds, situated in Alameda, were opened to the public early in the year 1868, and are the property of the Schutzen Loan and Building Society. They comprise between seven and eight acres of land, and contain all the necessary apparatus to make it a place of resort and picnic grounds. There are a dancing pavilion, swings, shooting-ranges, and other things of interest and attraction.

Oakland Nursery.

THE visitor will be amply paid for the time in making a visit to the large nursery of R. Groves, situated between Shell Mound Park and the Race Track. Take the San Pablo Avenue cars. Here will be found ferns and ornamental plants in great variety. Hundreds of varieties of roses, fruit-trees, and shrubs of numerous kinds have been shipped to various points on the coast. Mr. Groves' reputation for rose culture is unsurpassed, as well as his taste and success in the growth of an endless variety of plants, flowers, fruit and ornamental trees, especially adapted to this delightful and unsurpassed climate.

Public Squares or Parks.

THERE are eight squares and two plazas in Oakland, but only a few of these have been improved. Lafayette Square, on which is located the Observatory, has been laid out to lawn and graveled walks, fountains, and flowers, with the Observatory in the center. Jef-

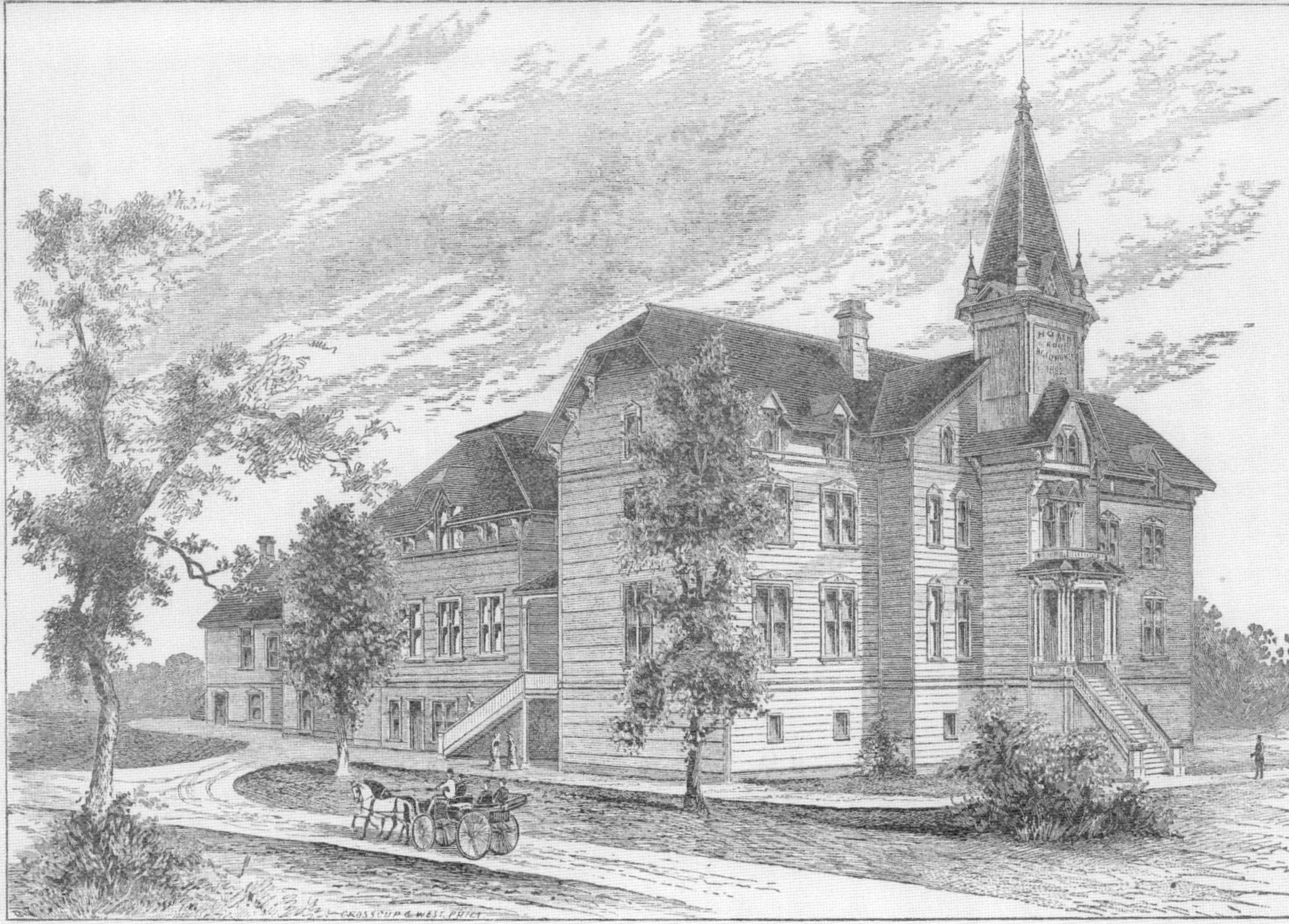

HOME FOR AGED WOMEN.

ferson Square has also been considerably improved, and is beautiful in its native live-oaks.

The squares are as follows:—

Franklin, bounded by Fourth, Franklin, Fifth, and Broadway; 300x200 ft.; valued at $75,000.

Harrison, bounded by Sixth, Alice, Seventh, and Harrison Streets; 300x200 ft.; valued at $17,000.

Independence, bounded by East Sixteenth Street, Eighteenth Avenue, East Nineteenth Street, and Sixteenth Avenue; 660x660 ft.; valued at $25,000.

Jefferson, bounded by Sixth, Jefferson, Seventh, and Grove Streets; 300x200 ft.; valued at $90,000.

Lafayette, bounded by Tenth, Jefferson, Eleventh, and Grove Streets; 300x200 ft.; valued at $28,000.

Madison, bounded by Eighth, Oak, Ninth, and Madison Streets; 300x200 ft.; valued at $28,000.

Oakland, bounded by Tenth, Alice, Eleventh, and Harrison Streets; 300x200 ft.; valued at $28,000.

Washington, bounded by Fourth, Broadway, Fifth, and Washington; 300x200 ft.; valued at $90,000.

Clinton Plaza, bounded by Twelfth, Street, Seventh Avenue, East Fourteenth Street, and Sixth Avenue; 300x160 ft.; valued at $6,000.

Caroline Square, between Second and Third Avenue, north of East Fifteenth Street; 300x300 ft.; valued at $14,000.

City Hall Park, 143x207 ft., and 422 ft. on Fourteenth Street and 276 ft. on San Pablo Avenue; valued at $140,000.

In May, 1859, Washington Square was given to the county, and, at a later period, Franklin Square, which was opposite, on condition that the county buildings, Court House and Hall of Records, be located there.

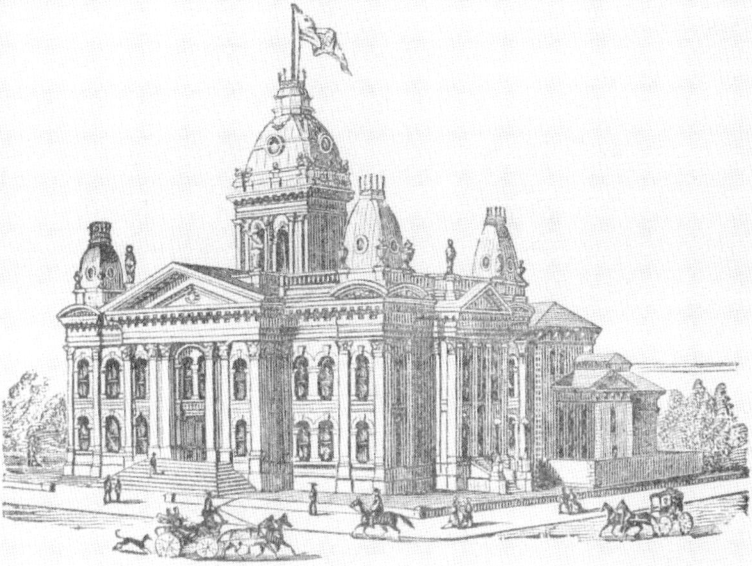

COUNTY COURT HOUSE.

Private Schools.

Private Schools.

BESIDES the public schools, the University and the Medical College, there are some twenty-four private schools, with about seven hundred pupils. Among the principal ones we may mention the Home School for Young Ladies; Notre Dame Academy. Alameda; Pagoda Hill Kindergarten; D. P. Sackett's School for Young Men; California Military Academy; Hopkins Academy; Oakland Business College; St. Joseph's Presentation Academy; Convent of Our Lady of the Sacred Heart; Miss Humphrey's School; St. Mary's Academy; St. Lawrence School; Harmon Seminary; Oakland Normal School; Miss Horton's School, and St. Joseph's Academy, conducted by the Christian Brothers.

Notre Dame Academy.

THIS institution conducted by the Sisters of Notre Dame—a branch of College of Notre Dame, San Jose—affords an opportunity of procuring for young girls, at a very moderate expense, a good moral and intellectual education.

The academy is favorably situated in Alameda near the bay. The climate of Alameda is not surpassed, and the facilities for reaching the place are frequent and convenient. The course of studies embraces the various branches of a solid and useful education. The scholastic year commences the second week in July, and ends the last of May.

It is situated on Chestnut Street, between San Antonio and San Jose Avenues, and easily reached by railroads or street-cars. We present our readers with a page view of this institution.

Sackett School.

ONE of the most substantial preparatory schools of California is the Sackett School, Hobart Street, Oakland. It was founded in 1878, by its present proprietor, Prof. D. P. Sackett. With modest beginnings the school slowly but surely came into prominence until it has twice become necessary to enlarge the building to accommodate the increasing patronage. Hand in hand with this increase of patronage has gone an enlargement of facilities offered to the students.

Three lines of street-cars pass within about a block of the school premises, but they are most directly reached by the Telegraph Avenue line from the Broadway railway station, the time from San Francisco being forty minutes.

The location of the school is central, and yet as retired and remote from the din and bustle of the city as though it were miles away in the country.

Attention is especially directed to the home-like and attractive grounds, and to the internal arrangement of the buildings looking to the convenience and comfort of the students.

The institution is pledged to furnish the most careful, intellectual, and moral training. The best instruction is provided by teachers of large experience and recognized ability. The foremost journal of our country has recently used the following language addressed to the school department of New York City: "Strengthen the *basis* of the school system before you increase the superstructure. Teach few things, but teach them so they will be *absolutely known*. First give the child what will be essential for the practical business of life, and a basis for self-improvement." This sentiment coincides exactly with the teaching and aims of this school. Thoroughness is insisted on, without which the student is practically helpless, and on which, as a foundation, all sound education must rest.

The school provides three distinct departments of instruction, viz., the Academic, including Classical, English, and Commerical courses; the Intermediate and the Primary. The schedule of studies is arranged to carry students from the earliest processes of education to the point where they shall have acquired the preparation necessary to enable them to enter the University of California, or any Eastern university or college; to fit them for the best scientific schools, or for business, as may be desired.

The recreation of the students is regular and wholesome. Aside from the usual outdoor games of foot-ball and base-ball, a gymnasium has been built, directly in the rear of the main building, which is equipped with most approved kinds of apparatus, consisting of ladders, rings, parallel bars, vaulting bars, Indian clubs, etc.

No substitute has yet been found for the voluntary, vigorous, daily exercise of the student in the open air. Health of body and grasp of mind alike depend upon this. Hence no pains have been spared to make the department of physical culture equal in its efficiency to the moral and the intellectual training of the school.

A reading and social room has also been provided, where the best dailies, scientific journals, and magazines will always be found.

Day scholars as well as boarding pupils are received into the school and share all of its advantages.

The present graduating class is the largest in the history of the school. It includes candidates for the Sophomore Class of our State University, for Yale College, and for active business life. The school as a whole. notwithstanding business depression, is larger than it was one year ago, thus showing the interest and sympathy of the people at large, which the institution richly deserves to have.

Pagoda Hill Kindergarten.

THE Pagoda Hill Kindergarten derived its name from the hill on which it was situated at the time of its opening, in January, 1883, a place among the foot-hills of Oakland, north of Temescal.

The hill was so named by the late J. Ross Browne, near whose residence was that of Miss Alice Phelps, the principal of the Kindergarten. The school was opened at the principal's own house, Jan-

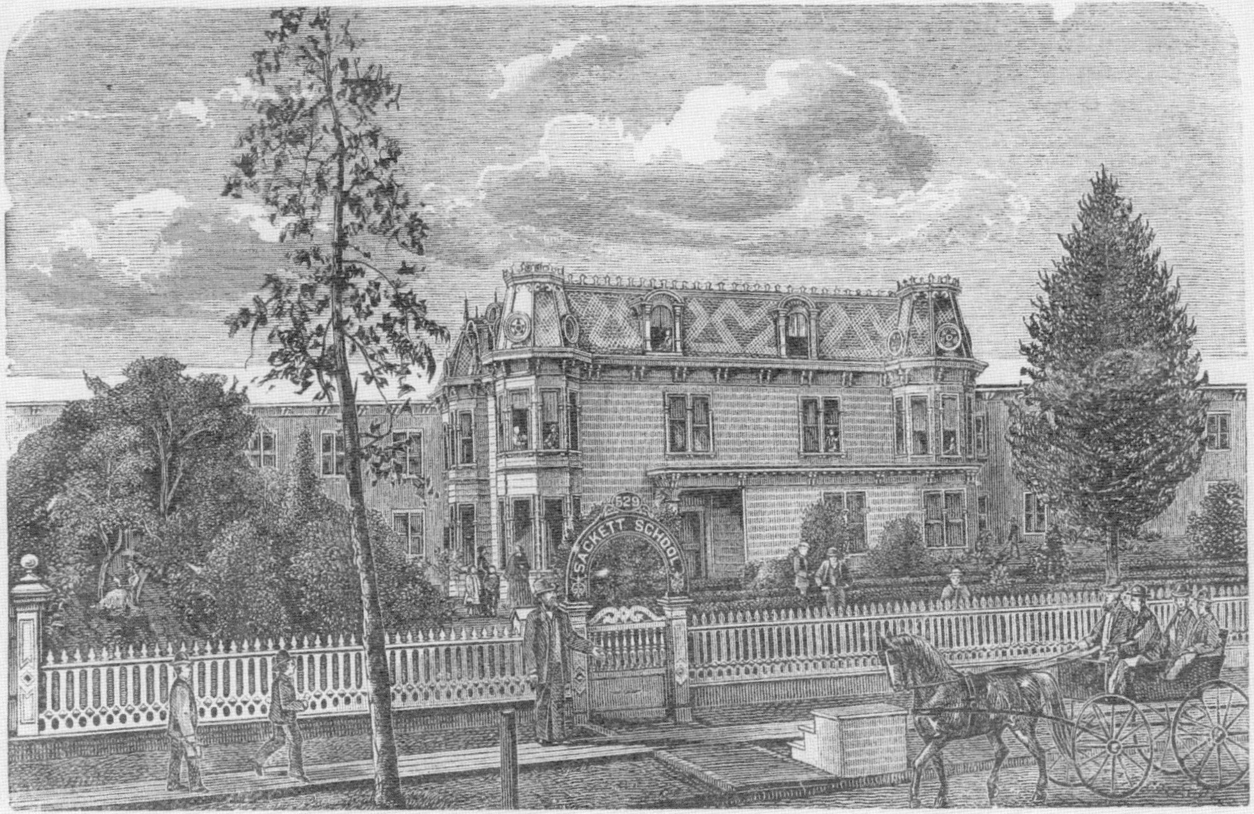
529
SACKETT SCHOOL

uary 2, 1883. Although twenty children had been promised, only seven were there on the morning of the first day, all living in the immediate vicinity.

Within a month, applications came for children living in Oakland, and they were brought to the school and taken home in the family carriage. As the number increased, a larger conveyance became necessary, and in May a large and comfortable bus was running between Oakland and Pagoda Hill, and was soon well filled with children from all parts of Oakland. Although the situation on the hill was a most delightful one, and the ride to and from the city one of great benefit to the little travelers, it soon became evident, from the increasing numbers, that it would be impossible to accommodate them all, either in the omnibus or at the house. Accordingly, in January of the next year the school was opened at 1513 Telegraph Avenue, Oakland, in a large, sunny house, well adapted for the purpose, and, in a short time, between fifty and sixty little ones were in daily attendance.

The present term began July 13, 1885, and the number enrolled, thirty-five, the older children who were in attendance the year before having gone to public schools.

The omnibus leaves the house at 7:30 A. M., to gather up the children, a teacher always being present to care for them. Two trips are made, the first to take in children from one part of town, who are left at the house about 8:30 o'clock; the second trip is made to the opposite side of town, for the remaining children. The second load reaches the house at 9:30, the hour for opening.

There are two teachers in the Kindergarten, one the principal, Miss M. A. Phelps, the other, her assistant, Miss Anna Warner, who has been with Miss Phelps from the opening of the school. Both are graduates of the California Kindergarten Training School, of San Francisco. Mrs. C. B. Phelps, the mother of the principal, is of material assistance in caring for the children, always attending them in the trips to and from school.

A cordial invitation is given to the public to visit the Kindergarten. Visitors are welcome on any day at any hour between 9:30 A. M. and 3:00 P. M.

For any further particulars see circular, which can be procured at the Kindergarten, 1513 Telegraph Avenue, Oakland.

Hopkins Academy.

REV. H. E. JEWETT, PRINCIPAL.

THE academy buildings stand upon a low hill in the city of Oakland, on a line with Thirty-fourth Street, between Telegraph Avenue and Broadway. The grounds comprise several acres, a portion of which is laid out in a lawn and drives, and a portion reserved for a play-ground. The location is healthful, retired, and beautiful. It may be reached by either the Telegraph Avenue or the Broadway and Piedmont line of horse-cars. The carriage entrance is on Webster Street.

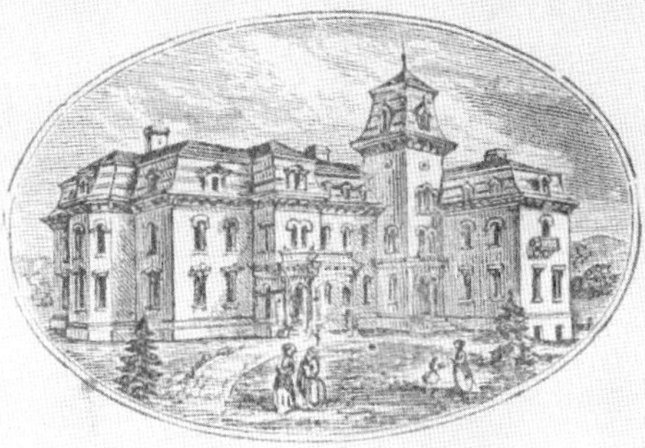

HOPKINS ACADEMY.

Hopkins Academy, like Phillips Academy, in Andover, Massachusetts, has been founded by Christian men as a fitting school for college and for business life.

It shapes its curriculum to meet the requirements of admission to any college

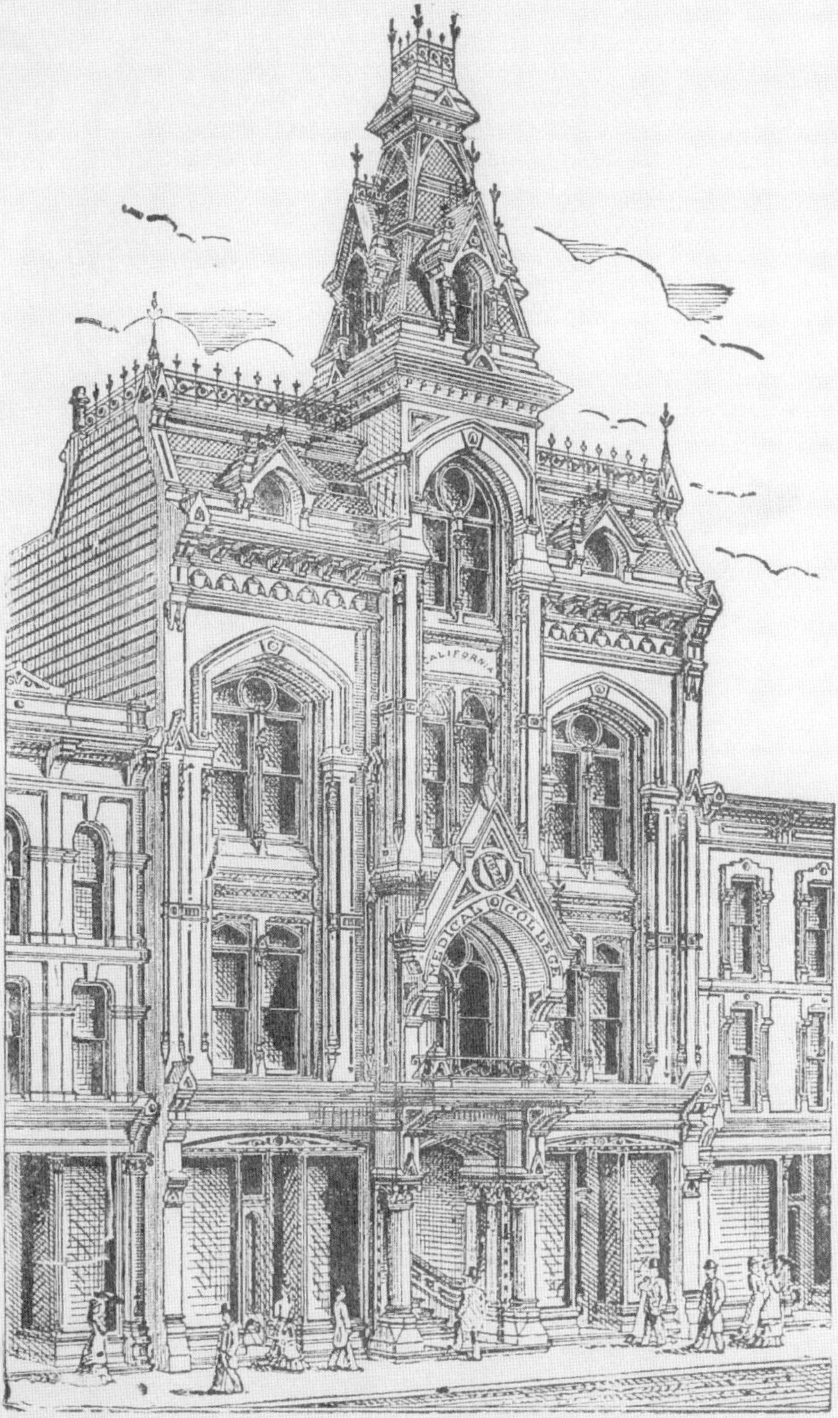

MEDICAL COLLEGE, CLAY STREET, BET. TENTH AND ELEVENTH STREETS, OAKLAND, CAL.

East or West, to which young men graduating from it may desire to apply for admission. The course of study, as usually followed, recognizes the requirements for admission to our own State institution, the University of California, but any one entering the academy having in view entrance to one of the older colleges, such as Yale, Harvard, Amherst, Williams, Dartmouth, etc., will be fitted for the institution of his choice.

Those who have business life in view will be directed in their studies along a practical business course.

To meet the needs of younger pupils a preparatory department is provided for young boys, and for those whose previous advantages have been limited.

Believing that mental discipline is not the whole of education, this institution, in its relation to its pupils, exalts moral principle and Christian faith. It seeks to promote high scholarship, practical knowledge, and Christian character. Physical culture, by means of manly sports and friendly competitions in field games, is largely encouraged. A gymnasium, well equipped with apparatus, is open daily to the members of the school.

The institution takes its name in recognition of the generous gifts of Mr. Moses Hopkins, of San Francisco, who, with others, has placed the school upon a firm financial foundation.

CALENDAR FOR 1886, FIFTEENTH YEAR.

Second term begins Tuesday, A. M., January 5, 1886.

Quarterly recess, March 12–15.

Year closes Friday, May 21.

Field Day, April 30, 1886.

Graduating Exercises, May 21, 1886.

SPENCERIAN BUSINESS COLLEGE is located at 1069 Broadway. The methods used are those practiced in the largest and best schools of the East. The rooms are centrally located, well arranged and lighted. Nothing is taught in the abstract. Principles are applied as they are developed, and everything is thorough.

Convent of Our Lady of the Sacred Heart.

THIS institution was established in the year 1868, by the Sisters of the Holy Name of Jesus and Mary. To the Rev. M. King, pastor of the Church of the Immaculate Conception, is due much credit for material aid and assistance rendered the institution at its inception. In 1873-74 a substantial building, three stories in height, and one hundred and ten feet long by seventy-five feet wide, was erected on Webster Street, near the head of Lake Merritt. The interior arrangement of this building meets every demand of a complete boarding-school.

The basement contains a gymnasium. The first floor contains parlors, library, and music rooms. On the second story are class-rooms, and in every part of the building modern appliances and improvements are to be seen.

Owing to its proximity to Lake Merritt, facilities are afforded the pupils for that pleasurable exercise, boating.

In addition to the branches usually taught in schools of a similar grade, the art of cooking, as a study, here finds a place in the curriculum.

The Harmon Seminary.

THE Harmon Seminary for young ladies is situated on Atherton Street, Berkeley, near the State University. The building is a fine, commodious, three-story villa, erected in 1882 and especially planned for a home-like school.

Both boarding and day pupils are received, and all ages are provided for. The courses of instruction are several, including a full seminary course, leading to a graduation diploma, also courses to preparation for the University, and elective courses in English and French literature, science, vocal and instrumental music, etc. In music, art, and modern languages, the instructors are the foremost San Francisco masters. The regular instruction in the ordinary branches is by teachers of recognized ability and skill. The discipline of the school is firm and watchful, yet cordial and kindly. Every effort is made to secure the comfort and good health of the pupil, as well as intellectual advancement. The sanitary condition of the buildings and surroundings is unexceptional. The institution is patronized by a large number of the leading families of Berkeley and vicinity, who send their daughters as day pupils, and the boarding pupils come from all parts of the coast. A catalogue is published, which gives full description of the seminary. The principals are Misses Harmon, Berkeley, California.

St. Joseph's Presentation Convent.

THIS flourishing institution was built and founded by the late lamented Mother Mary Teresa Comerford, in the year 1878, for the purpose of gratuitously educating girls. It is a large and handsome building, on the north, south, and west of which is a spacious. well-cultivated fruit and flower garden. The property on which this useful institution stands was donated to the founders by James Magee, who was also one of the most liberal contributors towards the erection of this commodious convent.

Opposite the convent, and fronting Addison Street, is the residence of the Very Reverend Pierce Michael Comerford, late vicar-general and apostolic missionary of the Mauritius, in the Indian Ocean. This pretty residence was erected by him in the year 1879, and he has since beautified it by many improvements. In the same year he became rector of the Parish of St. Joseph, in which position he has labored zealously and effectually for the welfare of his parishioners. In 1880 he erected St. Peter's free school for boys, which has a very steady attendance of pupils, taught by the nuns of the convent. And lastly, in the summer of 1883, he erected St. Joseph's handsome gothic church northeast of the convent. It is a small but perfectly symmetrical building, and when finished will be one of the prettiest edifices of the kind in this country.

California Medical College.

THIS college was organized May 17, 1878, by J. Watson Webb, M. D., and is located on Clay Street, between Tenth and Eleventh Streets, within five minutes' walk of the City Hall and Court House, and two blocks west of Broadway. It is about thirty minutes' travel from San Francisco by the half-hour ferry plying between the two cities.

The plan of the building excels any similar institution west of Chicago. It is four stories in height. On the second floor are a magnificent hall, and three suits of offices. On the third floor are the amphitheater, a museum, library, and laboratory. The dissecting room, the best appointed on the coast, is spacious and thoroughly ventilated by means of the dome.

This college is organized as the exponent of liberal and progressive medicine and surgery, and aims to present to the student medical science in all its breadth.

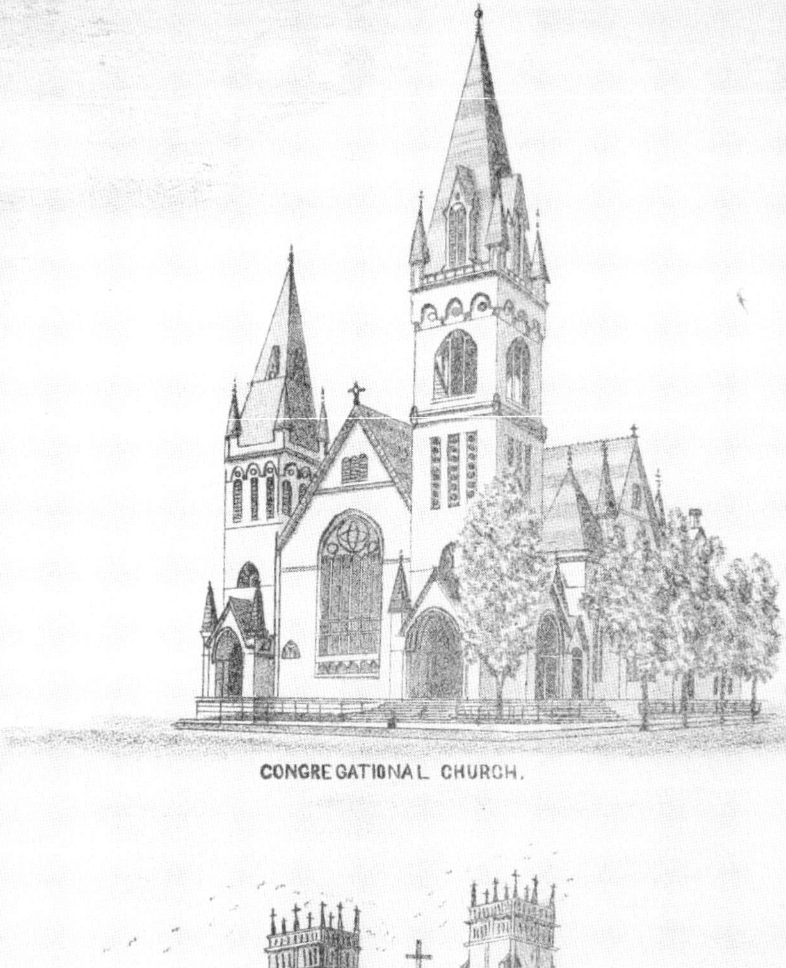

CONGREGATIONAL CHURCH.

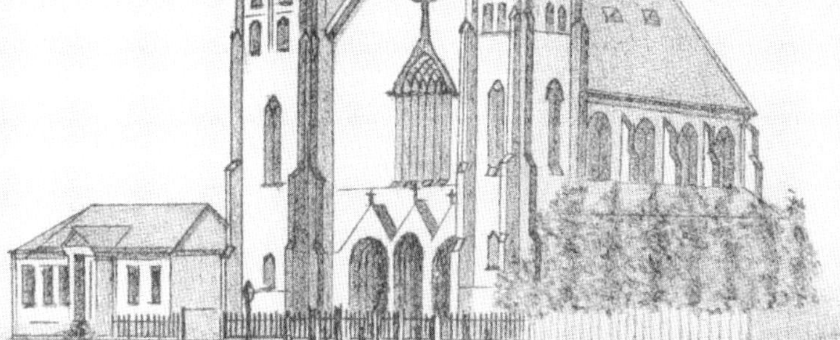

CATHOLIC CHURCH

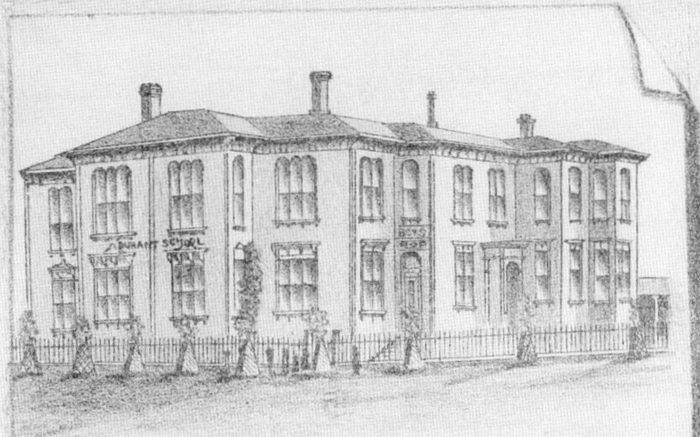

DURANT SCHOOL, COR 28TH & WEST STS.

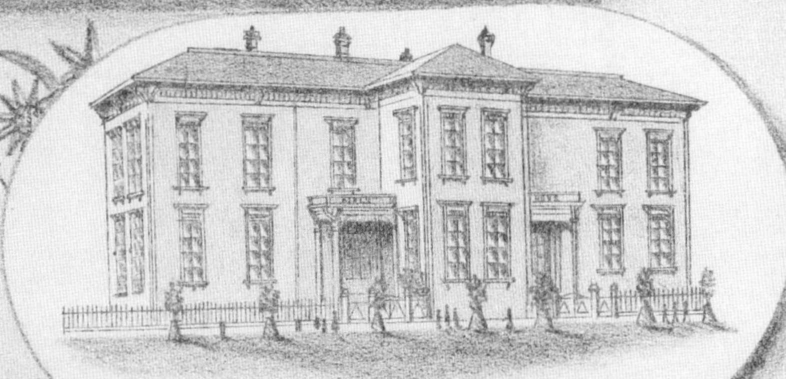

TOMPKINS SCHOOL COR 5TH & LINDEN STS.

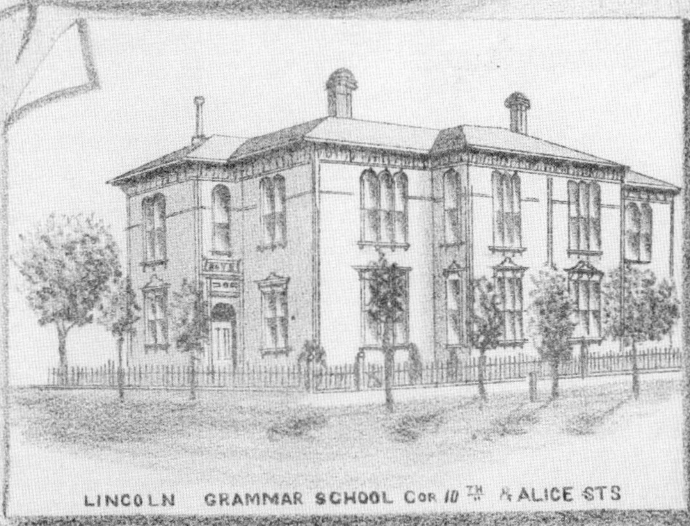

LINCOLN GRAMMAR SCHOOL COR 10TH & ALICE STS

They recognize truth wherever found, irrespective of sect or school, and adopt every scientific discovery and rational idea that tends to promote the healing art.

The sole aim of the college is to educate good, practical physicians and surgeons. Its course will be free from all exclusiveness and bigotry, and will accept students with reference solely to their attainments, and not with reference to the school or preceptors that may have taught them.

The Faculty consists of ten able physicians and professors. The officers now are: President, D. MacLean, M. D., San Francisco; First Vice-President, Colin Campbell, Oakland; Second Vice-President, G. G. Gere, M. D., San Francisco; Treasurer, J. P. Webb, M. D., Oakland; Secretary, H. T. Webster, M. D., Oakland.

Field's Seminary or the Home School.

1825 TELEGRAPH AVENUE.

THIS flourishing school was founded in the autumn of 1872, by Miss Harriet N. Field. It was intended to meet the demand for a school which should give its pupils, while acquiring a thorough education, the advantages of a highly cultured Christian home. Its aim has always been to combine with careful mental training, the best physical, moral, social, and religious development.

The school, on the corner of Telegraph Avenue and Knox Place, is beautifully located, commanding, in front, a fine view to the east and south, and in the rear, the bay and the Golden Gate.

The grounds are 140x400 feet. In front of the buildings is a large, well-kept lawn, making the place very attractive. In the rear, there is ample room for outdoor sports. The buildings, four in number, the main building, the school building, the cottage, and the gymnasium, are so connected that the covered walk furnishes a good place for a promenade in rainy weather.

The main building, three stories high, contains the parlors, reception room or office, a well-furnished library (to which the young ladies have free access), the music rooms, young ladies' rooms, dining-room and kitchen. The school building contains the assembly room and the recitation rooms of the academic department. The cottage contains the preparatory rooms, the laboratory, and a class room for the sciences. The gymnasium is of good size, and has sufficient apparatus to make physical exercise a pleasure. The studio, which is in the main building, contains a large cast of the Venus da Milo, several small casts, and a goodly number of aids to art study.

The seminary has a good collection of minerals and zoological specimens.

In every department the school is well equipped, and those who have it in charge are making additions which promise even better things for the future.

The course of study embraces a thorough knowledge of the English branches, a good education in the sciences, an extended course of history, and the best facilities for acquiring the ancient and modern languages, and a knowledge of music. Some branches are taught by lectures, and others by the use of textbooks. The best and latest methods of instruction are employed. Pupils are prepared for the University of California, or for any college.

The street-cars marked "State University" pass the gate.

State University.

The University of California.

WHEN California framed a constitution, she laid the foundation of her government so broad as to include a University, furnishing a culture complete in extent and available to all.

In 1853, Congress gave to the States seventy-two sections of land for the establishment of a fund for seminaries of learning, and ten sections of land to provide suitable buildings for such institutions as that provision might call into being. In 1862, through the Morrill Act, a special gift of land was made for the purpose of establishing schools of agriculture and the mechanic arts. This being apportioned *pro rata*, gave to California a magnificent domain of 150,000 acres.

The land found a good market, bringing five dollars an acre; a result only achieved by one other State. It has all been paid for, and passed under the control of the buyers. It was then flush times in California, and the demand for money permitted the investment of all the spare funds at ten per cent.

Trustees were appointed to control the inchoate College of Agriculture and Mechanic Arts, who met in Sacramento, June 10, 1867, and decided that it should be located somewhere in Alameda County.

This brought the scheme within the sphere of the College of California in charge of Mr. Henry Durant. The College of California had accumulated considerable property by gift or purchase, a part of which comprised one hundred and sixty acres of land north of Oakland, in the foot-hills of Contra Costa County. The time seemed to Dr. Durant opportune for uniting his languishing institution with the well-endowed Agricultural and Mechanical College, and making of the two a great practical school, satisfactory to the scientist and the average citizen. Therefore, the domain in the foot-hills was transferred to the Agricultural College, on the sole condition that it should maintain a Department of Letters. Of this union of ideas came the University as it exists.

As is custom in older countries, and a very good custom it is, the University has received gifts from private parties, some of them of more than ordinary importance: The Lick gift, for a grand observatory and telescope, amounting in value to over $700,000; the Harmon Gymnasium, with whose benefits and their donor all Oaklanders are well acquainted.

The University Grounds.

WHEN one reaches Berkeley the most conspicuous objects he sees are the buildings erected by the State on the University grounds.

Prof. Soulé said: "It is in area 200 acres; is watered by numerous springs in the hills, and the collection and disposal of this will furnish hereafter abundant study and practice to the engineering student. With the spring water and surface water saved, the grounds could be thoroughly irrigated throughout the year, and made to blossom as the rose. The lower portion of the grounds is flat and moist throughout the year, and will nourish

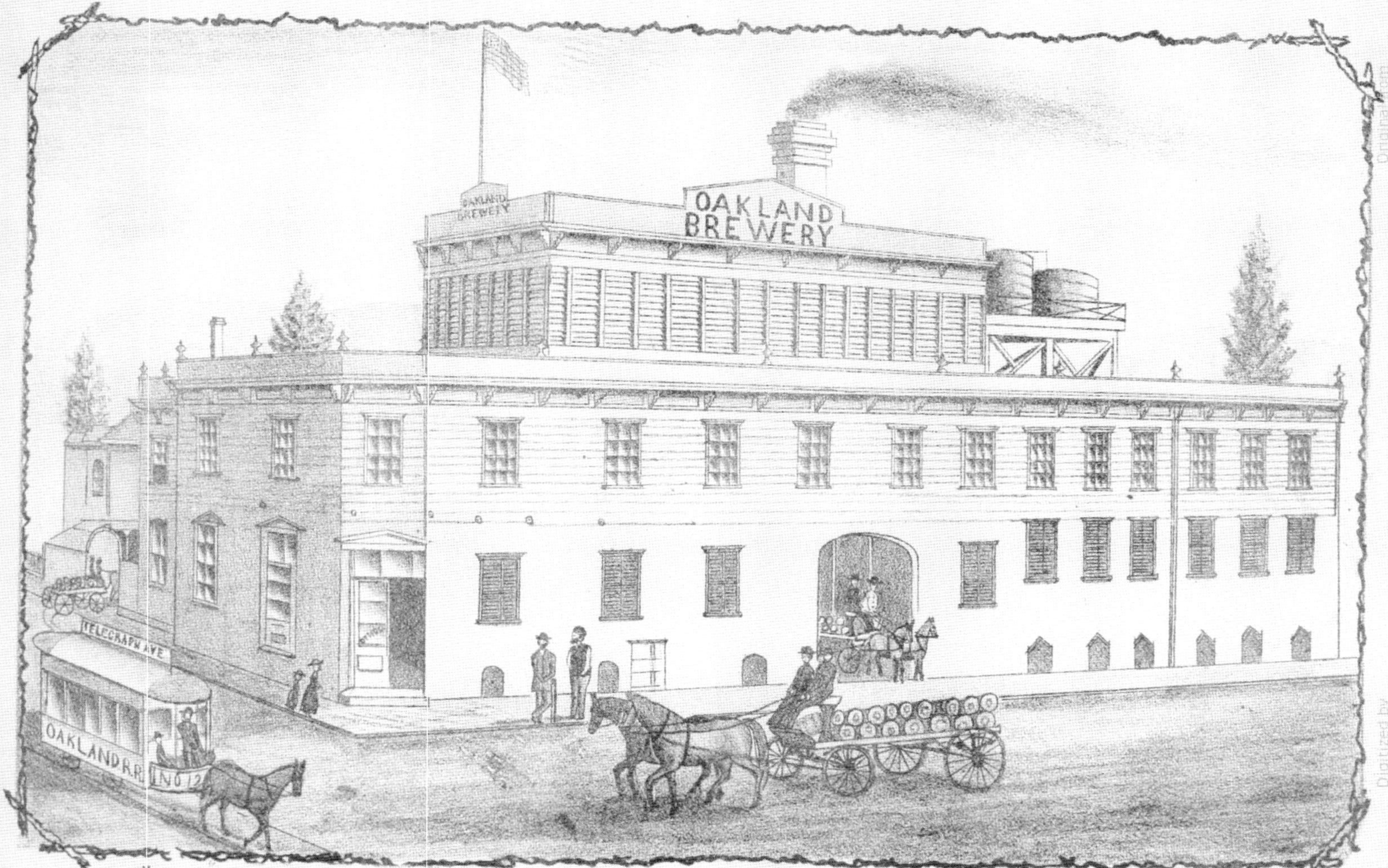

"OAKLAND BREWERY" TELEGRAPH AVE. & DURANT ST.

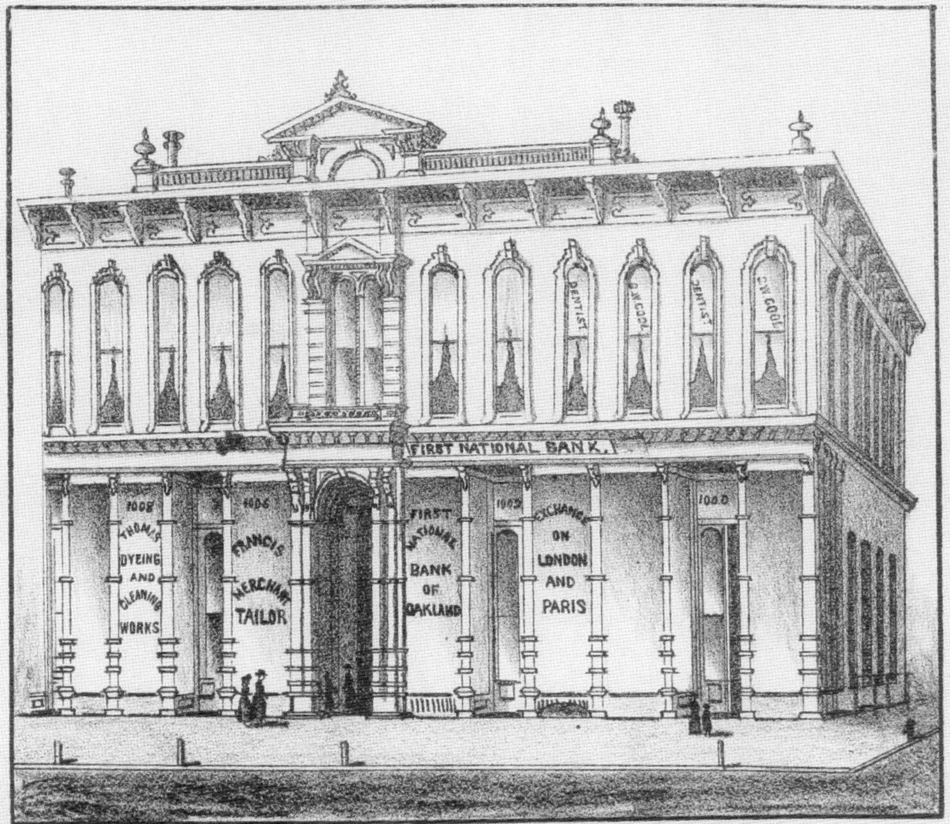

BUILDING OCCUPIED BY THE FIRST NATIONAL BANK OF OAKLAND.

such trees, flowers, and shrubs as require such soil.

There is a higher plateau, upon which the various buildings have been or are to be located, forming the *campus* proper. Beyond, toward the Monte Diablo Range, the ground rises into hills, the highest of which is 884 feet above tide-water, and 584 feet above the base of the south college. The average height of the tract is 400 feet above tide-water. The hilly portion could be well utilized for forestry.

The University is supplied with water from a reservoir of 38,000 gallons capacity, situated at the foot of Strawberry Cañon, and at an elevation of 205 feet above the basement of the south college. It will carry water entirely over any building contemplated. Other springs of large resources will be reclaimed and brought in from time to time.

Strawberry Creek is for a large portion of the year a beautifully clear stream; during the winter it discharges an enormous quantity of water, and runs between steep banks ten to fifteen feet in depth, and with a span from thirty to one hundred feet. Along it are found many shady, quiet nooks, gracious to the scholar, philosopher, and naturalist. The soil of the lower portion of the site is a deep, rich adobe, capable of being wrought into a soil of great productiveness; on the plateau it is a lighter kind. On the hills there is a thin soil of decomposed shale rock, etc. It would be difficult to find within so small an area as the University site a spot with so many varieties and capabilities in the way of soils, irrigation, and exposure."

The College of California had caused the property to be carefully examined by Frederick Law Olmstead, the well-known landscape engineer, before its transfer. He preferred such division and ornamentation as would preserve the natural features and flowing outlines of the place, a plan that has since been somewhat varied.

The grounds were afterward laid out by William Hammond Hall, under the directions of the Regents. The design is simple, involving winding drives, with entrances on the south, north, and west, serpentine walks, and a rather sharply defined terrace for the main buildings.

The open portions, dotted with fine specimens of live-oak, have, though untouched, a finished park-like appearance, and are gay with wild poppies, buttercups, primroses, and blue lilies through winter and spring. The improved places are filled with evergreen and deciduous trees, shrubs, plants, and flowers from every quarter of the globe. A conservatory occupies one of the warmest nooks.

The fields of the Agricultural Department are near the western entrance, and are, with their specimens of imported fruits, grains, and trees, undergoing a process of experimental culture, of the greatest interest to the farmer and botanist.

No modern college has grounds like these. The German universities are usually in crowded cities, and without external attractions. The English universities have lawns that are ill-kept, and a few trees poorly cared for. The American colleges have not found it easy to cultivate handsome surroundings, on account of a severe climate and ungrateful soil. Cambridge has a lawn and trees. Yale has its elms and public green. The New York colleges are much the same. The Southern colleges might do more in their softer climate, but their grounds are neglected and forlorn. None are so favored in climate, universal capacity of production, and beauty of outlook as this. Art might do much to aid nature, but even without art nature was never more attractive.

The University grounds are yearly being improved by new and attractive features that add to the beauty of location.

The University Buildings.

THE buildings are sufficiently spacious and convenient for the present needs of the University. The two largest stand on a terrace more than three hundred feet above tide-water, and command an unrestricted outlook over the bay and surrounding hills. They may be regarded as the historic structures, the nucleus of the group. The corner-stone of the Agricultural College, called South Hall, was laid in August, 1872, with public ceremonies. The corner-stone of the North Hall was laid in the spring of 1873.

The architecture of South Hall is simple, but handsome. The material is brick trimmed with gray stone. In construction it is solid and durable. It is 152 feet long by 50 feet wide, has four stories and 34 rooms, six of the rooms being 32x48 feet, and several others 20x20 feet. In its basement are the Chemical Laboratory and the Agricultural Department. On the first floor are the rooms at present occupied by the library, the secretary's office, and the instruction rooms of the College of Chemistry; on the floor above are the lecture hall, the museum, and other rooms needed by the Scientific Department.

The north building is 166 feet long by 60 feet wide. It has four stories divided into 28 compartments, an assembly room 43x58, a philosophical lecture room 39x50, the University printing office, students' reading rooms, and various recitation rooms.

Back of them, and irregularly placed on the hillside, stand two buildings of later construction,—the Bacon Art and Library Building, and the College of Mining and Mechanic Arts. The first is named from Henry Douglass Bacon, of Oakland, who gave to the University his excellent collection of paintings, sculpture, and miscellaneous works of art, a library of several thousand volumes, and $25,000 to erect suitable buildings to contain these treasures, provided the State would add $25,000 in furtherance of the project. The State appreciated the value and intelligence of the gift, and furnished the amount required. Its outside is prepossessing, being of brick unobtrusively ornamented with stone. The architectural style followed within and without is the later forms of gothic. There are, properly, two buildings in one. That fronting the west is rectangular; the rear building is semi-circular. The front portion is 88x38 feet. The center of the façade rises into a tower 102 feet in height. The interior arrangements are well designed. There are broad lobbies and stairways, an elevator, reading rooms, committee rooms, store rooms, and a large art gallery well lighted from the top. The rotunda of the library portion is 69 feet in diameter and 57 feet in height. It will hold 90,000 volumes. The only other building of importance is a large and well-furnished gymnasium, built by A. K. P. Harmon, of Oakland, which can, if needed, be used for literary exercises.

While the several other colleges of the State University are clustered at Berkeley, its Medical Department is, for obvious reasons, situated in San Francisco. The Medical College Building, known as "Toland Hall," in honor of its illustrious founder, is one of the most complete and stately in the country. It is located near North Beach, overlooking the Golden Gate and the Berkeley buildings, a locality favoring the health and industrious habits of the students.

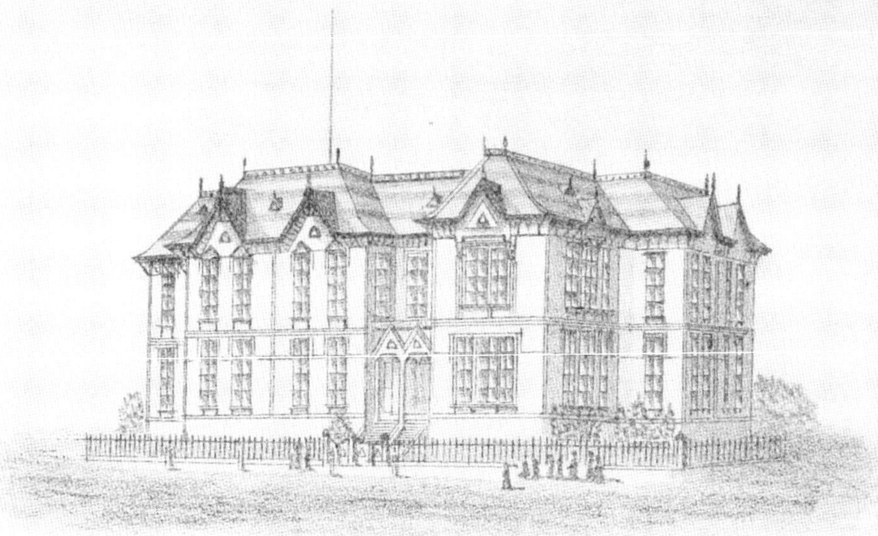

COLE SCHOOL, 10TH ST.

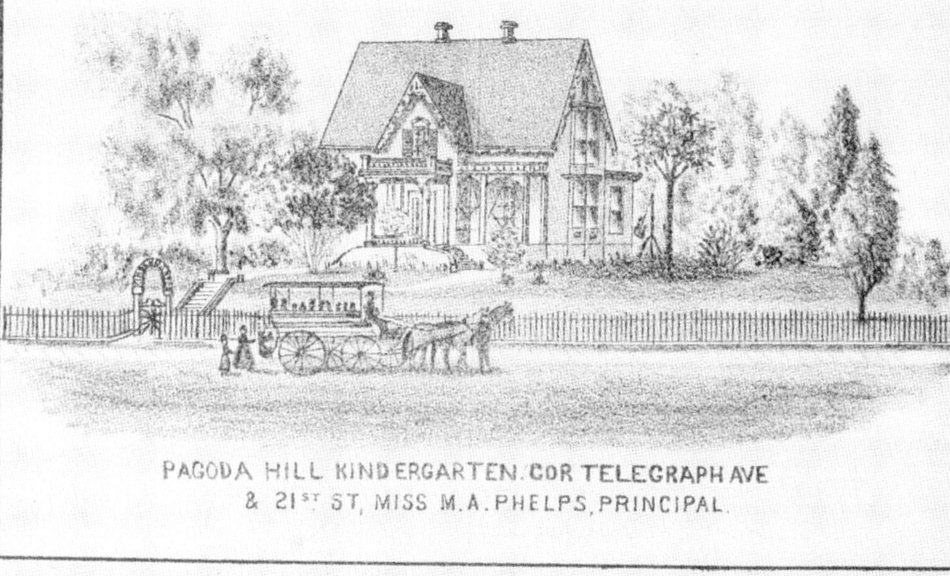

PAGODA HILL KINDERGARTEN. COR TELEGRAPH AVE & 21ST ST, MISS M.A. PHELPS, PRINCIPAL.

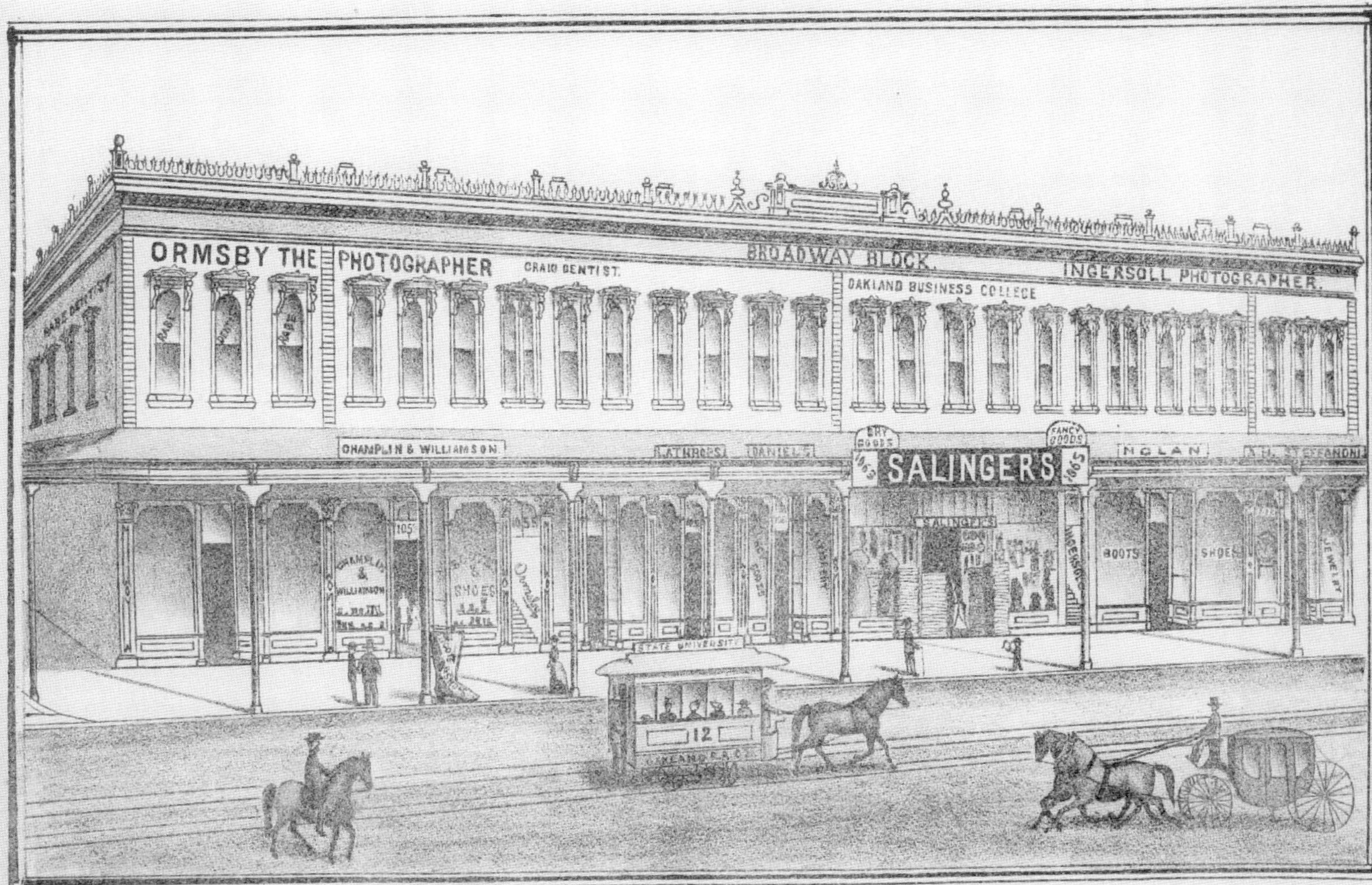

WEST SIDE BROADWAY FROM 11TH TO 12TH STS., OAKLAND, CAL.

Benevolent and Charitable Institutions.

Institution for Deaf, Dumb and Blind.

SITUATED at the base of the higher hills at Berkeley is the above-named institution. There being plenty of ground, the architect has put up a series of buildings, with plenty of space, light, and ventilation about each. Thus the dining-room, with its kitchen appurtenances, and the sleeping apartment of the help, stands by itself, the dormitories by themselves, the schools in one block, and the work-shops in another. Between and around these are broad, graveled walks, and flower beds; before them, the ground slopes gently down, by lovely residences and green fields, to the bay, while behind them the Berkeley hills rise steeply up, dotted here and there with groves of the blue-leaved eucalyptus. The Berkeley train stops at Dwight Way Station, from which a planked sidewalk leads up through a mile and a half of beautiful country road, and though the road were twice as long and twice as rough, the journey up it would be well repaid.

The present institution occupies the site of another, which was burned down some years ago. The original institution was founded by the ladies of San Francisco, on March 17, 1860, by the opening of a school in a little house on Tehama Street, with three pupils—two girls and one boy—under the charge of H. B. Crandall, an intelligent and well-educated deaf mute. The school for the blind was commenced in the following October, with four pupils—two boys and two girls. On the 11th of December, a public examination was held. Application was made to the Legislature for State assistance; this was granted to the extent of $10,000. The lady managers purchased the fifty-vara lot on the corner of Mission and Sparks Streets—a junction on the other side of the Bernal Heights—deeded it to the State, and thereon erected a substantial brick building, which it is believed has since been incorporated in St. Mary's College. In the first six months, the California institution increased to twenty-two pupils, and the first buildings erected, which were burned. Afterward, the present commodious ones were erected on an entirely different plan from the first ones. From that on, the institution grew and attracted public attention, and the Berkeley site was secured.

The Industrial Home for the Blind is located on Telegraph Avenue. Here they work at trades and are, in a measure, self-supporting. As the institution has lately started, we have no figures on its success.

Young Men's Christian Association.

THIS society was organized July 24, 1879, and continued until December 31, holding only religious services. E. S. Fowler, of San Francisco, was then called and accepted the position of General Secretary, when more definite work was planned and carried on for young men. They now have the finest rooms in the United States, outside of an association, owning their own building, and are doing a grand work for young men.

Prominent business men were interested in the work, and were appointed as members of the Board of Directors, fourteen in number. They were divided into four committees, as follows: Financial, Library and Rooms, Lecture and Entertainment, and Publication.

The upper part of a large building on Broadway, between Seventh and Eighth Streets, in the center of the city, was rented for fifty dollars per month, and fitted up at a cost of about seven hundred dollars, which made it pleasant and attractive. The audience room will seat comfortably about four hundred people. The reading-room is well supplied with reading-matter, is cheerful and attractive and adjoins the office, which is also the library, and contains nearly one thousand well-selected books.

The association is now conducting twelve religious meetings each week, with wonderful success, among which is a noonday meeting that has been the means of doing very much good.

Reading-rooms are open from 8 A. M. to 10 P. M.; Sundays, from 9 to 10:30 A. M.; 12:30 to 7:15 P. M. Young men are cordially invited to visit the rooms during their leisure hours, day or evening. The General Secretary may be found at the rooms at all hours, willing to give advice and assistance to young men in need of friendly aid.

Parlors are open day and evening for social intercourse. It offers free to every young man, reading and conversational rooms, writing material, directory of good boarding-houses, visitation in sickness, aid in obtaining employment, social companionship, course of free lectures. All young men are invited. Strangers are especially welcome. Any young man of good moral character may obtain an annual ticket for $2.00, ladies same price. For membership, or further information, apply to the General Secretary, at the rooms, 865 Broadway.

J. M. Buffington is president of the Young Men's Christian Association of Oakland, and has recently been re-elected to that important office, for the third time. His earnest convictions and devotion to theological principles have made him prominent in the religious as in the mining world. He has ever taken a deep interest in the Sunday-school cause, and for half a century has been a constant and enthusiastic laborer in this field of religious work.

In 1857, Mr. Buffington removed to San Francisco and engaged in the lumber trade until 1862, when he entered upon his present avocation—that of mining secretary. While Mr. Buffington has become a prominent figure in mining circles, and has mixed much with those who seek to obtain from mother earth her treasures of gold and silver, yet has he not forgotten the training of his childhood and youth, or the beneficent teachings of a pious and God-fearing mother.

The *Alta* says: The Hon. J. M. Buffington, of Oakland, gave the first of a series of parlor business talks to young men of San Francisco. Mr. Buffington was greeted by a crowded and enthusiastic

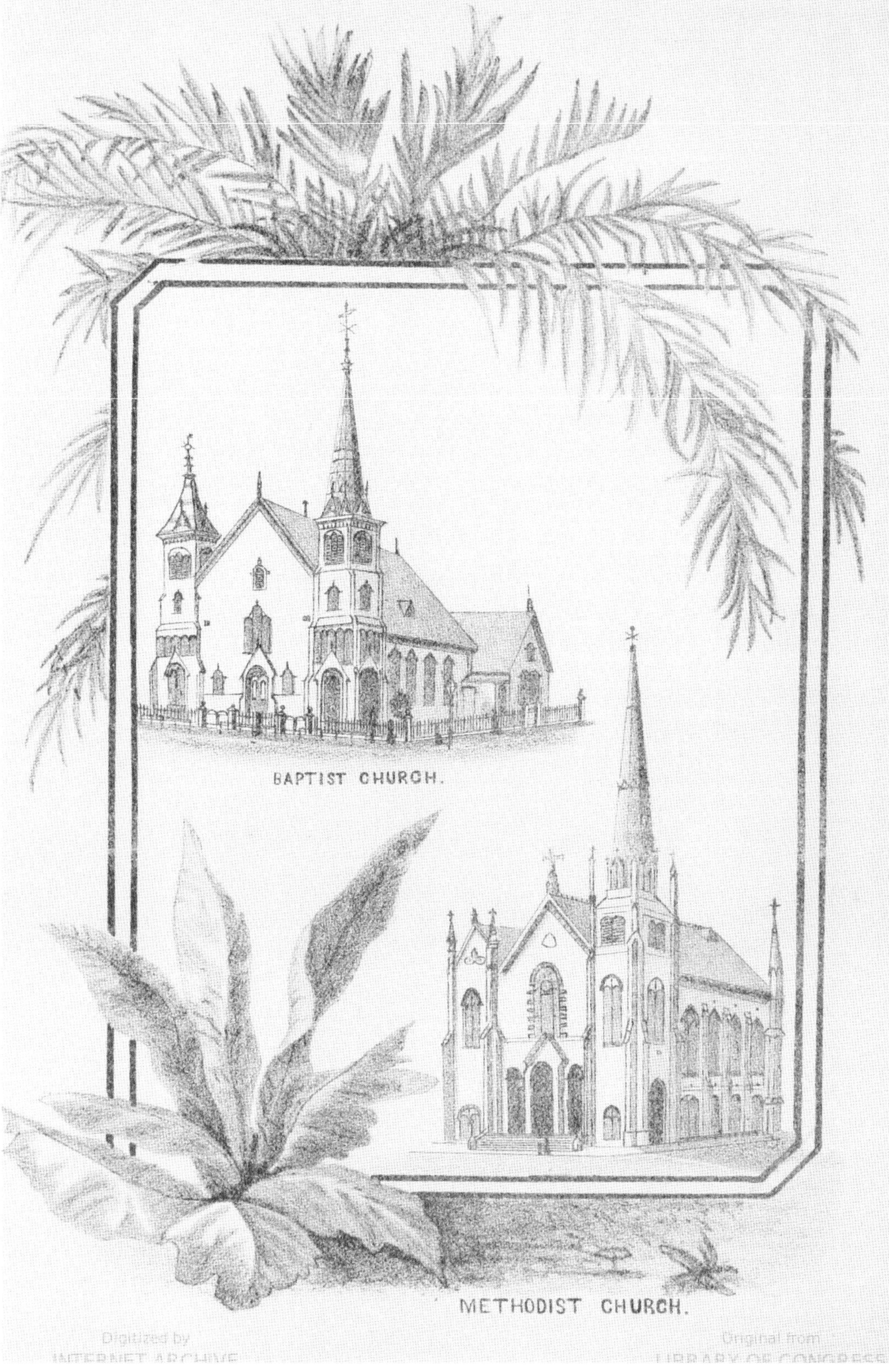

BAPTIST CHURCH.

METHODIST CHURCH.

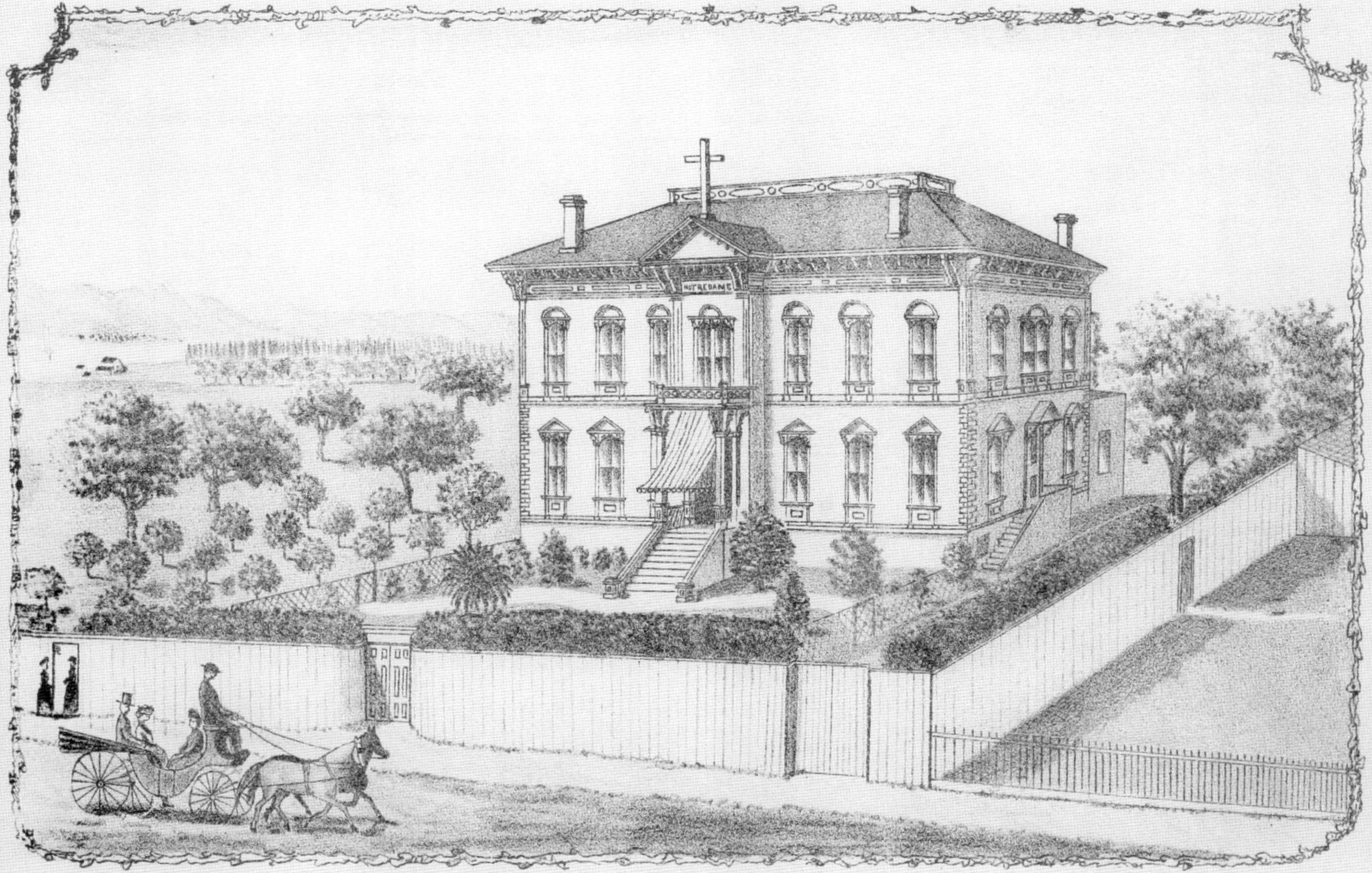

NOTRE DAME ACADEMY. ALAMEDA. CAL.

parlor of young men, who listened with rapt attention throughout to the speaker's graphic, interesting, and detailed account of the shades and shadows of the early days among the pioneers of our chosen State.

Ladies' Relief Society.

TEN acres of beautiful land, comprising fruitful field, dimpled pasture, and tasteful garden, situated halfway between Oakland and Berkeley, about two miles from either, form the domain of the Ladies' Relief Society of Oakland. On these valuable premises stand to-day two "Homes"—a home for children and a home for aged women. The ladies of this society have supported the Children's Home for twelve years; they have built and occupied the Aged Women's Home within twelve months.

The society was organized in 1872 for the relief of needy women and children. The ladies of the society have taken care, in 10 years, of 417 beneficiaries, chiefly children; also, that they owned a commodious home situated on premises 10 acres in extent, which cost $16,000 in the original purchase, and $4,000 more in repairs, and which was absolutely free of incumbrance. In this "Home" the ladies supported at that date (May, 1881) a family of 70 souls, of which 6 were employes, the rest children, at an expense of $446.60 per month.

Work on the Home for Aged Women was begun in June, 1882, and the building was completed in October of the same year. The corner-stone was laid with appropriate ceremonies on the 22d of July, and the city of Oakland made it a gala day. A thousand invitations were issued, and refreshments were served free on the grounds by the ladies of the board. A band of music was in attendance, and the society's kind friend, Governor Perkins, was president of the day. Rev. Dr. Akerley and Rev. Dr. McClure conducted the religious exercises, while Hon. C. N. Fox and Harry J. W. Dam, Esq., were respectively orator and poet of the occasion. The whole scene was a moving panorama of children, youth, and middle-age, of comings and goings and greetings, of vehicles arriving and departing, of booths and refreshment tables overflowing with cheerful occupants, and of exploring parties making acquaintance with grounds and buildings, while on the air came bursts of music and sounds of laughter.

Homeopathic Hospital.

A MEETING was held November 15, 1877, to organize a hospital and dispensary for the city of Oakland, at which a constitution and by-laws were adopted, and signed by forty benevolent ladies. The organization was called the Oakland Homeopathic Hospital and Dispensary Association. These ladies had long felt the necessity of such an undertaking, as the county hospital is some ten miles distant. In order to raise a fund immediately, eighteen ladies became life members, paying into the treasury fifty dollars each. The city council courteously declined to assist the ladies; but, on application to the supervisors of the county, an appropriation of forty dollars per month was made, on condition that they receive all the patients the supervisors might send. This virtually made this a receiving hospital for the city of Oakland.

The founders of the society were prudent, making a small beginning, securing the services of a competent matron, but furnishing only by degrees, as the rooms were needed.

The second year was begun with $600 in the treasury, and the hospital barely furnished. The succeeding years have come and gone, showing many and varied states of the exchequer, and bringing care and some success to the interested ladies.

In 1883 they moved into a commodious building, No. 1057 Alice Street, and during the past year have nearly paid the indebtedness on the building.

Woman's Christian Association of Oakland.

THIS society was organized October 5, 1877, its objects being "to carry Christian sympathy, love, and help to all families in our midst who may need such ministrations." The officers of the association are a president, vice-president, secretary, assistant secretary, corresponding secretary, and an executive committee of seven or more persons. Membership may be had by any lady paying the sum of one dollar annually, while the payment of twenty-five dollars constitutes life membership. For the conduct of its benefits there are four departments, viz.: Fruit and Flower Mission, Sheltering Home, Industrial Committee, with head-quarters at the rooms of the association, at No. 1274 Franklin Street; and the Helping Hand School at the corner of Twenty-second and Market Streets. The association now consists of 300 members, 5 life members, and 51 sustaining members.

The California Sheltering home.

THIS charitable institution was organized in April, 1881, and was originally situated on Chestnut Street, but was afterwards removed to No. 1274 Franklin Street. It is one of the branches of the Ladies' Christian Association. The object of the home is to render aid and provide a temporary home for destitute women and children who have no habitation. In this place a number of motherless children have been kindly cared for until other homes could be provided for them. Two aged women, strangers to the city, have enjoyed the hospitalities of the home for a season, until means could be provided to send them to their native places. Sixty persons in all have been members of the Home, while the number of families during the last year averaged twelve. These two associations cannot be too well patronized, fulfilling as they do woman's mission upon earth—the doing good to her fellow-beings.

Other Organizations.

HEBREW BENEVOLENT SOCIETY was organized in July, 1861. It meets the first Sunday of each month, and its work is that of charity.

DIANA OF CALIFORNIA, a Danish society, was organized in 1882. Its object is to assist and relieve its members, to establish a relief fund for widows and orphans of deceased members, to assist and obtain employment for its members when in need, to improve its members socially and materially, and to create a spirit of harmony amongst the Danes in California.

FRUIT AND FLOWER MISSION is located on Franklin Street, between Ninth and Tenth. The object of the Mission is to carry flowers, delicacies, and clothing to the poor; Miss Nellie Smith, President.

HELPING HAND SCHOOL is located corner Twenty-second and Market Streets. The object of the school is to teach children to sew.

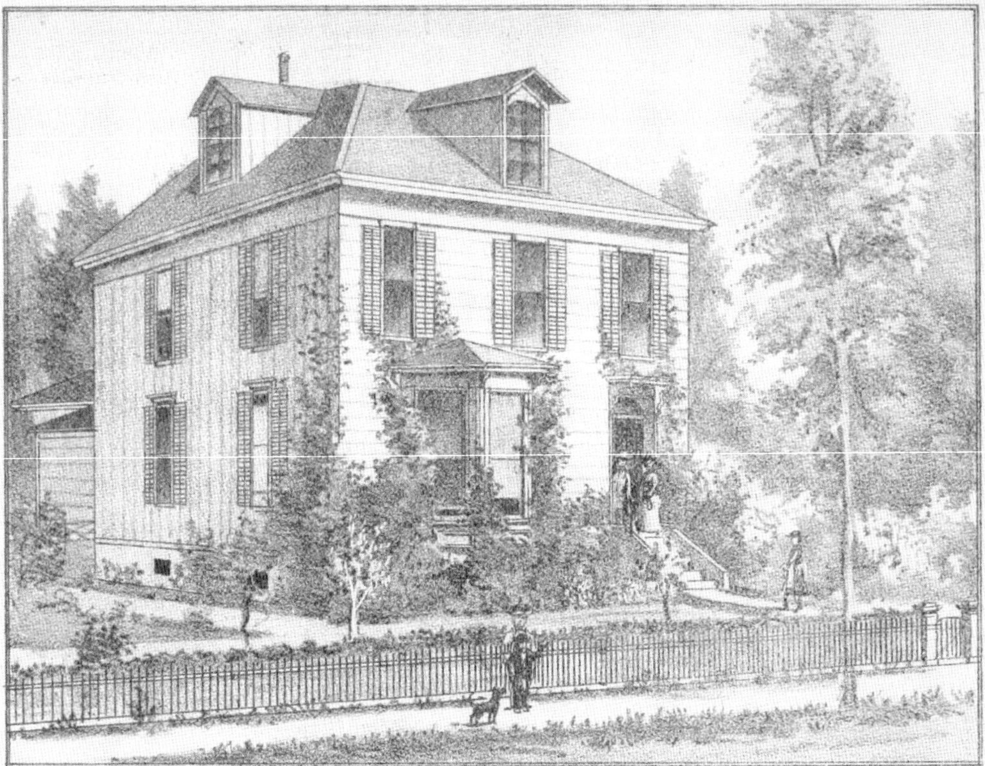

RESIDENCE OF JUDGE WALDO. M. YORK. COR. OF VINE & ARCH. BERKELEY CAL.

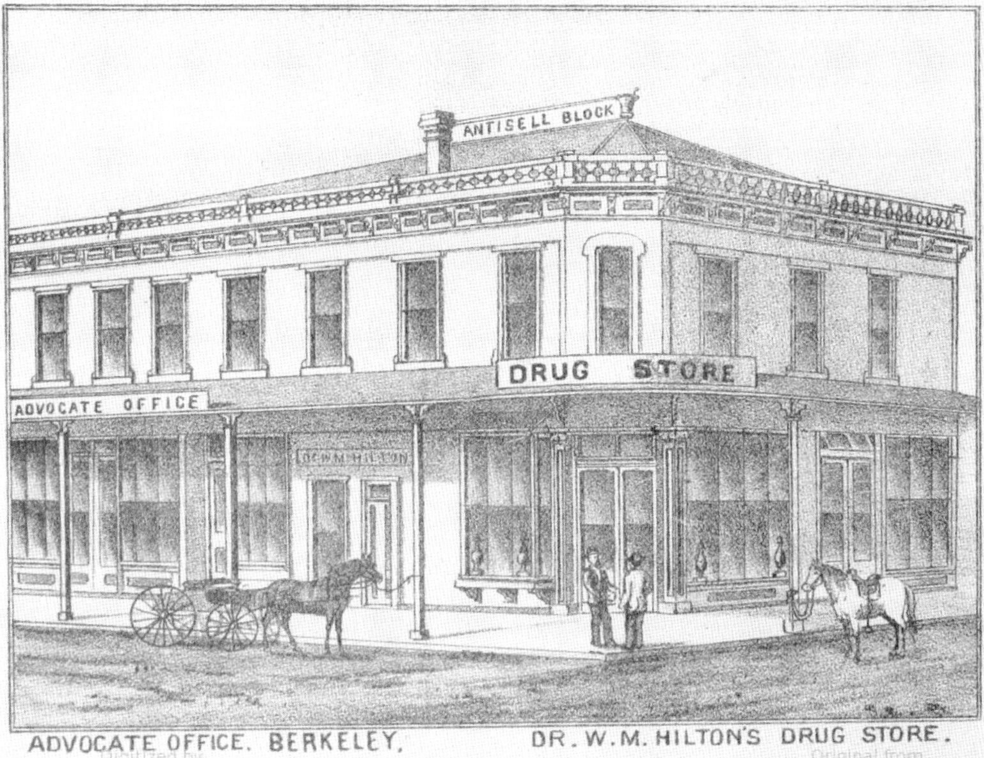

ADVOCATE OFFICE. BERKELEY. DR. W. M. HILTON'S DRUG STORE.

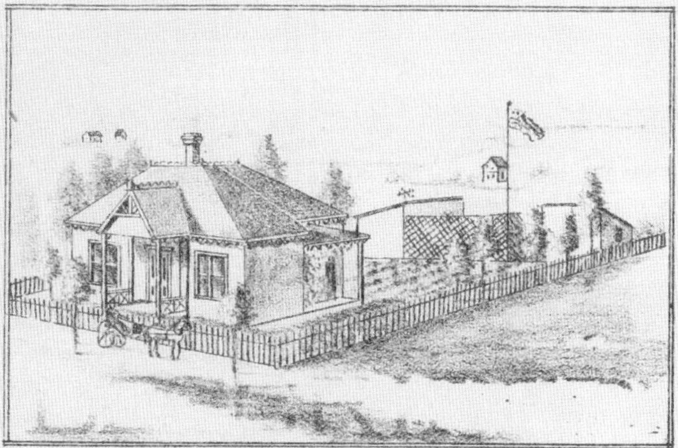

"ALBION COTTAGE" ADDISON ST. BERKELEY.
PROPERTY OF FRANK MOORE. ESQ.

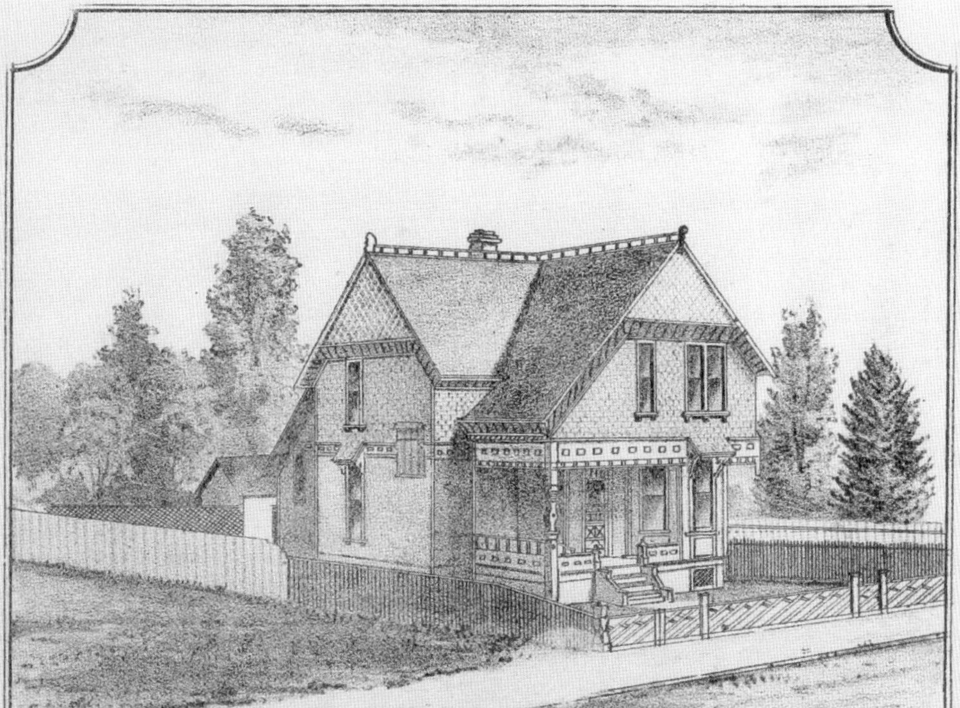

"EASTLAKE COTTAGE", A. H. BROAD. BUILDER. BANCROFT WAY. BERKELEY.

OAKLAND BENEVOLENT SOCIETY was organized June 7, 1869; located at No. 516 Fifteenth Street, John I. Tay, Secretary; the object of the association is to provide food and clothing for the poor. About 300 persons receive aid monthly.

SHELTERING HOME is located at 1274 Franklin Street. It gives a temporary home for the poor until they are able to find work.

OAKLAND HOSPITAL.—This is located on Clay Street, and is conducted by Dr. Woolsey as a private hospital.

WOMAN'S CHRISTIAN TEMPERANCE UNION.—The work of this society may be estimated by the following subjects and committees:—

Juvenile Work, Mrs. S. C. Borland; Press, Mrs. H. H. Havens; Woman's Christian Temperance Union, Mrs. S. G. Chamberlain; Evangelistic Work, Mrs. Gray; Bible Readings, Mrs. W. M. Sublette, including managers of corporations to require total abstinence in their employes, Mrs. Caleb Saddler; Sabbath-school Work, Mrs. Noyes. Drawing-room Work — In Oakland, Mrs. J. C. Ainsworth. In East Oakland, Fruitvale, and Highland Park, Mrs. Mathews. Coffee House and Reading-room, Mrs. Gaskill. Prison, Police Station, and Intemperance among Women, Mrs. Gove. Foreign Work, Mrs. Dr. Bradway. Legislative Work, Mrs. E. W. Marston. Presenting Temperance in the High Schools of Learning, Mrs. G. S. Abbott. Ecclesiastical Educational, Sunday-school and other bodies, C. A. Buekle, M. D.

Parish of Sacred heart.

THIS parish was established in 1876 at North Temescal. Rev. Lawrence Serda was made pastor, and on the 17th of December of the same year, the Most Rev. Joseph S. Alemany, Archbishop of San Francisco, assisted by several of the clergy, dedicated the neat church edifice, which had been built during the year. It was dedicated to the Sacred Heart of Jesus. Two years later the parochial residence was built, in which the clergy of the parish now reside, next to the church on Evoy Avenue, near Grove Street. In 1880 another large building was erected next to the parochial residence. Its second story is used as a hall for meetings of the various Catholic societies of the parish, also for the Sunday-school, lectures, concerts, fairs, etc. The first story is divided into four rooms, spacious, beautifully lighted, and well-ventilated, used for school purposes.

This building was dedicated to the Almighty God, under the invocation of Saint Lawrence, on the 27th of June, 1880, by Most Rev. Joseph S. Alemany, assisted by the rector and several other priests. The school opened with fifty-six pupils, and by the zealous exertions of the pastor and the excellent education imparted by the teachers, this number was increased to over a hundred before the end of one year. It is now attended by about 150 young girls varying in age from six years to nineteen years.

It is a Catholic school, intended principally for the Catholic girls of the parish. Pupils of other denominations also are received, but are not obliged to recite Catholic prayers, nor learn Catholic doctrine, unless they choose to do so, with the express consent of their parents.

The school is taught by the Sisters of the Holy Names of Jesus and Mary, and superintended by the rector of the parish. Reverend Father Serda and his assistant, Rev. John A. Lally, with the co-operation of their parishioners, are now preparing to erect a school for the boys of the parish, to be taught by Christian Brothers, and to commence in July, 1886.

Public and Private Buildings.

Handsome Buildings.

OAKLAND has superior buildings for public use. The Court House, City Hall, Public Library, Hall of Records, and others are well constructed and ornamental.

There are handsome business blocks on Washington, Broadway, and Franklin, which comprise the principal business streets; but Broadway is the main business center, from which all the business radiates.

The Bank of Savings, on corner of Twelfth and Broadway, and the Union Savings Bank, on corner of Ninth and Broadway, are substantial and well-constructed edifices. The Everts' Block, on Broadway, has the most handsome and attractive finish.

The new Coleman Block, on corner of Broadway and Twelfth Street, has a fine and showy exterior finish, and cost about $70,000. The corner store has been elegantly and elaborately fitted up by Messrs. Kelsey & Flint as a drug store. They have for many years occupied the opposite corner where, by using great care in selecting pure articles, they have established a large trade. They keep the choicest toilet preparations and fancy articles.

The Home Insurance Block, corner Ninth and Washington Streets, is a grand building. Numerous other business blocks on Broadway are an ornament to any street of any city.

The Masonic Temple, described elsewhere, is one of the grand buildings of the city.

Henry Matthews' large frame building, on Washington and Thirteenth Streets, is three stories high, stores below and rooms on the upper floors, and cost $10,000.

Weber's Hotel, corner Twelfth and Franklin Streets, is built new, entirely of brick, and perfectly fire-proof. It has only been opened since the 1st of September, this year. The prices are very reasonable for rooms and board. It is near the railroad, South Pacific Coast, and in close communication to Seventh Street Depot.

Court House and Hall of Records.

THE County Court House is located on the west side of Broadway, occupying the block between Fourth and Fifth Streets. The present building was completed in June, 1875. The structure cost per contract price, $148,550; the furniture and fixtures about $66,500. It is fire-proof. The material is brick, stone, and iron. A handsome lawn surrounds the building, surrounded by an iron fence and patent stone sidewalk. The county jail is within the inclosure, which occupies a square.

The Hall of Records is located on the east side of Broadway, between Fourth and Fifth Streets. The building is earthquake and fire-proof. The work on the erection of the building was begun about May, 1879. The building cost about $70,000, the furniture and fixtures about $60,000.

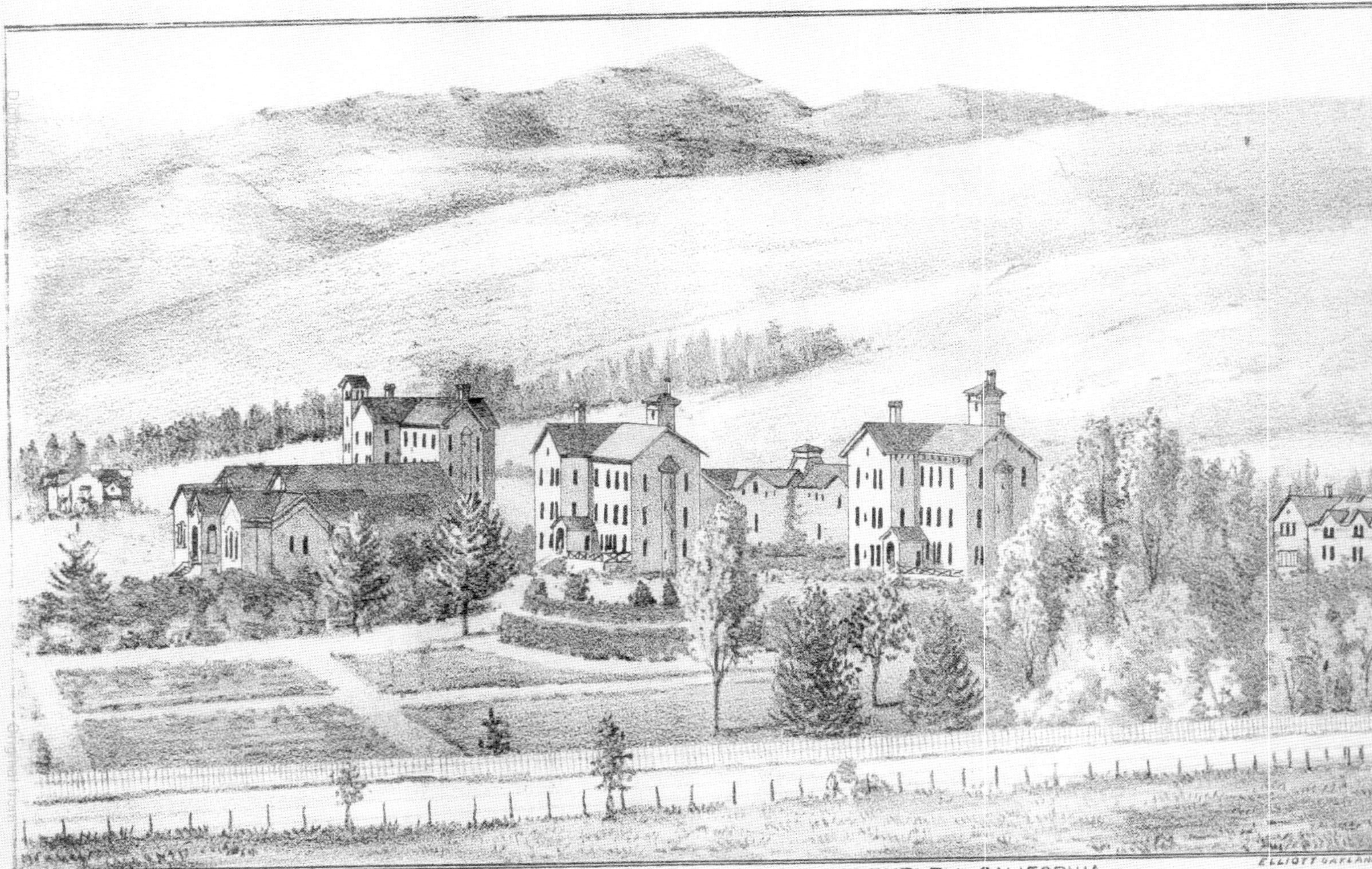

ASYLUM FOR THE DEAF, DUMB, AND BLIND. BERKELEY CALIFORNIA.

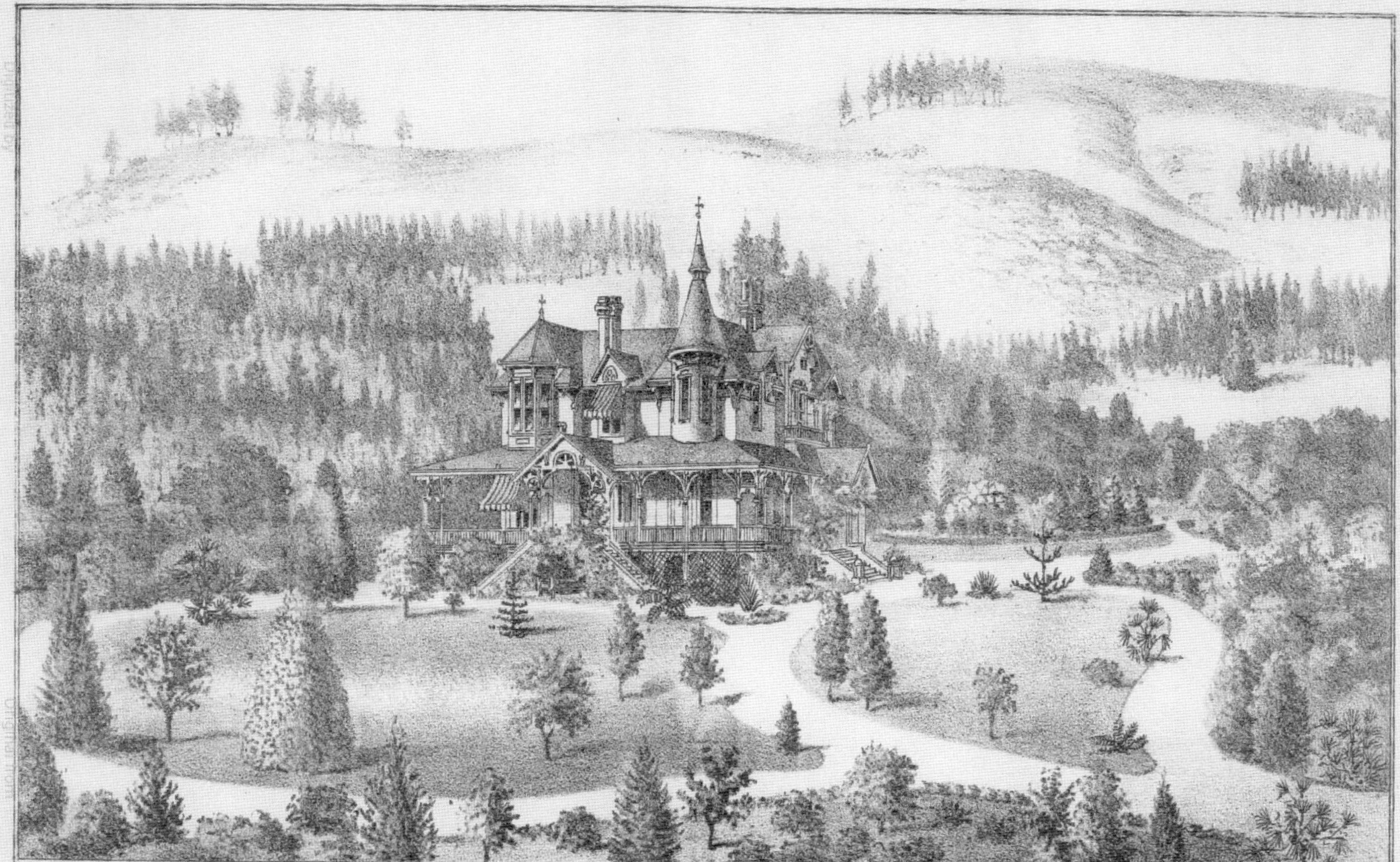

"BELLEROSE" CLAREMONT AVENUE, RESIDENCE OF JOHN GARBER.

ELLIOTT, OAKLAND.

City Hall.

THE City Hall is located in a triangular piece of ground finely laid out at the head of Washington Street. It was erected in October, 1868, at a cost of about $80,000. The three upper stories were of wood, while the basement was stone. On August 25, 1877, at 9:15 P. M., the building was destroyed by fire, causing a loss of about $40,000. The fire originated in the northwest corner of the building. The City Hall was rebuilt during the summer and fall of 1878, at a cost of about $23,000. Beautiful grass plots surround the structure.

It affords ample accommodations for the various city offices, and is creditable to the city. It has been appropriately furnished, and there are suitable safeguards against future conflagrations. A convenient office has been fitted up for the Mayor, and we may here observe that Mayor Playther has kept ordinary office hours except when called to other parts of the city by public business. The necessity for this has been made evident by the great number of persons who call to lodge information upon various matters of general interest, and also to ascertain points in which citizens are interested. There is quite enough business to occupy the time of the Mayor for several hours each day in his office.

Oakland Observatory.

DURING the month of May, 1883, A. Chabot, president of the Contra Costa Water Company, donated $3,000 to the city of Oakland for the erection of an astronomical observatory, and the purchase of an eight-inch telescope. The matter was placed in the hands of the School Department, and the Board of Education selected Lafayette Square as the site. On the 21st of May, at 3 P. M., the corner-stone was laid with appropriate ceremonies.

The square has been laid out in walks and grass plots, and set out to many beautiful flowers and shrubs. A few of the native live-oaks have kindly been spared, and, as mementoes of Oakland's name, should ever remain.

Armory Hall.

THIS drill-hall, or armory, was erected in 1883, on the corner of Central Avenue and Washington Street.

The drill-hall is a splendid apartment, 100x60 feet in dimensions, with ante-rooms for officers and men, besides assembly rooms and parlors. The Oakland Light Cavalry were mustered into the service of the State, September 23, 1878, with forty-nine rank and file, but their membership has reached ninety. There are now sixty-two effective members on the roll. This may be said to be the *corps d'élite* of Oakland, and, as such, takes a just pride in presenting a most creditable demeanor at every public parade. They are a fine body of men, generally good horsemen, and have a distinguished military appearance in their handsome and becoming uniforms. The social entertainments given by the corps are remarkable for their high standard of excellence and rank among the events of Oakland's social world.

Masonic Temple.

THE temple is semi-Gothic in style, and is 65x105 feet, and constructed of brick, granite, and San Jose sandstone. The main entrance, on Twelfth Street, is in the form of a Gothic portico of polished granite, supported by pillars of polished black granite, with the

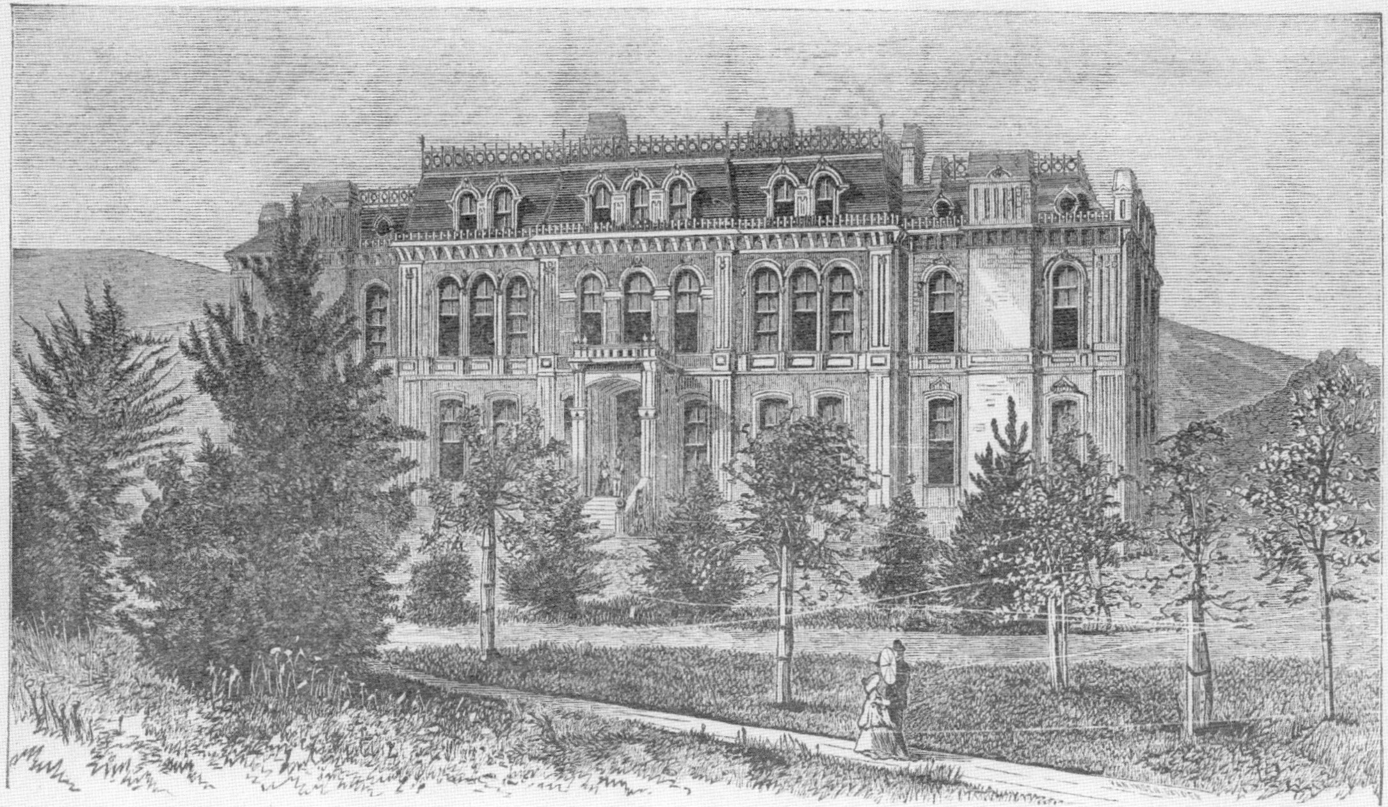

STATE UNIVERSITY (CENTRAL BUILDING), BERKELEY, CALIFORNIA.

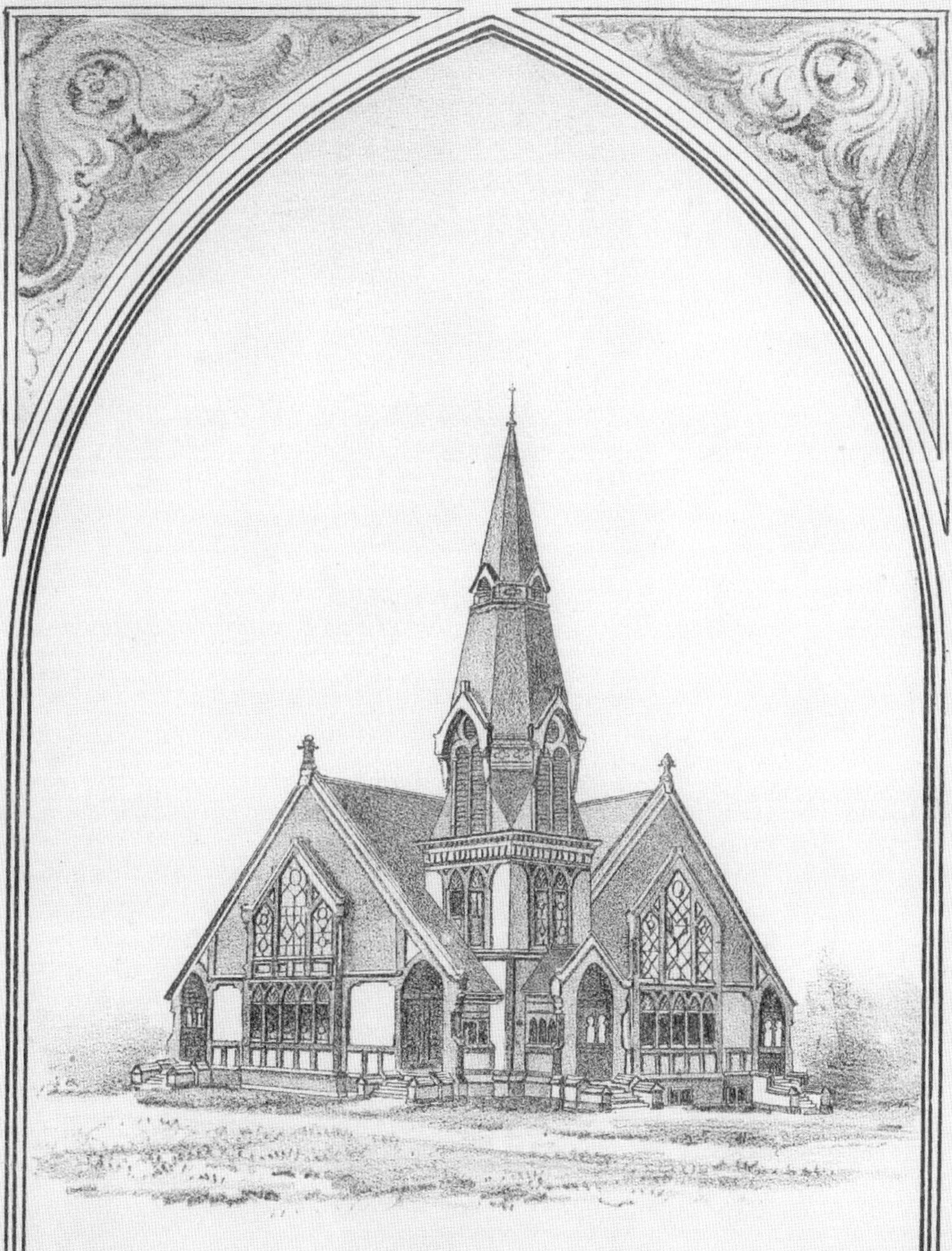

CONGREGATIONAL CHURCH. BERKELEY.

ELLIOTT, OAKLAND.

letters "G. T." cut in the massive arch over the gateway. The first floor contains a main hall 42x68 feet, with a banqueting hall adjoining, 18x68. Ladies' and gents' rooms are also attached. On the second floor, which is constructed with special reference for the meetings of the various Masonic bodies, the main hall, or lodge room, is 42x60 feet with 25 foot ceiling and a central dome reaching six feet higher. This floor has also a banqueting hall, with tyler's room, coat, committee, and preparation rooms, also armory rooms for the Knights Templar. The cost of the lot and building, with furniture, is fully $100,000.

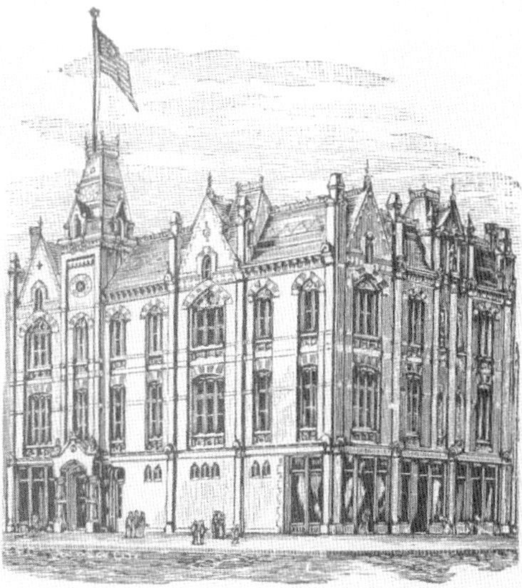

MASONIC TEMPLE.

The corner-stone of the temple was laid, with appropriate ceremonies, January 10, 1880, by W. N. Trayler, Grand Master of the Grand Lodge of free and accepted Masons.

The Oakland Masonic Temple Association was incorporated June 25, 1878, with a capital of $100,000, divided into 10,000 shares of $10.00 each. The directors are: F. K. Shattuck, A. Chabot, N. W. Spaulding, Geo. Patterson, R. C. Gaskill, John Crellin, C. E. Gillett, James Lentell, A. W. Bishop, J. B. Merritt, Daniel E. Hayes. The officers are: F. K. Shattuck, President; A. Chabot, Vice-President; C. E. Gillett, Secretary; V. D. Moody, Treasurer.

Prominent Halls and Buildings.

THE following gives the location of most of the prominent public buildings and halls:—

City Hall, head of Washington Street.

Hall of Records, Broadway, between Fourth and Fifth Streets.

Kohler's Hall, northwest corner Seventh and Chester Streets.

Masonic Hall, northwest corner Twelfth and Washington Streets.

Odd Fellows' Hall, northwest corner of Eleventh and Franklin Streets.

Pythian Hall, 1058 Broadway.

Schimmelpfennig's Hall, Twelfth Street, between Fifteenth and Sixteenth Avenues.

Ancient Order of United Workmen, southeast corner Twelfth and Franklin Streets.

Medical Hall, west side of Clay, between Tenth and Eleventh Streets.

Germania Hall, east side of Webster, between Sixth and Seventh Streets.

The Harmon Gymnasium, University Grounds, Berkeley.

Light Cavalry Hall, corner Washington and Twelfth Streets.

Public Library Building, on City Hall Square.

Court House, on Broadway, between Fifth and Sixth Streets.

Odd Fellows' Hall, Berkeley, on Shattuck Avenue.

Dietz Opera House, northeast corner Twelfth and Webster Streets.

Oakland Theater (Colosseum) is between Webster and Alice Streets.

Park Theater, opposite City Hall, on Fourteenth Street.

Neptune Gardens, Alameda near Third Avenue.

Home Mutual Insurance Company.

THE Alameda Branch of the above-named company, occupies rooms in the Union National Bank Building, corner of Broadway and Ninth Street. This company is in a sound financial condition, having been in successful operation for over twenty years and has accumulated nearly $300,000 additional assets after paying twelve per cent annual dividends. Its total cash assets are $856,658.22, as returned to the Insurance Department. All losses are liberally adjusted and promptly paid.

21ST ANNUAL EXHIBIT, JANUARY 1, 1885.

Premiums Since Organization	$5,021,759 59
Losses Since Organization	2,118,501 84
Assets January 1, 1885	856,658 22
Surplus for Policy Holders	825,963 68
Income, 1884	484,616 73
Capital Paid Up (Gold)	300,000 00
Re-insurance Reserve	275,157 07
Net Surplus over Everything	250,806 61

The officers are: J. F. Houghton, President; J. L. N. Shepard, Vice-President; Chas. R. Story, Secretary; R. H. Magill, General Agent.

Prominent hotels.

THE principal hotels are the Galindo, on Eighth Street, near Broadway; the Centennial House, northeast corner Fourteenth and Clay; Eureka, southwest corner Seventh and Washington; Newland House, northeast corner Seventh and Washington; the Arlington, 474 Ninth Street; Tubbs' Hotel, East Twelfth Street, between Fourth and Fifth Avenues; Winsor House, southwest corner Ninth and Washington; Blake House, Washington and Twelfth; Winter's Hotel, 1236 Broadway; Piedmont Hotel, Piedmont; Park Hotel, Park and Enincal Avenue, Alameda; Union Hotel, Thirteenth Avenue, East Oakland.

GALINDO HOTEL.—The largest and most pleasantly located hotel in Oakland is the Galindo, on Eighth Street. Over 200 guests may be comfortably accommodated at any one time, and the popularity of the management is sufficient to keep it full during the year. Transient visitors to this city cannot find a more commodious or pleasantly situated hotel in Alameda County, or a house more convenient of access, as regards transportation to and from San Francisco and the various lines of travel.

The table is always supplied with all the delicacies of the season, provided by a competent caterer. The proprietor has had a wide experience in the business of hotel-keeping, and understands how to render his guests comfortable. The proprietor is B. Wright.

TUBBS' HOTEL.—Cars pass the door ever fifteen minutes connecting with trains at Broadway and East Oakland, and a few minutes' walk is sufficient to reach Clinton Station, where the local trains pass east and west every half hour. Extensive and beautiful grounds surround the hotel, and Lake Merritt, a large and beautiful sheet of placid water, laves the western side of the grounds.

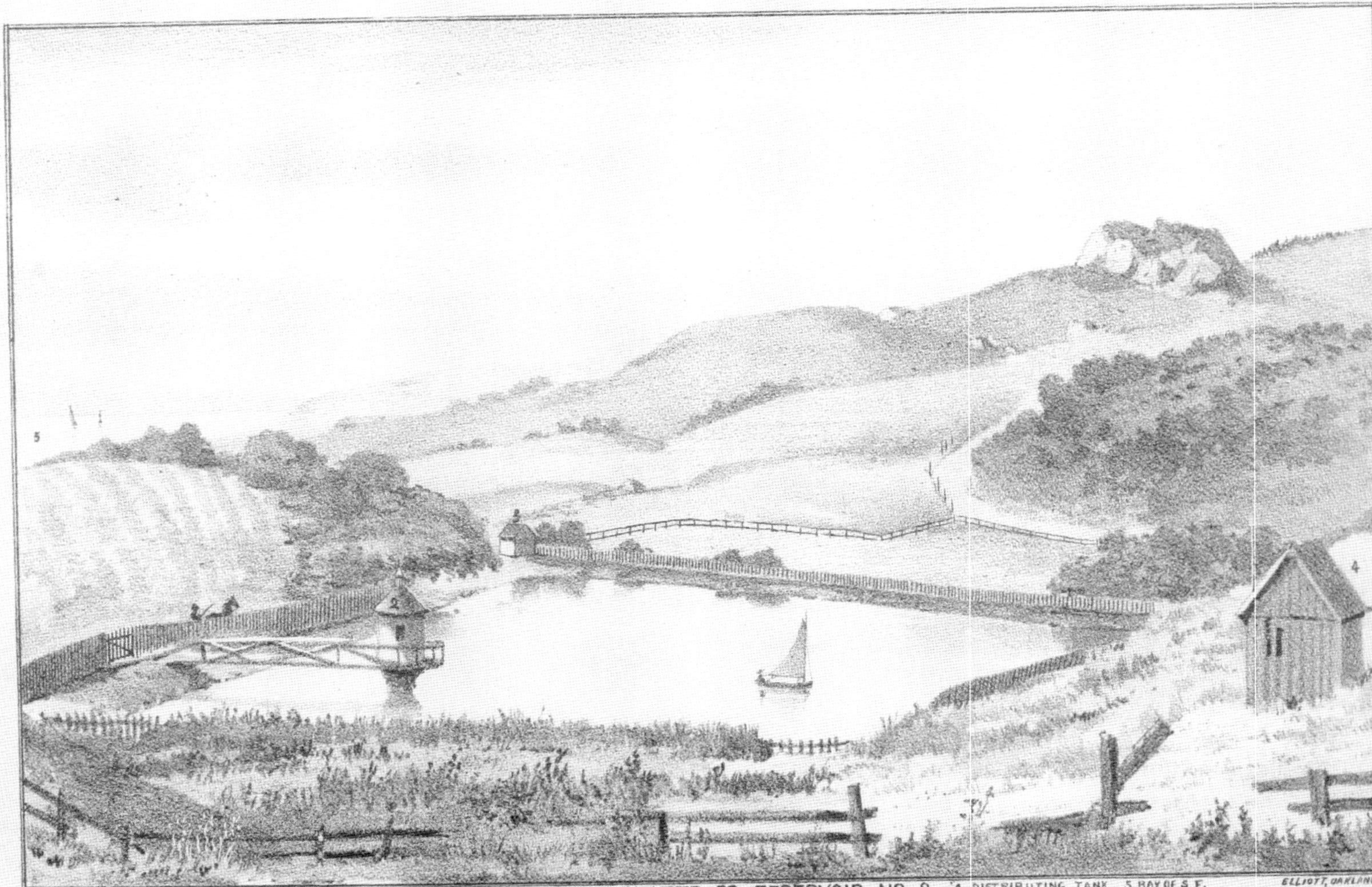

1. RESERVOIR 2. OUTLET TOWER 3. TOOL HOUSE. ALAMEDA WATER CO. RESERVOIR NO. 2. 4. DISTRIBUTING. TANK 5. BAY OF S. F. ELLIOTT, OAKLAND.

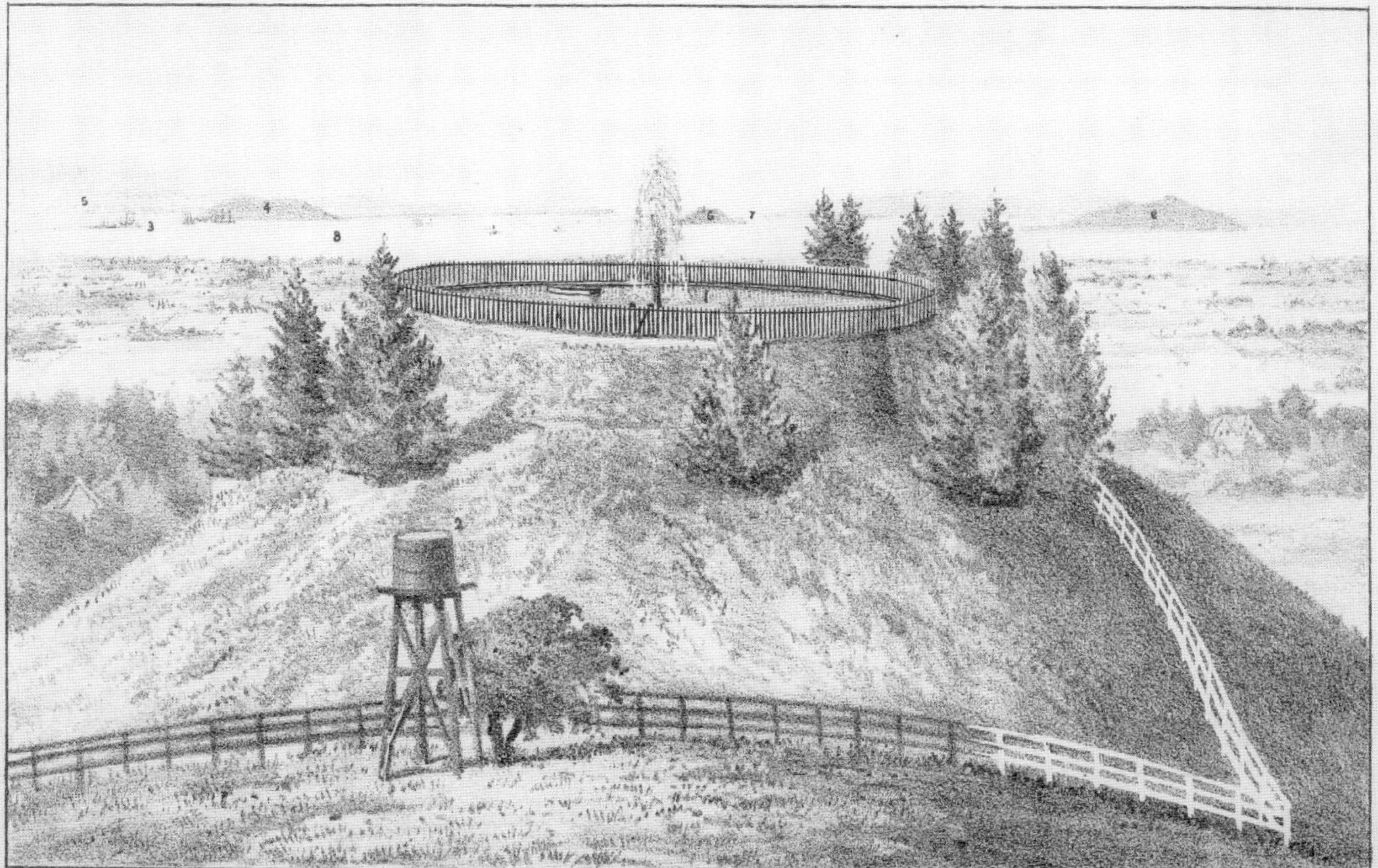

2. PRIVATE TANK. 4. GOAT ISLAND. 3. C.P.R.R. WHARF. 5. SAN FRANCISCO. ALAMEDA WATER CO'S DISTRIBUTING RESERVOIR NO.1. 6. FORT ALCATRAZ. 7. GOLDEN GATE. 8. BAY OF S.F. 9. ANGEL ISLAND

ELLIOTT, OAKLAND.

Banks and Banking.

THE OAKLAND BANK OF SAVINGS has one of the most substantial brick buildings in the city, on the corner of Broadway and Twelfth Street. The building was erected in 1876. Its capital and reserve paid in is $500,000. The directors are: Francis Blake, Henry Rogers, W. E. Miller, R. E. Cole, Samuel Merritt, Israel Lawton, W. A. Aldrich, E. C. Sessions, E. A. Haines. E. C. Sessions, President, and W. W. Garthwaite, Secretary.

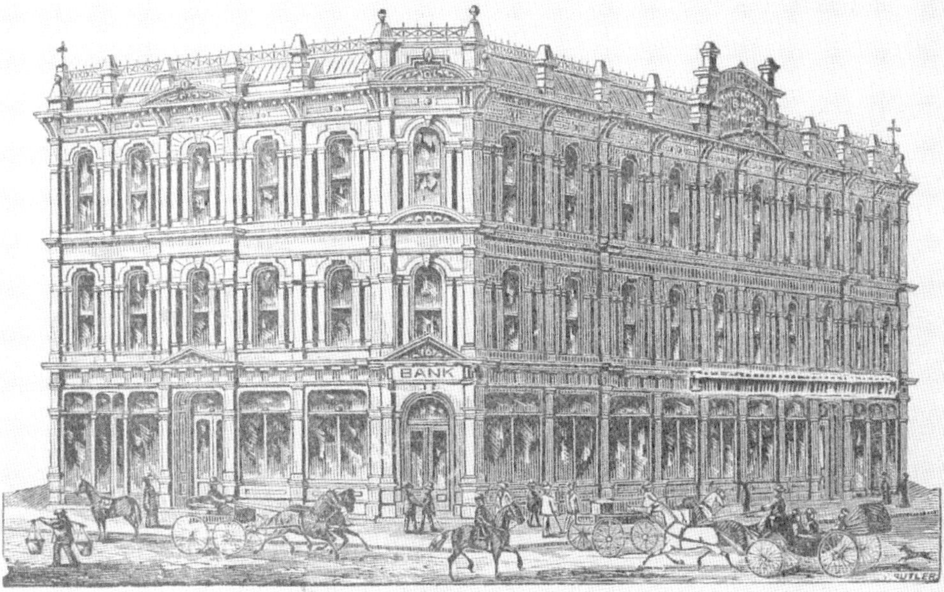

OAKLAND BANK OF SAVINGS, CORNER BROADWAY AND TWELFTH STREET.

The bank was organized August 13, 1867, with a capital stock of $150,000, which was increased to $300,000, and by further action of the stockholders was increased to $1,000,000. The bank draws directly on Dublin, Paris, and London.

The bank has recently erected in the building at large expense a steel fire and burglar-proof safe-deposit vault. The object in view is the furnishing at a moderate charge of a safe and convenient place for the keeping of valuables.

There are many purposes for which such a place of deposit in Oakland will prove, as in other cities, to be a matter of great convenience to ladies as well as to business men, such as the storage of diamonds, jewelry, silverware, valuable mementoes, bank-books, notes and mortgages, stocks, bonds, deeds, wills, marriage records, and other valuable papers and articles.

Five hundred small safes inside of the main vault are offered at a low rental, to which access can be had as frequently as desired. Diamonds and jewelry can be withdrawn one day and re-deposited the next. Tin boxes to fit the safes are furnished, which may, for the purposes of packing, be taken to the residence or can be examined at leisure, free from observation, in the private room furnished for use of ladies exclusively.

Large packages of silverware, or other bulky articles, to which access is only required at rare intervals. are stowed in a separate compartment in the main vault.

All business entirely confidential. The only keys to the safes are delivered to the renter, and it is not possible for any person other than the renter or some person designated by him, to have access to the safe or to know of its contents.

Union Savings Bank.

THE UNION SAVINGS BANK of Oakland began business in July, 1869, near the corner of Broadway and Eighth Streets, the President being A. C. Henry, and the Cashier, H. A. Palmer. The capital stock was originally $150,000, which, in a few years, was increased to $450,000. In 1871 the present building at the corner of Ninth Street and Broadway was constructed, whither they moved on the 1st of May of that year. In 1875 the bank was reorganized under the Civil Code, when it separated its commercial from its saving business, and transferred the former to the Union National Gold Bank, with the same management. saving the election of Hon. J. West Martin as President in the place of A. C. Henry. The status of the bank is most satisfactory. The present capital, fully paid, is $200,000, with a reserve fund of $100,000. The directors of the bank are: J. West Martin, R. W. Kirkham, A. C. Henry, Hiram Tubbs, D. Henshaw Ward, R. S. Farrelly, H. A. Palmer, Socrates Huff, W. W. Crane, Jr., A. A. Moore. President, J. West Martin; Vice-President and Treasurer, H. A. Palmer. The bank does a purely "savings" business, investing its funds in mortgages, etc.

"Union Savings Bank Building" is illustrated in this work, and situated on the corner of Broadway and Ninth Street.

Union National Bank.

UNION NATIONAL BANK institution was organized July 1, 1875, under the National Banking Act of the United States, and succeeded to the commercial business of the Union Savings Bank. The first officers were: A. C. Henry, President; H. A. Palmer, Cashier. The bank remained under the first management until October 1, 1881, when Mr. Henry was succeeded on his resignation by H. A. Palmer, who was elected to the presidency, and Charles E. Palmer, Cashier. On March 8, 1881, the institution was changed, under the Act of Congress, to the Union National Bank, transacting its business in the same building as does the Union Savings Bank, the organization of officers being identical with it save as regards the President and Cashier.

First National Bank.

THE First National Bank was originally organized as the First National Gold Bank in May, 1875. In 1876 V. D. Moody was elected to the presidency under whom, and with the same name, it was conducted. In 1878 Mr. Twombly was elected Cashier. On March 8, 1880, the institution was reorganized, under the style of the First National Bank of Oakland, with the same management, and in February, 1883, moved to No. 1002 Broadway, where they are now located. Financially the bank has been a success.

Its officers are: V. D. Moody, President; J. E. Ruggles, Vice-President; A. D. Thomson, Cashier. Board of Directors: A. Chabot, J. E. Ruggles, G. J. Ainsworth, A. J. Snyder, W. P. Jones, V. D. Moody, F. K. Shattuck, J. C. Ainsworth, L. C. Morehouse. The bank transacts a general commercial banking business.

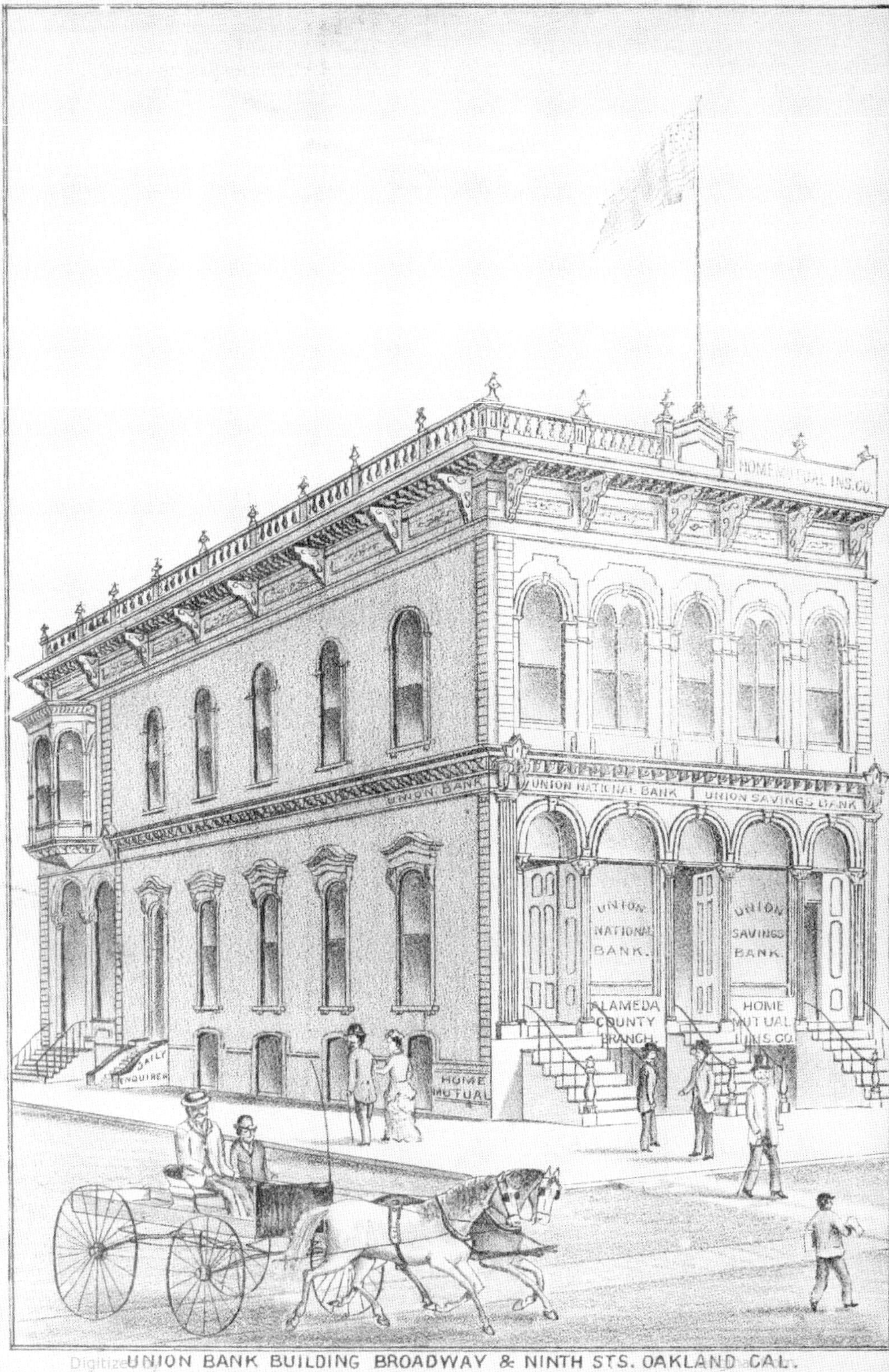

UNION BANK BUILDING BROADWAY & NINTH STS. OAKLAND CAL.

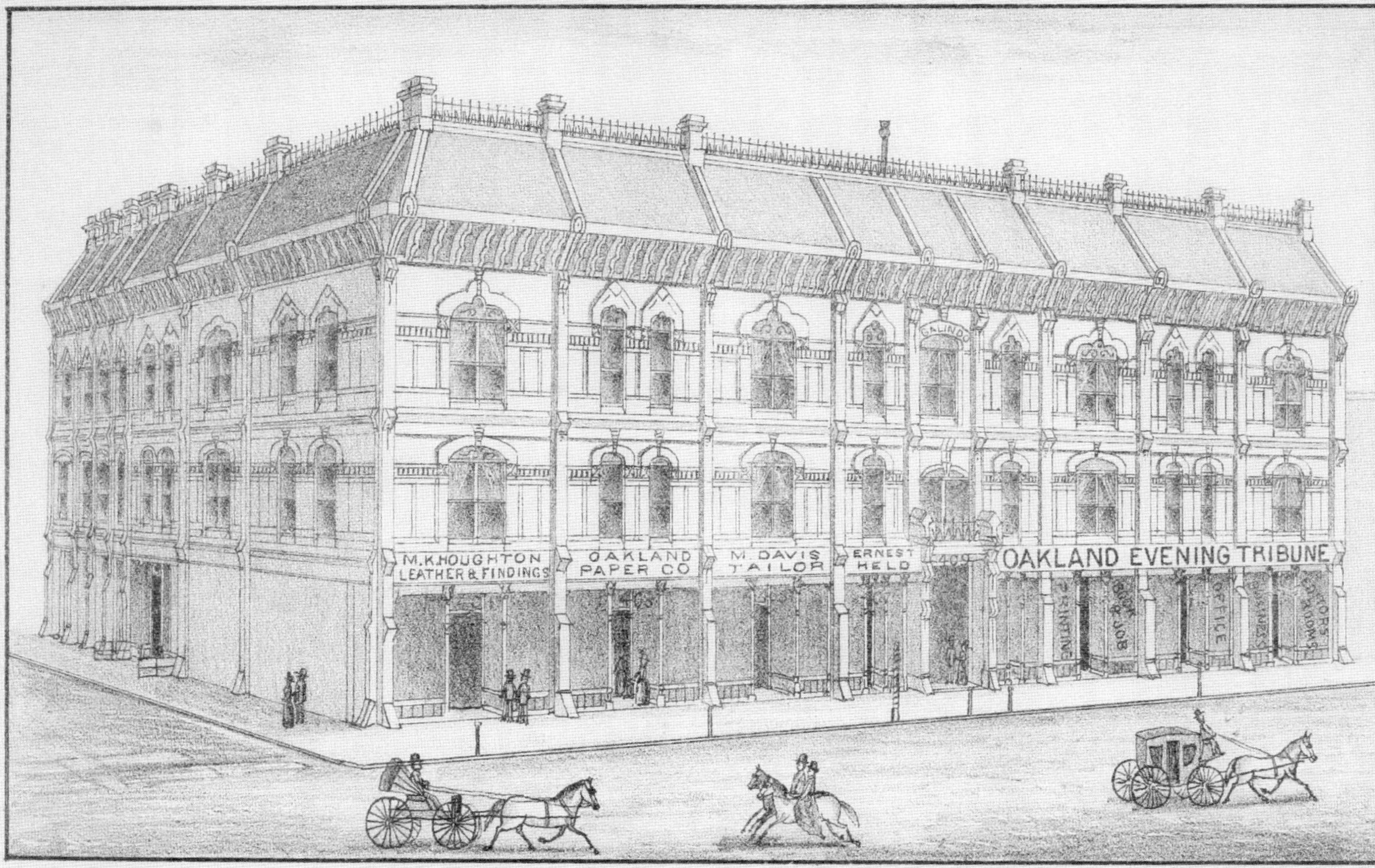

GALINDO HOTEL, B. WRIGHT, PROPRIETOR.

Means of Communication.

Oakland Ferries.

MUCH enthusiasm was evinced in Oakland on August 2, 1862, on the commencement of the ferry railroad, and the initial steps being taken towards the construction of the wharf, proceedings which caused an immediate advance of about fifty per cent in the value of real estate. On September 2, 1863, the railroad ferry went into operation, with the following time-table, which is produced simply as a matter of comparison between now and then:—

Leave San Francisco at 7 A. M., 9 A. M., 11 A. M., 2:30 P. M., 4:30 P. M., 6:30 P. M.

Leave Oakland at 6 A. M., 8 A. M., 10 A. M., 1 P. M., 3:30 P. M., 5:30 P. M.

In regard to the ferries no better service exists anywhere. The mole and depot by the Central Pacific Railroad have added materially to the comfort of passengers on the main local line, while the creek route has its fair share of patronage. Add to these the boon conferred by the South Pacific Coast Railroad Company and their excellent line of ferry-boats which, landing on the Alameda side of the San Antonio Creek, transfer their passengers by a local line over Webster Street Bridge into the heart of the city, gives us travel nowhere excelled.

The crowning glory of Oakland is the depot and ferry-house of the Central Pacific Railroad, and which is the largest and completest structure of the kind at present in the world, an illustration of which is herewith presented.

Rapid and Safe Transit.

MEANS of communication between Oakland and the metropolis are of the most admirable kind. The Central Pacific or Broad Gauge has five large and elegantly equipped ferry-boats, three of which are in constant use, and two held as reserve in case of accident. One of these runs to the foot of Broadway, and is used largely for freight and carriage travel. Two run to the terminal depot at the end of the mole and connect with the half-hourly trains to the several Oakland stations, to Berkeley and Alameda.

Twenty minutes after the boat leaves the wharf in San Francisco it arrives at the mole. Twenty minutes later the trains connecting with it have reached the furthest stations in Oakland, Alameda, and Berkeley, having deposited their passengers at a score of neat little stations along the line.

The local system of the Central Pacific, including its branches to East Berkeley and West Berkeley, is about twenty miles in length, and represents, with terminal depot, mole, buildings of all kinds, track, boats, and rolling stock, a capital of not less than $3,000,000. The boats and rolling stocks required for the service may be tabulated as follows:—

Passenger Coaches	75
Locomotives	15
Boats	5
Trains (daily average)	190

Central Pacific Terminal Depot.

THE buildings comprising the depot cover nearly four acres and a half. They have a frontage on the bay of 240 feet, and a total length of 1,050 feet. Their architectural design is simple yet symmetrical and pleasing, the main point considered in their construction being the convenience of travelers and quickness and ease of transfer. The stairways are broad, the waiting-rooms large and well lighted, the floors smooth and solid, and all furnishings and appointments neat and appropriate.

The structure includes five buildings grouped according to a general design—a main central building with which four others are aligned. Of these the two larger begin at the eastern end of the central structure and extend on either side of it down the arms of the slip. They are each 720 feet in length by 60 feet in width. They are for the accommodation of the local travel alone. The main structure, whose western end is in a line with the end of the mole, is 450 feet long by 120 feet broad and 60 feet high. Its seaward elevation is flanked by two towers 85 feet in height.

The second floor is occupied in great part by the main waiting-room, an immense apartment extending the full width of the building, 120 feet, and having a length of 70 feet, with a height of nearly 50 feet. It will accommodate 3,500 people.

Light is admitted from the top as well as from windows on all sides, which afford a view of the vast interior, the broad expanse of the bay, and of San Francisco.

The roofs are of iron and glass, through which the light is admitted so freely as fairly to flood the spacious interior. All the rooms are warmed by steam, though the climate requires but a slight degree of artificial heat. Though the building accommodates the overland and State travel, it is chiefly the result of the suburban needs of San Francisco and Oakland.

The mole and Terminal Depot have cost not far from $1,500,000, and it is safe to say that, considering this vast expenditure, and the value of the tracks and appurtenances of these local roads, no similar amount, outside of London, has been expended anywhere in the world to facilitate intercourse between any large city and its immediate suburbs. Over 600,000,000 passengers annually pass over this ferry.

The "Mole."

THE western terminal station of the Central Pacific Railroad rests upon a pier of earthwork and rock running out into San Francisco Bay from its eastern shore a distance of one and a quarter miles, having a wharf and ferry slip at its western extremity. The mole reaches to a height of ten feet above high tide, with a width sufficient for a double-track railroad and a passenger depot, to be 200 feet wide and 900 feet long. The material, 1,000,000 cubic yards of rock, was transported in cars, a distance of nearly thirty miles. Work was commenced in June, 1879, and completed in 1881.

Four parallel tracks extend from the Oakland shore, a distance of 4,800 feet, and thence to the terminus; additional tracks (twelve in all) are laid, ten of which pass through the depot building. From the western end of the rock-pier extends the pile-work forming the ferry-slip, and foundation for a portion of the main wings of the depot building. The slip is 600 feet in length by 177 feet in width at its entrance, and has a sufficient depth of water for the largest ferry-steamers at the lowest tides.

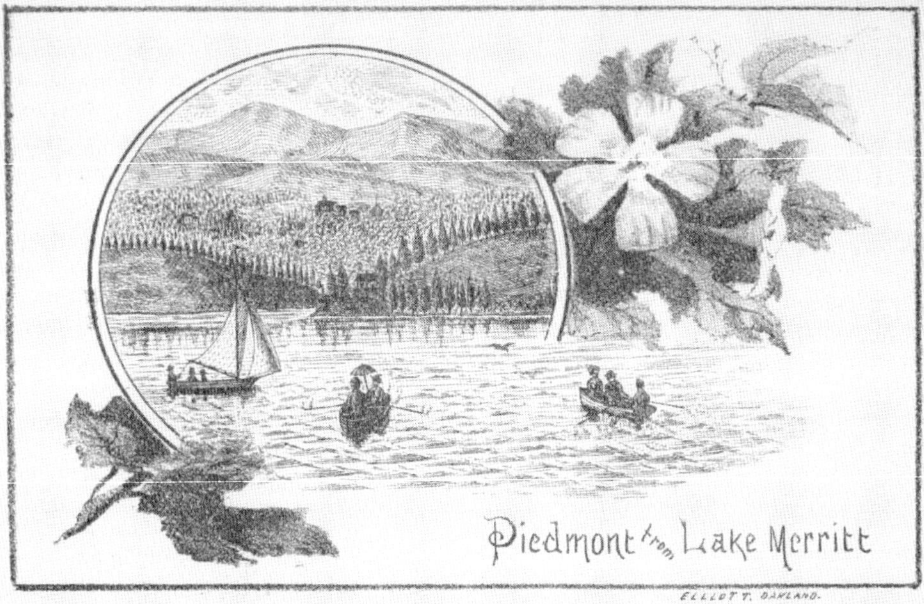

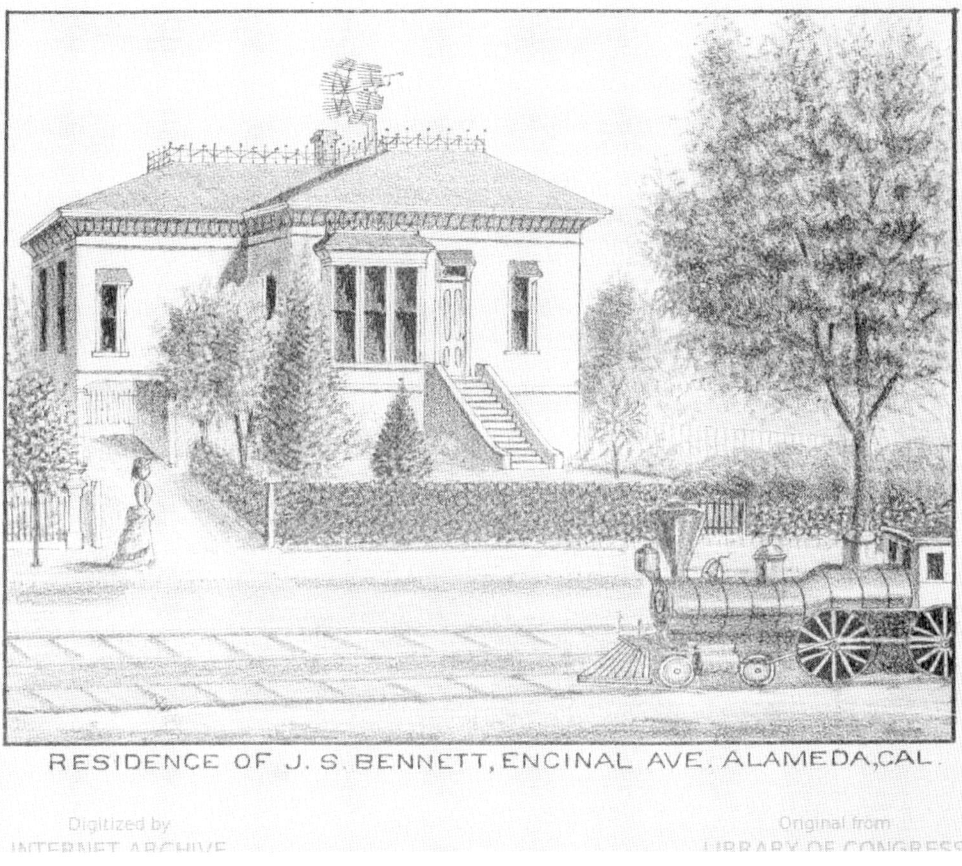

RESIDENCE OF J. S. BENNETT, ENCINAL AVE. ALAMEDA, CAL.

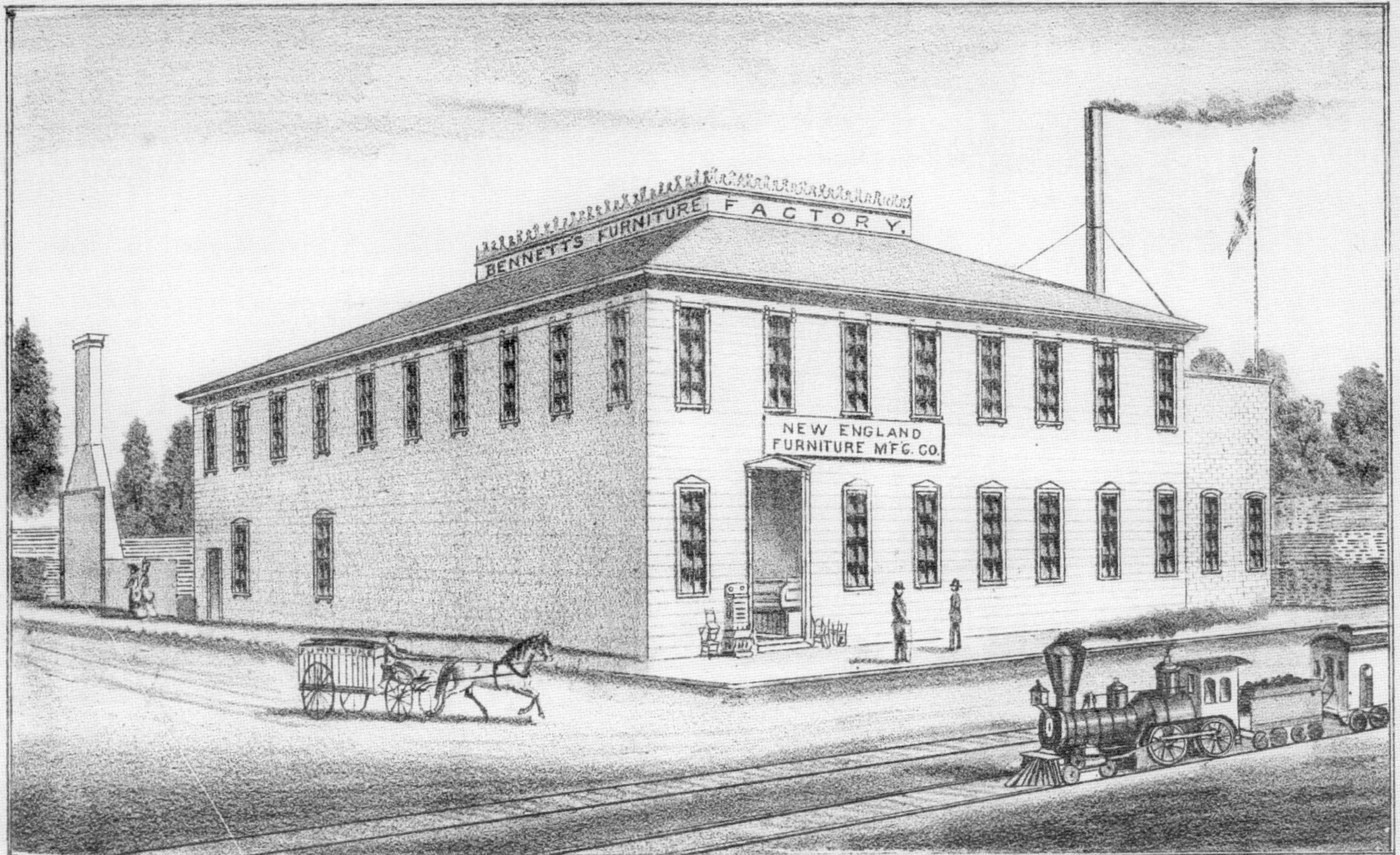

J.S. BENNETT. FURNITURE FACTORY. COR. WALNUT & ENCINAL AVE. ALAMEDA CAL.
WAREROOMS 401 & 403 12TH ST. OAKLAND. CAL

ELLIOTT, LITH OAK. CAL.

Free Railroad Rides.

THE Central Pacific Railroad is probably the only railroad in the world that furnishes *free rides* to all that wish to travel in or through the city. Every half-hour during the day long trains of passenger cars, going either way on Seventh Street, are patronized by all classes, rich and poor, white or black, American or Chinese, without cost. The length of this free ride is from the West Oakland Station along Seventh Street about five miles to East Oakland. People can get on and off at any of the following stations:—

West Oakland, corner Wood and Seventh; *Center*, corner Seventh and Center; *Adeline*, corner Seventh and Adeline; *Market*, corner Seventh and Market; *Broadway*, Seventh, between Washington and Broadway; *Oak*, Seventh and Oak; *Clinton*, foot of Fifth Avenue; *East Oakland*, foot of Thirteenth Avenue; *Fruitvale*, and *Melrose*.

South Pacific Railroad.

THE South Pacific Coast Railroad Company, or the Narrow Gauge as it is popularly called, has three large and fast boats, which run to Alameda and connect with a train to Fourteenth Street in Oakland. The trains run along the south training wall of Oakland Harbor and crossing the estuary at Webster Street continue up to Fourteenth Street. This route is some minutes quicker than the old route, and when extended beyond its present limits will be a very popular line. It first began business in 1878 and has rapidly increased in favor. Nothing can be more invigorating to the tired and perplexed merchant, or to the weary clerk and mechanic, than this short daily excursion by water, to which is added a brief trip by rail among orchards, gardens, cottages, and beautiful homes.

This road also contributes its share of trade, tapping, as it does, the fertile valleys of Santa Clara and the rich country bordering the line between this point and Santa Cruz. This road is a favorite mode of transport for excursionists desiring to reach the famous summer resorts of Santa Cruz and the intermediate points of Felton and the Big Trees.

The future of Oakland as a terminal point is full of great possibilities, and with an increase of trade and population will rival any similar point in the country. The depots of the various lines are expensive structures, built with a view to public convenience and easy transfer of passengers and freight.

This road also runs trains every half-hour directly from Oakland to Alameda. This is the popular route to Alameda Baths and Neptune Gardens.

Street-Car Lines.

THERE are eight horse-car railroads in this city which have an aggregate length of about thirty-five miles. Nearly all lines connect at the corner of Seventh Street and Broadway on arrival of trains.

Oakland and Alameda cars leave Broadway at Seventh Street for Park Street, Alameda; time, thirty-five minutes. These cars carry passengers to the Neptune Gardens and Baths.

Highland Park and Fruitvale cars leave East Oakland for Fruitvale, passing through Highland Park and stopping at the Hermitage.

San Pablo Avenue line of cars leave Broadway and run along San Pablo Avenue to the Fair Grounds and Race Track to the section of the city called Emeryville.

Telegraph Avenue street-car line leaves Broadway and Seventh Streets every seven minutes for Temescal; there connection is made with the steam dummy for Berkeley and the University.

Broadway and Piedmont cars run from Seventh and Washington to Mountain View Cemetery and Piedmont; running time, twenty-five minutes. This is a very popular line. Passengers reach Blair's Park by this route. Cars leave on arrival of trains at Broadway Station.

Fourteenth street-car line runs from Seventh and Washington to Sixteenth Street Depot, also Wood Street, Point Station; running time, twenty minutes. Leave Seventh and Washington every half-hour.

Oakland, Brooklyn, and Fruitvale street-cars run from Seventh and Broadway to Thirteenth Avenue, East Oakland; running time, twenty minutes. These cars pass Tubbs' Hotel and Lake Merritt Boat House.

Market street-cars run from the junction of Market and the Central Pacific Railroad, along Market and Adeline to Thirty-second Street.

The City Council of Oakland has granted a franchise to J. G. Fair, Esq., the San Francisco capitalist, to operate a street railroad by cable or animal power from Broadway and Seventh Streets through Grove Street.

One of the important and convenient ways of reaching Berkeley is by means of the Telegraph Avenue Street Railway and Dummy line. This road begins at Seventh and Broadway, where it makes close connection with the local train of the Central Pacific Railroad, and, running the length of Telegraph Avenue, connects with the Dummy line at Temescal, which has its terminus at the University Grounds. The trip from Broadway to the University is made in about forty minutes. A trip over this line gives one a fine view of the Golden Gate, and many of the beautiful residences which line the way.

The cars begin their trips at 5:35 A. M., and run till 12:35 P. M. During the busy hours cars run every seven minutes.

Broadway and Piedmont Cars.

THE Broadway and Piedmont Street Railroad connects Piedmont with the Broadway Station. A ride upon it during the pleasant weather of winter or in the early spring is like a delightful excursion into the country. It winds up to its destination through green fields belonging to Walter Blair, its builder, through blooming orchards and tree-bordered avenues, across or through which the cities by the sea and far-off villages and hills are visible. Horse railroads are usually prosaic means of traveling, but a trip by this one has the veritable air of romance, and no visit to Oakland is complete without it. Branches of this road connect with Oakland Point and Alameda.

This is the line that passes the entrance of Blair's Park, a beautiful resort lately opened and free to visitors.

Alameda and Oakland Cars.

IT may be interesting to the public generally to know that, aside from the steam cars that make hourly and half-hourly trips from Oakland to Alameda, there is the Oakland and Alameda horse-car line that makes its regular trips every half-hour during the day, connecting at Seventh and Broadway with the Central Pacific Railroad local trains to and from San Francisco.

The cars run from Oakland to the Alameda Baths (fare five cents), giving passengers the shortest, cheapest, and most direct route to these resorts.

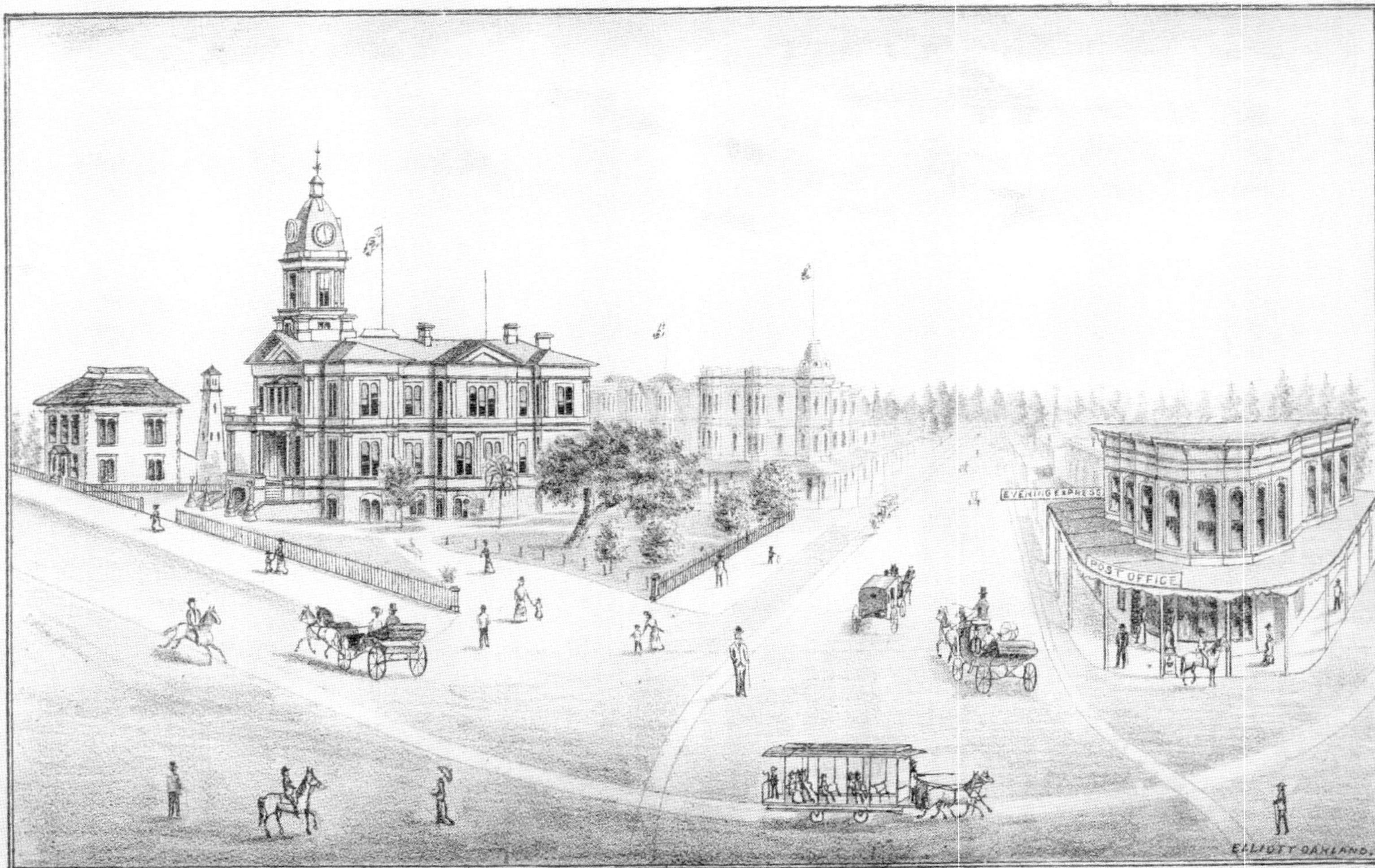

"LIBRARY." "14TH. STREET." "CITY HALL." STREET VIEW IN OAKLAND. "SAN PABLO AVENUE." "POST OFFICE." "BROADWAY."

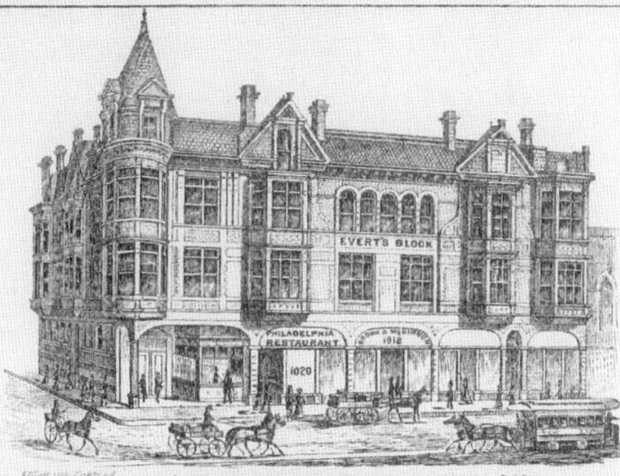

EVERT'S BLOCK BROADWAY & 11TH STREETS. OAK.

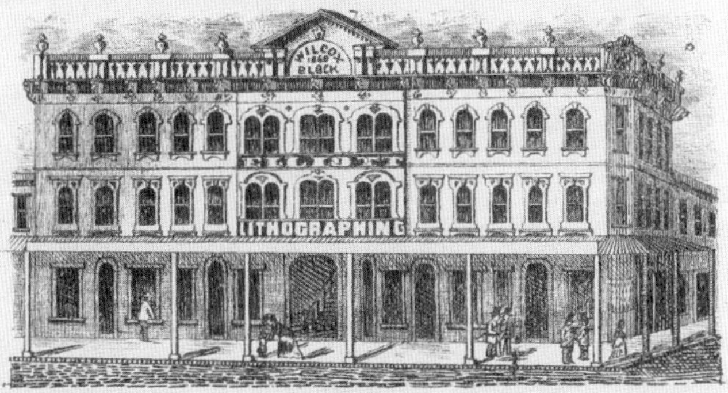

ELLIOTT LITHOGRAPHING ESTABLISHMENT 921 BROADWAY. OAK.

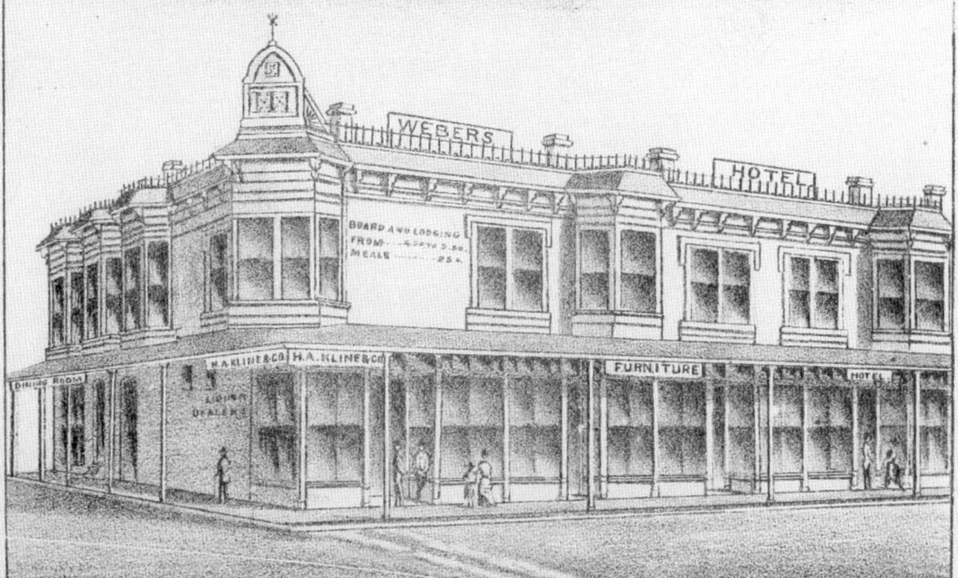

SALE ROOMS OF ALAMEDA FURNITURE FACTORY 12TH & FRANKLIN ST. OAK.

East Oakland.

East Oakland.

EAST OAKLAND was a separate township until 1872, when it, by vote of the inhabitants, became a part of Oakland and constitutes the Seventh Ward. East Oakland, or, as it is commonly called, Brooklyn, is that part of Oakland lying east of Lake Merritt.

Brooklyn, in addition to being a delightful residence locality, shows signs of greater business activity than almost any place of its size in California. The manufacturing interests are as follows: The only cotton mill in the State, a jute sack factory, employing about four hundred and fifty men, two tanneries, two breweries, a steam flouring-mill, an extensive terra-cotta manufactory, two potteries, a planing-mill, sash, door, and blind factory, and a number of wagon manufactories and repair shops.

There are several railway stations along the Central Pacific within the township, and, with the street railroads and excellent carriage drives, all parts are made accessible, and many of the inhabitants of Brooklyn transact daily their business in San Francisco. Brooklyn is accounted one of the most desirable suburbs of San Francisco, and in summer many business men of that city resort hither on account of the quiet and picturesque retreats here afforded

There are many large residences and numerous pretty cottages. Of these we have been permitted to represent in this work those of Geo. R. Williams, 1113 Eighth Avenue, and G. E. Yates, 1354 Tenth Avenue. These are representative handsome homes, which abound in that section.

Fruitvale is two miles and a half from East Oakland, and connected therewith by a horse railroad. It lies embowered in the hills just where Sausal Creek emerges from the Coast Range. An intervening ridge excludes the sea wind and creates an atmosphere of almost perpetual summer. A lonely valley in the heart of the Sierra could hardly have an air of greater quiet and repose. The residents are principally retired merchants, and persons engaged in raising fruit. A visit to these vineyards and cherry orchards is one of the attractions of Oakland. It is the fame of its fruit that has given name to the locality.

Highland Park.

HIGHLAND PARK is on elevated ground not far from the Brooklyn Station. It is one of the two points, in the neighborhood of Oakland, where the local road approaches the hills. It is therefore near the city, and yet in the heart of the country. Fifteen minutes' walk from the station and five minutes' ride on the street railroad, brings the visitor into the midst of shady cañons and green hills covered with eucalyptus, cypress, and locust, villas surrounded by neat lawns, and all the evidences of city refinement joined with rural comfort.

Ten years ago, when E. C. Sessions, the owner of the tract, began his improvements, it presented the smooth, round outlines of all the foot-hill region. He had it laid out after the best principles of landscape gardening, and resolved that it should not be parted with, except to persons who would build well and continue the generous system of ornamentation which he had inaugurated. The protective rules he established have been enforced.

The property is sold in ample subdivisions, or lots, none of which have less than 100 feet front. The smallest are therefore large enough to contain large houses with lawn, garden, and the usual suburban accessories. The residences are built on the crests or higher portions of the hills, with grounds sloping into the depressions, so that Oakland, San Francisco, and the ample features of the broad landscape, can be seen from every tower and balcony. The water is brought into every house from one of the reservoirs of the Contra Costa Water Company. All can have gas who desire it. The public schools are within a few blocks, and speedy means of communication permit the daily attendance of residents at any one of the private schools of Oakland or Berkeley.

Lake Merritt.

THIS fine sheet of water is located within the limits of the city. It separates the central portion of East Oakland, covers an area of 240 acres, and is nearly five miles in circumference. It is a clear and wholesome sheet of water, a rare ornament to the city, and a beautiful feature of the landscape. Persons living along the lake provide their own boats for family use. It is a popular resort, and on summer afternoons its surface is dotted with the white sails of small crafts. Boats can be hired at boat-houses situated at the Twelfth Street crossing. Horse-cars pass along Twelfth Street and take passengers directly to the boat-house.

A magnificent boulevard is about being constructed around the lake. This will give a drive of somewhat over three miles, rivaling in completeness and picturesque loveliness anything artificial in the world. The plans provide for the construction of a boulevard 150 feet wide, nearly the entire distance to be taken up as follows: Next to the shore a side-walk, 10 feet in width; then a single horse-car track for cars going out; next to this two carriage ways, each 40 feet in width, the one divided from the other by a row of trees, so that people making the circuit from one direction will all travel the same way, those coming from the other direction passing on the other drive, thus avoiding any clashing or confusion, and in a large measure providing against accidents. Next to the carriage way is to be constructed a separate and distinct track, 24 feet wide, for the accommodation of equestrian parties; next to this a second horse-car track for returning cars. Another side-walk, next to the bulkhead and lake, will occupy the remainder of the width of the way.

The new boulevard would form a municipal pleasure-ground and breathing-place, equal for beauty of outline and capacity for improvement to any on the continent. When the improvements are completed, as they are sure to be within a few years, there will be nothing of the kind in the world which will excel in loveliness this little sheet of water with its splendid residences, its green lawns filled with semitropical shrubbery terraced to the water's edge, its distant prospect, its white sails glistening in the sunlight, and its circling lights glowing and glistening with fairy-like splendor at night.

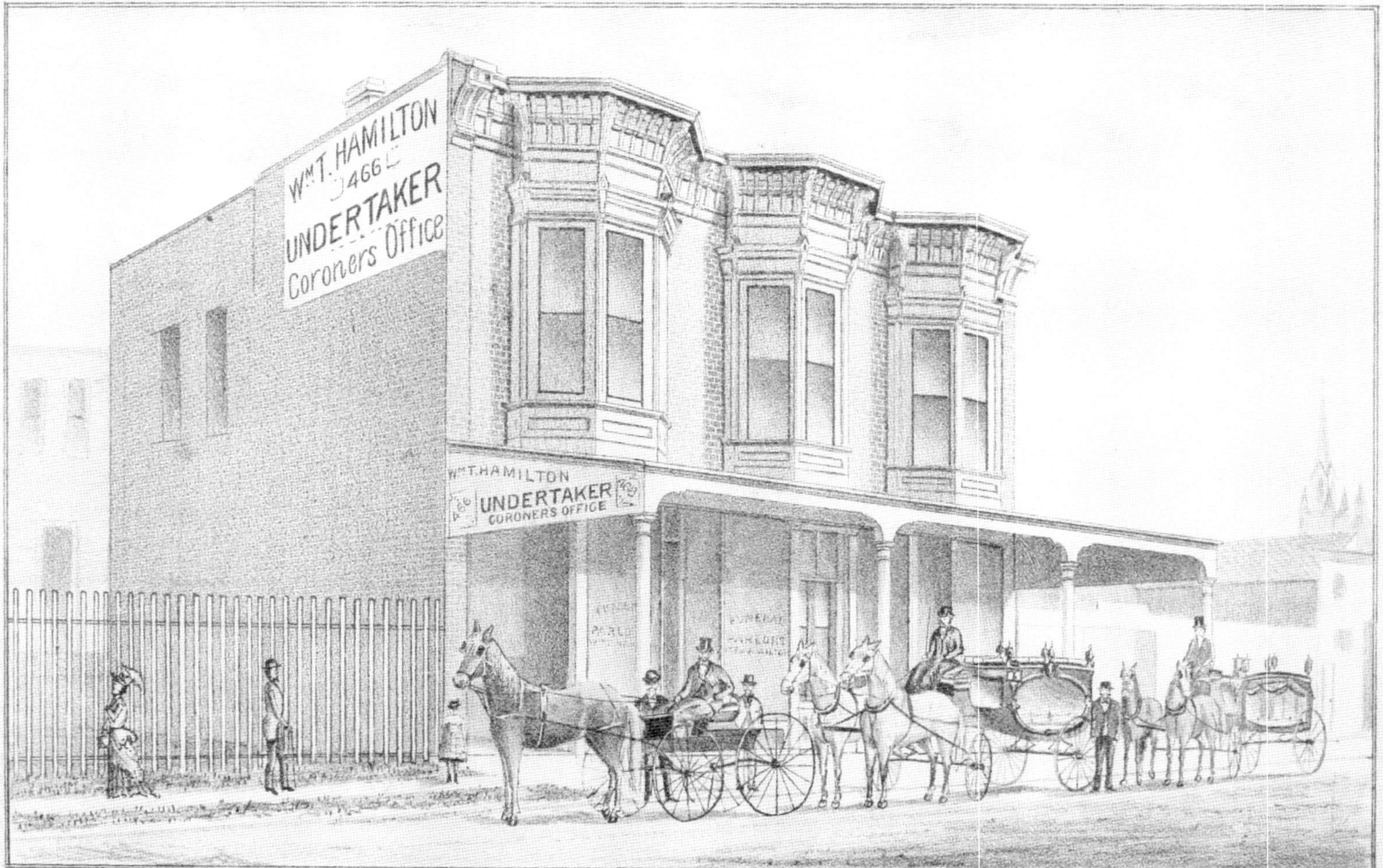

W.T. HAMILTON, UNDERTAKER, 466 & 468 13TH ST. OAKLAND, CAL.

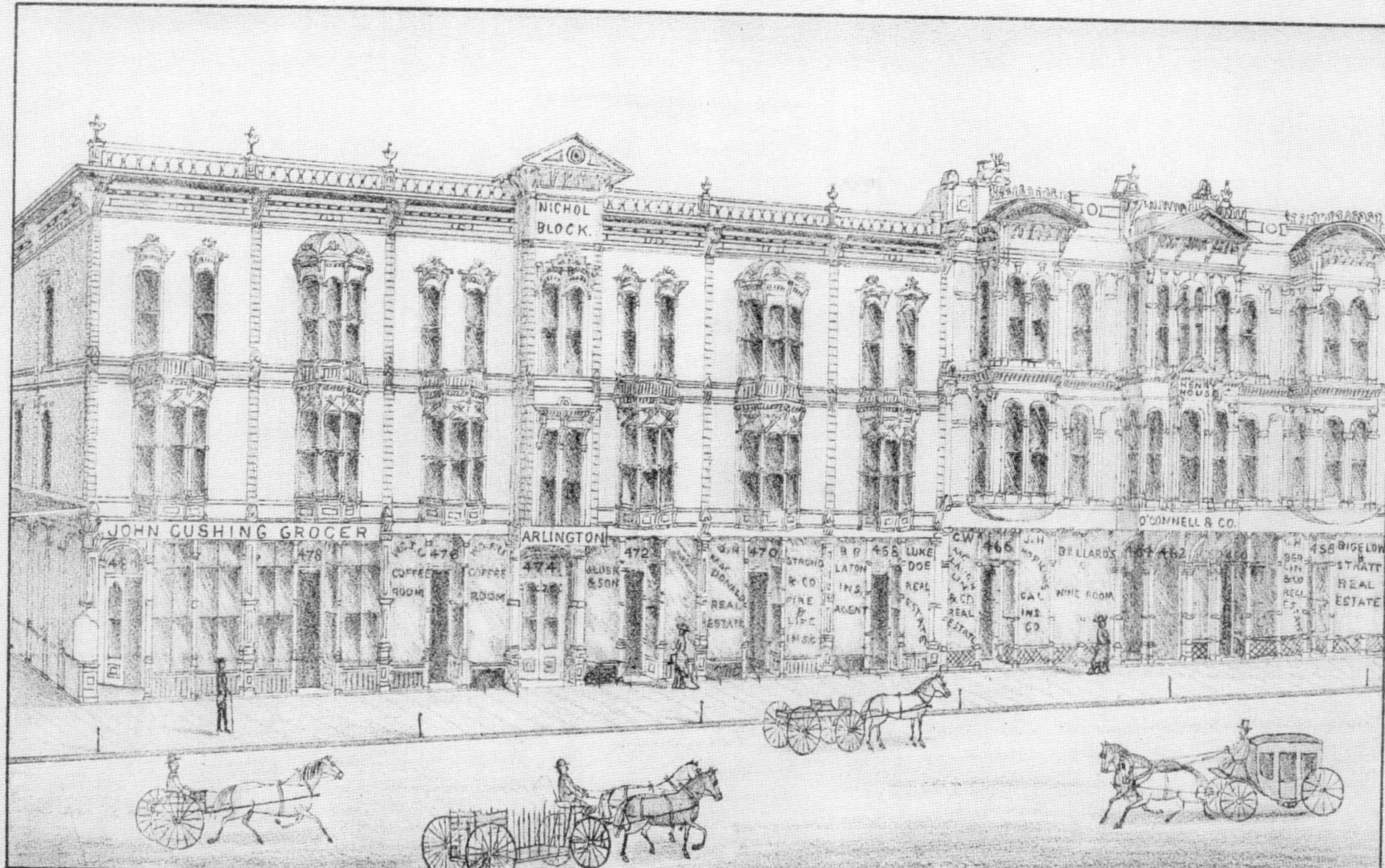

NINTH STREET, COR. WASHINGTON OAKLAND CAL.

ELLIOTT OAKLAND.

Municipal Matters.

City Officers.

THE city is governed by a board of seven councilmen selected from the different wards. The Mayor is elected by the people annually.

E. W. Playter is the present Mayor, having been elected in March last. In his first message he recommended that large retrenchments be made in expenses of running the city government, and in no way, said he, can we do more to promote the growth and prosperity of our fair city than by a rigid economy of administration.

The Mayor is a native of New Jersey, and came to this coast from Buffalo, New York, in 1852. He settled in Oakland in 1864, where he has resided since in the handsome residence illustrated in this work.

The Council is composed of the following members: J. L. Carothers, J. H. Smith, T. L. Barker, T. G. Harrison, John Hackett, James McGiveney, and Henry Hayes. Mr. Cutter is President of the Council. G. M. Fisher is City Clerk and Treasurer; James M. Dillon, Assessor, and C. T. Johns is City Attorney.

Police and Fire Department.

THE city is districted into some eleven districts, patrolled by eighteen regular police officers. One police officer is detailed to patrol all the local trains; there are two detectives; two sergeants, who patrol all over the city, keeping the officers in view at odd hours and places; one bailiff, two jailers, and one clerk. It will be observed that the territory embraced in several districts is of large extent, and it would be impossible for an officer to make more than one or two rounds in twelve hours. Yet this force has no difficulty in keeping an orderly city, and few disturbances of magnitude occur.

The Fire Department was organized March 13, 1869, and is at the present time composed of a chief engineer, two assistant engineers, and a superintendent of fire alarm and police telegraph, while its force consists of 4 steamers, 5 two-wheel hose-carts, carrying 3,700 feet of hose, 2 hook and ladder trucks, 64 officers and men, 182 hydrants, 5 cisterns, and 46 fire alarms. Water for the use of the department is supplied by the works of the Contra Costa Water Company.

Mayors of Oakland.

THE Mayors of Oakland, in the order of their election, are as follows, beginning with the year of incorporation of the city:—

1854. Horace W. Carpentier.	1870. A. Williams.
1855. Charles Campbell.	1871. U. W. Spaulding.
1856. S. H. Robinson.	1872. U. W. Spaulding.
1857. A. Williams.	1873. Henry Durant.
1858. A. Williams.	1874. Henry Durant.
1859. F. K. Shattuck.	1875. Mack Webber.
1860. J. P. M. Davis.	1876. E. H. Pardee.
1861. J. P. M. Davis.	1877. E. H. Pardee.
1862. George M. Blake.	1878. W. R. Andrus.
1863. W. H. Bovee.	1879. W. R. Andrus.
1864. Edward Gibbons.	1880. James E. Blethen.
1865. B. F. Ferris.	1881. James E. Blethen.
1866. J. W. Dwinelle.	1882. C. K. Robinson.
1867. W. W. Crane, Jr.	1883. J. West Martin.
1868. Samuel Merritt.	1884. A. C. Henry.
1869. John B. Felton.	1885. E. W. Playter.

Oakland Real Estate.

FOLLOWING is the estimated value of lands and buildings belonging to the city of Oakland, the estimate having been made by City Assessor Dillon:—

Property.	Land.	Bldgs.	Fur'e & Apprtus.
Prescott School	$ 7,600	$23,500	$4,500
Cole "	8,925	32,500	4,000
High "	10,700	33,000	7,000
Tompkins "	4,800	20,000	4,500
Grove Street School	6,500	3,000	1,000
Lafayette School	28,000	12,000	3,000
Durant "	4,000	29,500	3,700
Lincoln "	16,000	26,000	4,000
Harrison "		2,000	600
New Broadway School	7,000	10,000	1,500
Swett School	5,000	5,000	800
Franklin "	12,000	23,000	3,000
32d Street, lot	2,400		
17th and West, lot	3,200		
East 14th Street, lot	1,100		
Total School property	$110,225	$209,500	$36,100

Property.	Land.	Bldgs.	Fur'e & Apprtus.
City Hall	$140,000	$45,000	$10,000
Library Building		2,500	11,300
City Wharf	45,000	20,000	
Telegraph Dep't			21,400
Street Dep't			2,765
Fire Dep't Property	10,700	13,614	57,891
Lafayette Square	28,000		
Jefferson "	16,000		
Washington "	90,000		
Franklin "	75,000		
Harrison "	17,000		
Oakland "	28,000		
Lincoln "	28,000		
Plaza near Lake	6,000		
Clinton Square	14,000		
Independence Square	25,000		
Totals	$631,425	$290,614	$139,456

Total value of all property owned by the city ... $1,061,495
Total value of the school property ... 385,824

VALUATION OF PROPERTY.

The following is a tabulated statement of the assessment and tax levy of this city, from 1854 to 1885, inclusive. Copied from the *Tribune*:—

FISCAL YEAR.	VALUE OF PROPERTY.	RATE OF TAX.	REVENUE.
1854-55	$ 100,905	$1 50	$ 1,513 58
1855-6	428,662	1 50	6,429 93
1856-7	402,318	1 50	6,034 77
1857-8	354,275	1 50	5,314 13
1858-9	not comp.	1 50	not comp.
1859-60	not comp.	1 50	not comp.
1860-1	not comp.	1 50	not comp.
1861-2	not comp.	no rate	not comp.
1862-3	581,121	1 00	5,811 21
1863-4	794,121	1 00	7,941 12
1864-5	970,125	1 00	9,721 12
1865-6	1,107,949	1 00	12,187 44
1866-7	1,434,866	60	8,609 20
1867-8	1,832,438	1 00	18,344 28
1868-9	3,364,078	1 00	33,640 78
1869-70	4,257,204	1 25	53,215 05
1870-1	4,563,767	1 25	57,016 72
1871-2	5,215,704	1 50	78,235 56
1872-3	6,647,039	1 25	83,087 99
1873-4	18,528,303	70	129,698 12
1874-5	19,869,162	90	178,822 46
1875-6	22,200,706	88	195,366 21
1876-7	24,000,712	88	211,206 26
1877-8	28,845,028	88	227,436 23
1878-9	27,730,109	1 05	291,166 14
1879-80	28,348,778	1 09	309,001 68
1880-1	28,691,610	1 19	341,449 04
1881-2	28,238,631	1 05	296,526 40
1882-3	28,289,650	1 01	285,751 89
1883-4	28,353,338	80	226,861 32
1884-5	28,794,919	75	215,970 00
1885-6	29,217,050	98	286,327 77

The annexed table shows the condition of the City Clerk and Treasurer's accounts for the year ending August 31, 1885, and the city's financial expenses for one year:—

Total receipts for year ending Aug. 31, 1885	$501,940 27
Total disbursements from September, 1884, to August 31, 1885	457,953 06
Cash in the treasury on August 31, 1885, as per cash book	43,987 21
Grand total	$501,940 27

The following statement will give a good idea of the extent of the city, the distances reckoned from the post-office: Alameda, 3½ miles; Neptune Gardens, 2 miles; Berkeley, 4 miles; Fruitvale, 2¼ miles; Lake Merritt, ¾ mile; Lakeside, 2 miles; Mountain View Cemetery, 2½ miles; Piedmont Springs, 4 miles; Temescal, 2¼ miles; Emeryville, 2 miles; West Berkeley, 4½ miles; State University Buildings, 4 miles; Deaf and Dumb Institute, 3¾ miles; Blair's Park, 3 miles.

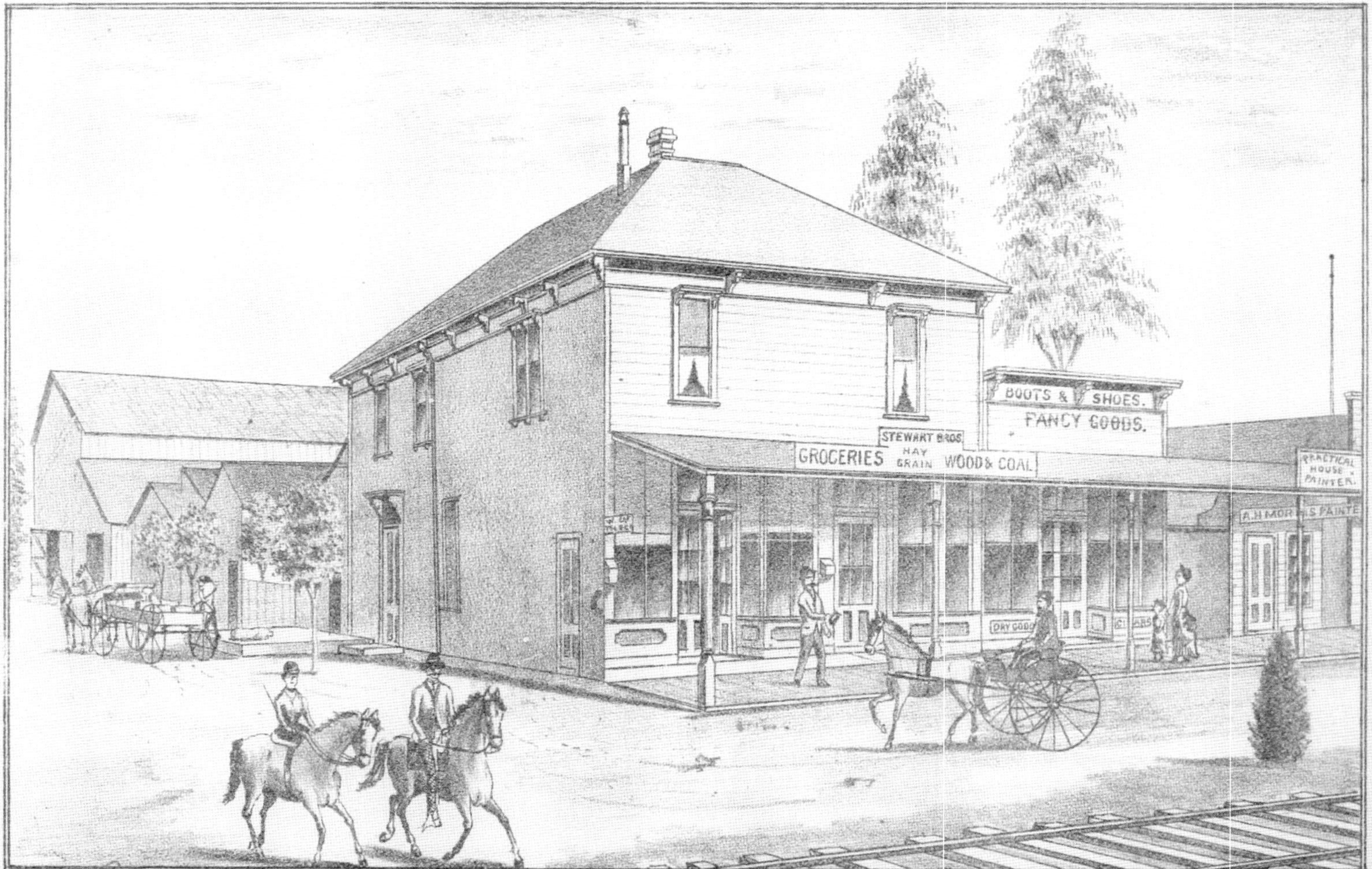

GENERAL MERCHANDISE STORE. PROPERTY OF J. K. & ROBT. STEWART. BERKELEY CAL.

ELLIOTT, LITH. OAK.

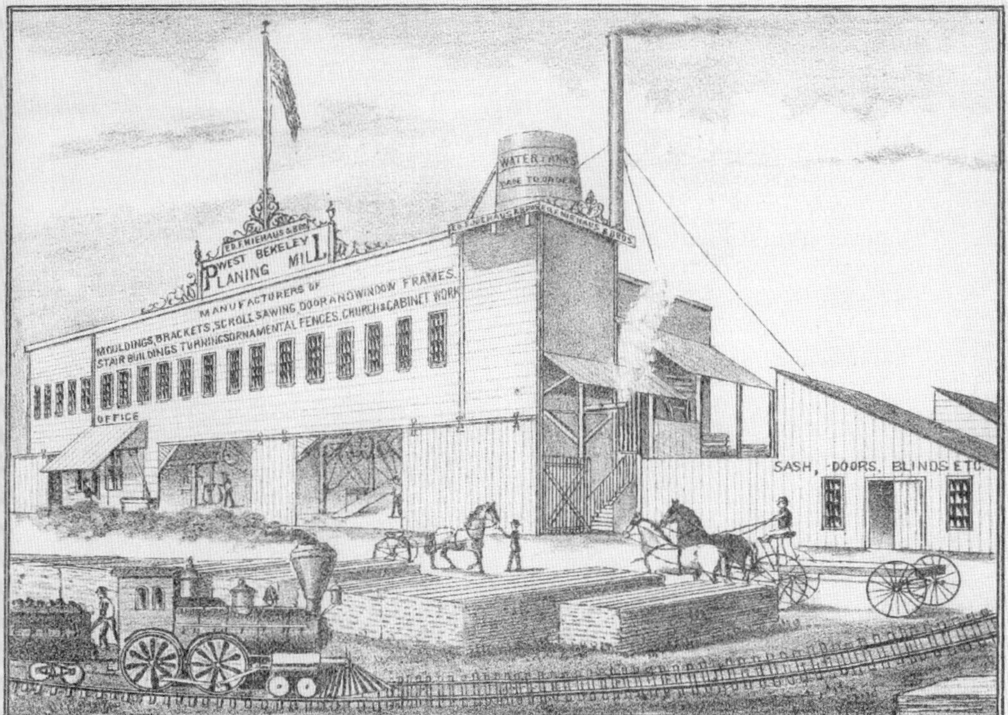

WEST BERKELEY PLANING MILL. ED. F. NIEHAUS & BROS.

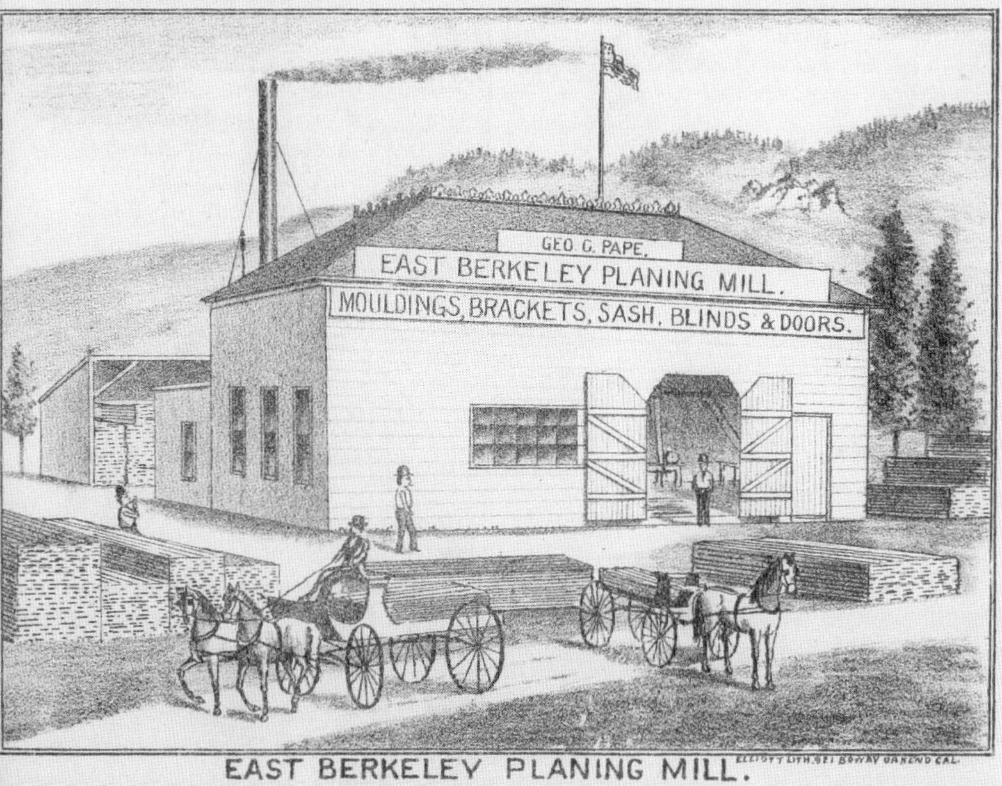

EAST BERKELEY PLANING MILL.

The City Wards.

THERE are seven wards in the city. Total area of land in city, 4,883 acres, or 7.629 square miles. The following are the boundaries and the number of acres in each ward.

FIRST—1,268 acres; bounded by northern boundary line of the city, Adeline Street, and water front (bay of San Francisco).

SECOND—764 acres; bounded by northern boundary line of the city, Cemetery Creek, Lake Merritt, Twentieth Street, and Adeline Street.

THIRD—302 acres; bounded by Twentieth, Broadway, Tenth, and Adeline Streets.

FOURTH—312 acres; bounded by Tenth Street, Broadway, estuary of San Antonio, and Adeline Street.

FIFTH—216 acres; bounded by Twentieth Street, Lake Merritt Estuary, Tenth Street, and Broadway.

SIXTH—236 acres; bounded by Tenth Street, estuary, and Broadway.

SEVENTH is what is called East Oakland.

Oakland of Old.

THIRTY years ago nearly all of Alameda County was included in Contra Costa. Courts were held at Martinez. In the evening the fandango was the great entertainment of the whole court—judge, jury, sheriff, and prisoners—all in the mazy dance. The major, from Oakland, waltzed on the floor with a buxom senorita.

A fandango room was usually surrounded with benches, and in an adjoining room a bar, where it was incumbent upon the dancers to take the value of a couple of dimes in liquor or lemonade after each dance, in compensation for the amusement. The music usually consisted of two Spanish harps, on which the Mexicans are adepts at playing. But times have greatly changed.

Oakland was incorporated March 25, 1854, with seven councilmen, mayor, etc.

In 1860 its population was 15,200. In 1880, 39,175, and estimated for 1885 at 46,000.

County Officers.

MEMBERS of Board of Supervisors:—Henry Dusterberry, District No. 1; Thomas Molloy, District No. 2; Bart Morgan, District No. 3; J. J. Hanifin, District No. 4; Wm. S. Pelouze, District No. 5. J. J. Hanifin, Chairman; Chas. T. Boardman, Clerk.

Judges of Superior Court—District No. 1, Noble Hamilton; District No. 2, E. M. Gibson; District No. 3, W. E. Greene.

Members of Assembly—W. H. Jordan, T. C. Morris, J. F. Black, Geo. W. Watson, Walter M. Haywood, F. J. Moffitt.

County Officers—County Clerk, Chas. T. Boardman; Auditor, Chas. T. Boardman; Recorder, F. D. Hinds; Treasurer and Tax Collector, J. A. Webster; Sheriff, W. E. Hale; Surveyor, George L. Nusbaumer; Superintendent of Public Instruction, P. M. Fisher.

Senators—Geo. E. Whitney and Henry Vrooman.

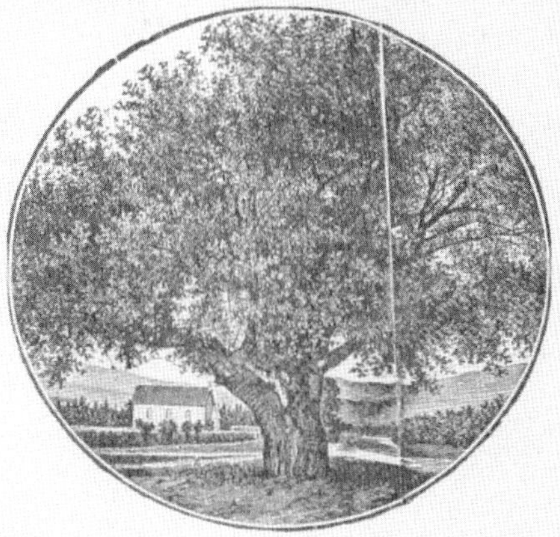

Literature and Art.

Art and Artists.

OAKLAND can lay claim to little in the way of variety of art work. It has some fine photographic establishments, among which is the fine gallery of W. W. Dames, which has been sketched and lithographed for this work. It is well worth a visit by those who admire artistic work.

The lithographic art has only one representative establishment in Oakland—that of W. W. Elliott, 921 Broadway, where several artists are constantly employed.

The Ebell Society is one of the most noted of literary organizations, which meets for mutual improvement of its members and other literary work.

Lithographic Business.

"HARDLY a month passes," says the Oakland *Times*, "that does not see the founding of some new and important business enterprise in this city. The latest of these is the opening of a lithographic printing establishment, by W. W. Elliott, at No. 921 Broadway. Mr. Elliott is well known on this coast, where he has for a number of years followed his profession. During this time he has published a number of excellent and beautiful works, descriptive and illustrative of more than half the counties in the State, as also of Idaho and Arizona. These works illustrate the scenery and resources of California admirably, and will no doubt attract much attention and add to the prosperity of the State.

"Mr. Elliott has printed maps of different localities, and his late issue of the only complete map of Idaho ever published, has met with a large demand in that locality and in the East. He has lately completed Nutting's Map of '100 miles around San Francisco.' A reporter of this paper who visited his establishment was shown a number of samples in the line of bank checks, letter heads, and various styles of business engraving and lithographing.

"Oakland business men who have the interests of their city at heart, will do well to consult Mr. Elliott before giving their orders to other parties. His work is quite as good as any and much superior to a good deal that is done in San Francisco. It is the only lithographing in this city."

Oakland Newspapers.

THERE are numerous daily, weekly, and monthly publications of ability, of which much might be said in favor. We give the following list:—

The Oakland *Evening Tribune* was started on Saturday, February 21, 1874, by Ben A. Dewes and George B. Staniford. It was of small size but good typo-

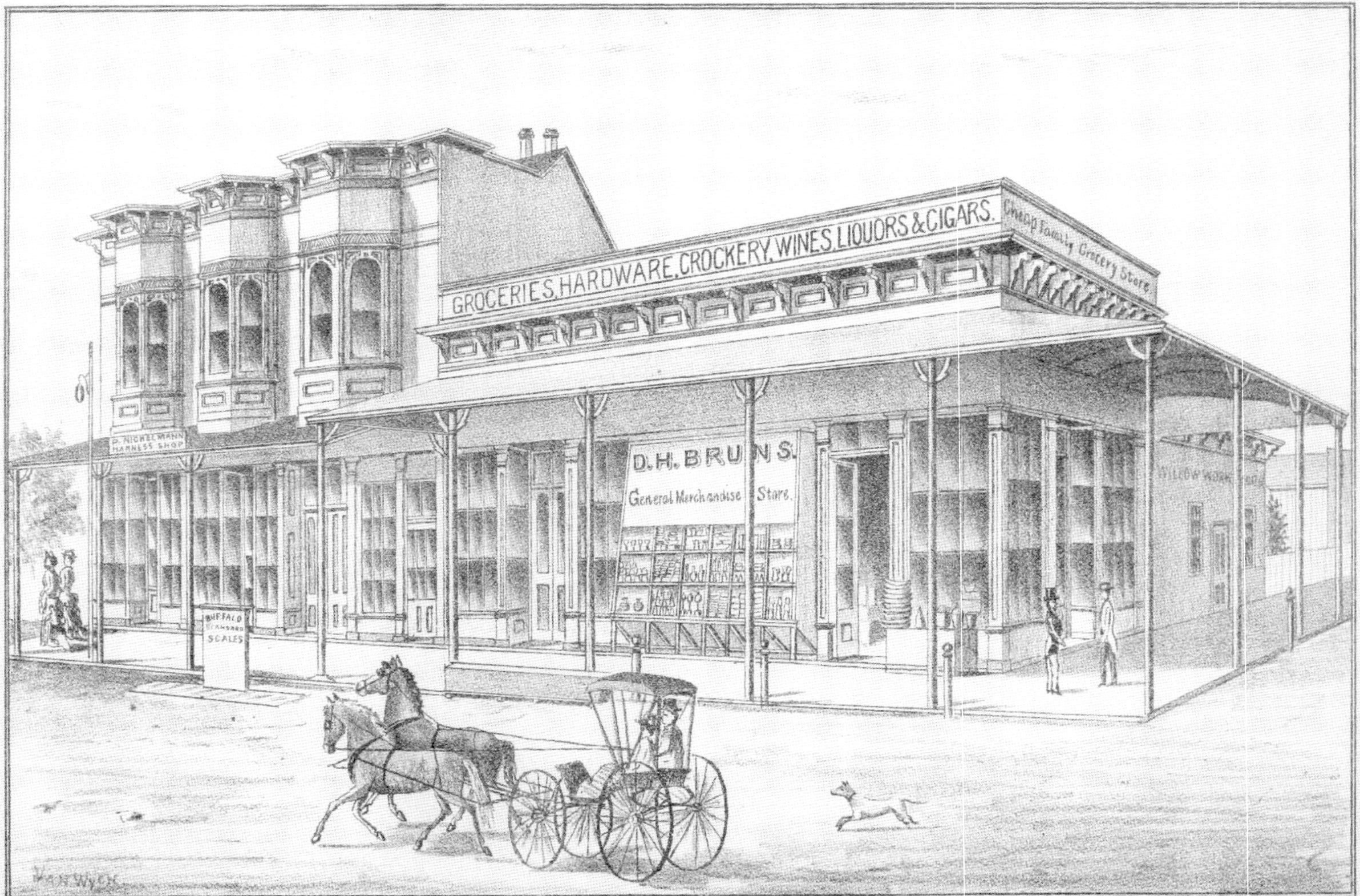

D. H. BRUN'S GENERAL MERCHANDISE STORE. WEST BERKELEY CAL.

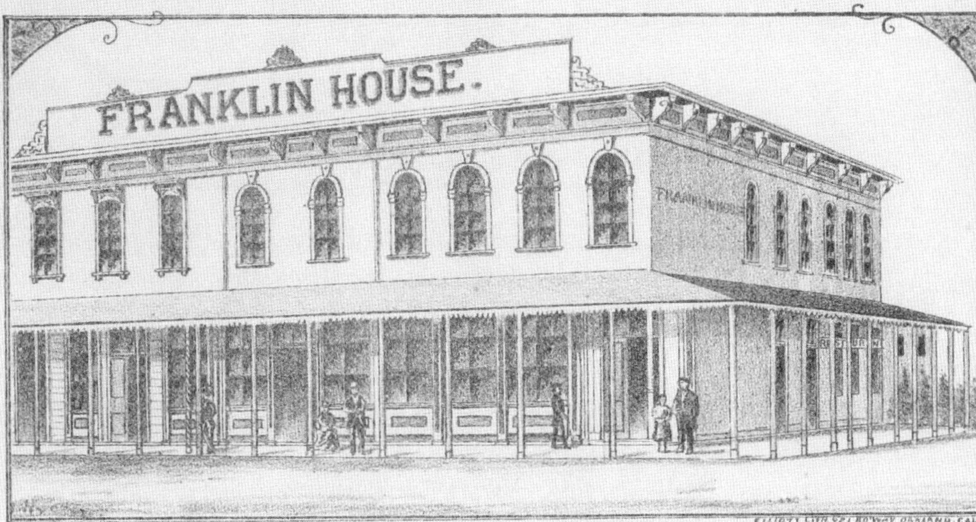

FRANKLIN HOUSE, WEST BERKELEY. CAL.

ELLIOTT, LITH. 921 BD'WAY OAKLAND. CAL.

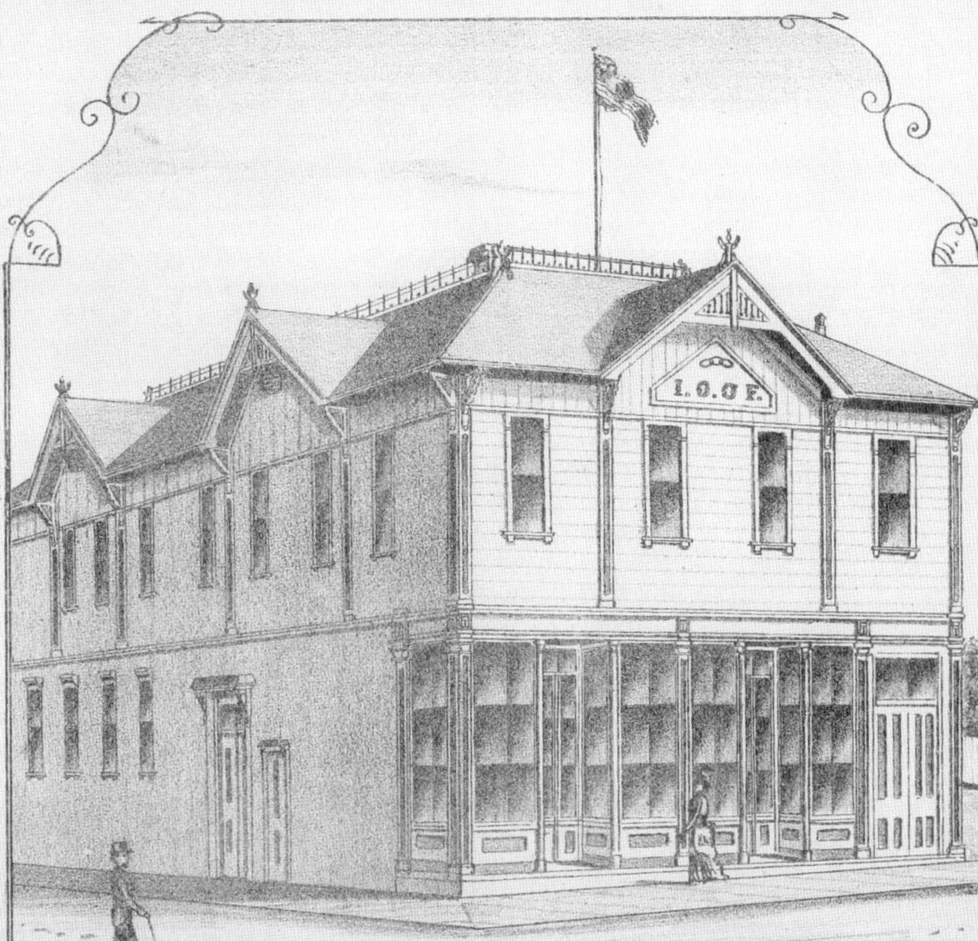

ODD FELLOWS HALL. BERKELEY, CAL.

graphical appearance. It was distributed free of charge, depending for support on its advertising patronage. The paper was soon increased in size, and owned and managed by different parties until July 24, 1876, William E. Dargie, the present manager of the paper, bought out Messrs. Staniford & Nightingill, and he still retains control. New life and energy were put in the paper, and the proper organization of the business departments was fully attended to, and especial attention given to that which was of interest to the people of Oakland and Alameda County. In addition to this much telegraphic and general news and well-selected miscellany were presented to its readers. Within a month after his purchase, Mr. Dargie succeeded in obtaining the Associated Press dispatches, which no other paper in Alameda County before or since has done. At the end of the first year the business and circulation of the paper rapidly increased.

On October 1, 1877, the *Tribune* was moved to more commodious quarters at 406 Twelfth Street, and a book bindery and job department were added. One of Hoe's double cylinder presses was purchased on which to print the paper, and a two-roller cylinder press was bought for the book and job department. On November 1, 1881, the *Tribune* was moved to its present central and roomy quarters at 413-417 Eighth Street. The *Tribune* has a circulation of about 5,000, and is found in nearly every household throughout Alameda County. It is Republican in politics, and is printed by the *Tribune* Publishing Company, W. E. Dargie, Manager, and T. T. Dargie, Secretary.

The Alameda *Encinal* is the pioneer paper of the county, having been established in September, 1869. It is a large and influential journal, with a good circulation. It is edited and published by F. K. Krauth, at 1520 Park Street, Alameda.

The Oakland *Times* is issued by the *Times* Publishing Company, an incorporation organized October, 1878, with $100,000 capital. It has published a daily and weekly issue continuously from that time to date. At the present it is, in politics, independent, criticising either party, and siding with neither. It has a regular circulation of over 2,000 copies. Mr. J. B. Wyman is editor, and W. R. Bentley, business manager.

The Oakland *Enquirer* was started about five years ago by the late Dan. W. Gelwicks, under the style of the Oakland *Independent*. The paper is now and has always been Democratic. About a year ago the plant came into the possession of Assemblyman Moffitt, who is now its sole editor and proprietor, and who has re-christened the paper the *Enquirer*. The office is located in the Union Bank Building, at the corner of Ninth and Broadway. It is published twice a week, has a large circulation, and is delivered by carriers for 25 cents a month.

The daily *Evening Express* has lately been established, and is in a flourishing condition. L. M. Allum is business manager, and W. W. McKaig, editor. It is quite outspoken in its views. Each department is under special and efficient supervision. The *Express* is a well-printed publication, containing all the latest telegraphic and local news, with well digested editorials and well-written articles on special subjects.

California Medical Journal is published monthly by H. T. Webster, M. D., and is a 48-page journal devoted to medicine.

The Berkeley *Advocate* is now in its ninth volume, and is published every week, by H. N. Marquand, who aims to give all the local news of its locality.

The *Berkeleyan* is in its nineteenth volume, and is published at the office of the Students' University Press. It is published fortnightly by an associated company of students of the University of California.

The *Occident* is also published weekly at the University of California.

The *Church and Sunday-school*, a little paper, issued by the pastors, Sunday-school, and yoke-fellows of the First Congregational Church of this city, is meeting with much deserved success.

The Brooklyn *Eagle* is a weekly paper published at 555 Twelfth Street, East Oakland. It is now in its second volume, and its editor and publisher is W. T. Bailey. It gives all the local news of the vicinity, and is thus made valuable to residents of that part of town.

West Oakland *Sentinel*, as its name implies, is published for the benefit of West Oakland. It is a large 8-page weekly, and is in its fourth volume. It is ably edited and managed, and is fearless in its expressions. Fonda & Co., 379 Tenth Street, are its publishers.

The Alameda semi-weekly *Argus* is issued at Alameda on Wednesdays and Saturdays. It is a 7-column journal, Republican in politics, and circulates very thoroughly among the 7,000 residents of the encinal of Alameda. It was established in 1877, and its founder, T. G. Daniells, is still the sole proprietor. It is one of the most prominent interior journals in the county.

The *Gnostic* is a 24-page monthly magazine, well printed, by Messrs. Fonda & Co., of 379 Tenth Street. It is devoted to Theosophy, Spiritualism, Occult Phenomena, and the Cultivation of the Higher Life. Its publishers and editors are George Chainey and Anna Kimball.

Practical Supplemental Studies, for use in public and private schools, is a 24-page monthly, published at 520 Fifteenth Street, Oakland, by J. B. McChesney & Co. Terms: one copy, one year (10 months), $1.25. Five copies or more, to one address, per copy, $1.00.

The *Signs of the Times*, a 16-page weekly paper, is devoted to the doctrines and interests of the denomination known as Seventh-day Adventists. It was instituted in 1874, and has had a remarkably successful career, its circulation reaching 25,000 copies weekly. It is published by the Pacific Press Publishing House, at $2.00 per year.

The *Herald of Truth*, an 8-page semi-monthly, is the organ of the Baptist Church, and the only Baptist paper issued in California. It is edited and published by Rev. G. S. Abbott, D. D., Superintendent of the American Baptist Publication Society's depository in Oakland. The subscription price of the *Herald* is $1.00 a year.

The *Holiness Evangelist* is an 8-page monthly journal, purporting to be "an independent paper in the interest of Bible Christianity." It is edited and published by Rev. A. Coplin, 1171 Broadway, Oakland, at 75 cents a year.

The Alameda *Reporter* is in its second volume, and is published at Alameda by the *Reporter* Publishing Co. A. Megahn is editor and manager.

The West Oakland *Home Journal* is published at West Oakland by M. L. Hanscom & Co., at 869 Wood Street. It gives much attention to local items, which is the chief value of a home journal.

The *Carrier Dove* is a monthly publication devoted to modern Spiritualism and edited by Mrs. J. Schlesinger, at 854½ Broadway.

Oakland *Ingleside* is published at 969 Broadway, by John M. Lathrop, who is manager.

Of amateur journals, there is published at Alameda the *Bumble Bee*. R. H. Magill, Jr., is the editor.

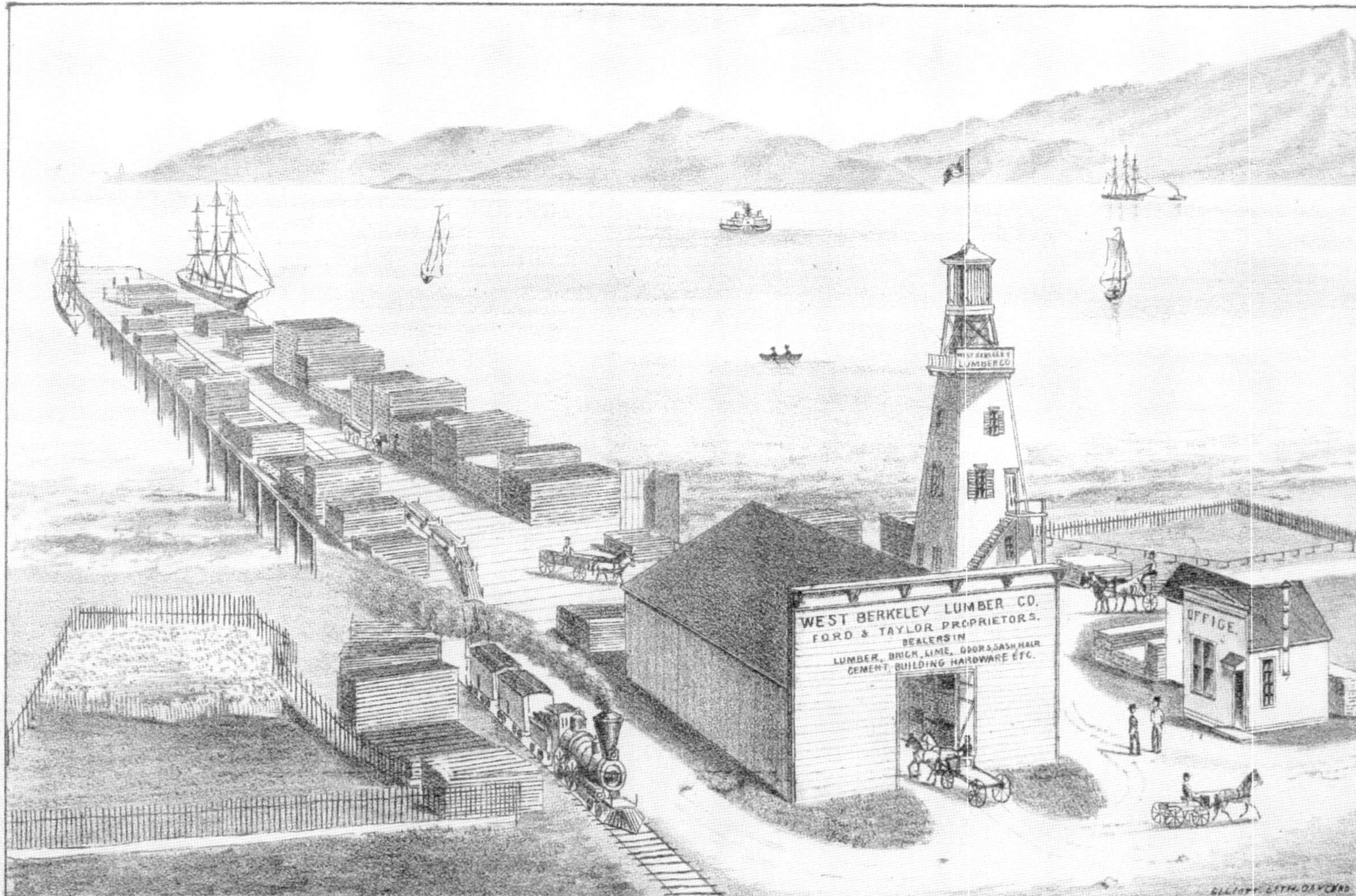

WEST BERKELEY LUMBER CO. WEST BERKELEY, CAL.

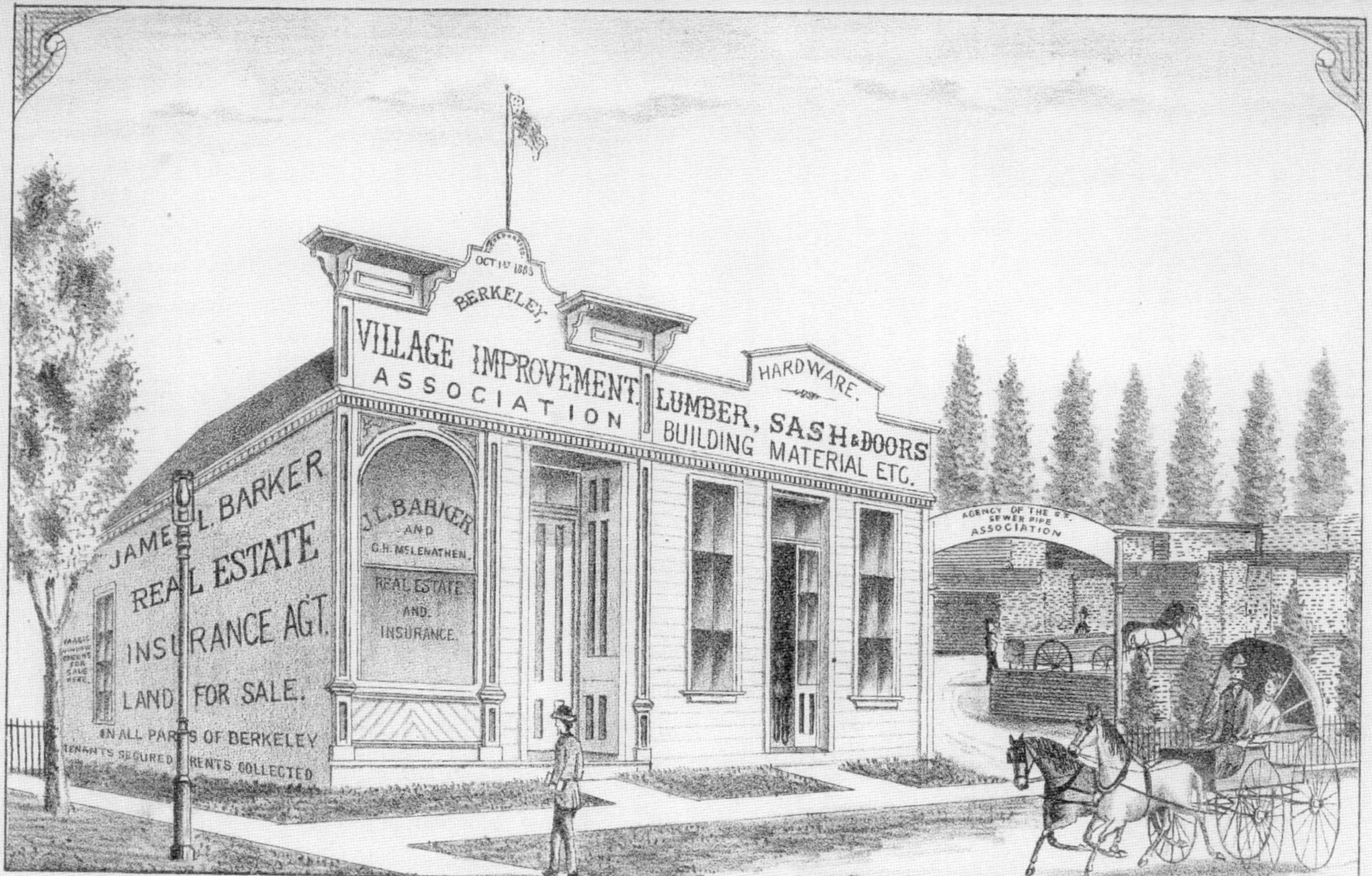

OFFICE AND LUMBER YARD OF THE BERKELEY VILLAGE IMPROVEMENT ASSOCIATION.

ELLIOTT OAK CAL.

The *Pacific Health Journal and Temperance Advocate* is a bi-monthly magazine of 24 pages, yet in its first year, but meeting with encouraging success. It is edited by Elder J. H. Waggoner, and published by the Pacific Press, at 50 cents a year.

The Pacific Press.

THIS popular publishing house is one of the prominent business features of Oakland. The property owned by the association is located on the corner of Twelfth and Castro Streets, and the commodious buildings are in keeping with that desirable and well-improved section of the city.

The business of the institution is varied and extensive. Here are published and sent forth the books and pamphlets of the denomination known as Seventh-day Adventists; and the well-known weekly paper, *The Signs of the Times*, which the proprietors claim circulates in every part of the world where the English language is spoken. Also, a variety of health and temperance works, and the *Pacific Health Journal and Temperance Advocate*, which is rapidly gaining popularity.

This house also issues valuable works of a secular character, the latest being a "History of California," beginning with the earliest voyages of the Spanish and English navigators to the Pacific Coast. The author is Theodore H. Hittell, Esq., of San Francisco, a pioneer and graphic writer of considerable note. This work is complete in two volumes of 800 pages each.

Aside from proprietary publications, this establishment does a general book and job printing business, book-binding, paper ruling, blank-book manufacturing, electrotyping, stereotyping, wood-engraving, etc. All the various departments are thoroughly equipped with the best facilities and first-class machinery.

There is also kept on hand a varied supply of books and stationery, including a fine line of Bibles of all sizes, and helps to Bible study, such as concordances, dictionaries, and commentaries. Also books for the family circle and Sabbath-school library, and valuable books sold only by subscription. Of the latter may be mentioned the "Home Hand-Book of Hygiene and Rational Medicine," a very large and complete manual of diseases and remedies; by J. H. Kellogg, M. D., of Michigan State Board of Health. Also "Parson's Hand-Book of Business and Social Forms," a comprehensive and reliable aid in all the ordinary walks of life.

The Pacific Press has had a successful career of over ten years, has kept pace with the characteristic enterprise of this growing city, and has done much towards spreading the fame of Oakland while building up its own extended reputation.

See page 63 for illustration of the building owned by this association.

Lithograph Work.

THE publisher of this book, W. W. Elliott, lithographer, Oakland, makes a specialty of getting up illustrated descriptive works, keeping constantly employed artists and engravers adapted to this line of work. He is also doing all kinds of letter and bill-heads, checks, drafts, and other lithographic work.

"One of the finest engraving establishments on this coast is that under the management of W. W. Elliott, at 921 Broadway, this city. There is no better work in the line executed anywhere than is turned out at this place, as any one can find out by visiting his rooms, and yet some Oakland people go to San Francisco to get this class of work done. Mr. Elliott's work goes into almost every county in the State."—*Evening Express.*

Berkeley.

Location of Berkeley.

BERKELEY has hitherto seemed retired from the observation of the tourist and pleasure-seeker. Its story has been untold, and its charms unsung, while its neighbors have noisily proclaimed their virtues in the ears of the world.

Seen from San Francisco on a bright spring afternoon, Berkeley seems a gray ribbon-like strip, drawn close in between the water and the hills. More nearly observed, it expands into a broad slope, or tilted plain, with a rise so gradual that, in crossing it, one attains a considerable elevation before he is aware that he has left the level of the ocean. Hence it has height without the effort of ascent, and those desirable accidents of height, pure air, and an ample prospect, which includes plain, valley, mountain, inlet, island, and nearly every other incidental feature of earth, water, and atmosphere, considered essential to fine landscape. This natural panorama of San Francisco Bay and the adjacent hills is specially remarkable.

The town of Berkeley lies on the eastern shore of San Francisco Bay, facing the Golden Gate. Behind it are the gentle acclivities of the Coast Range, broken by cañons which reach far into its solitudes.

Berkeley Residences.

AMONG the more conspicuous residences are those of the Messrs. H. A. and C. T. H. Palmer, situated at the entrance to Strawberry Cañon, on what Professor LeConte calls a terminal moraine, and at an elevation of not less than three hundred and fifty feet above tide-water. Houses and grounds are in excellent taste. The prospect from the point is superb. H. A. Palmer is the President of the Union Savings and Union National Banks of Oakland.

F. K. Shattuck a few years ago erected a beautiful residence on the avenue of the same name. The house is surrounded by trees, shrubbery, and flowers of many kinds, to which constant additions are made. Our artist has made an illustration of this place, which gives some idea of its immediate surroundings.

Among our illustrations is the residence of J. L. Barker, on Dwight Way. This fine house is surrounded with a great variety of choice shrubbery and ornamental trees. Walks and carriage drives are laid out with taste and care.

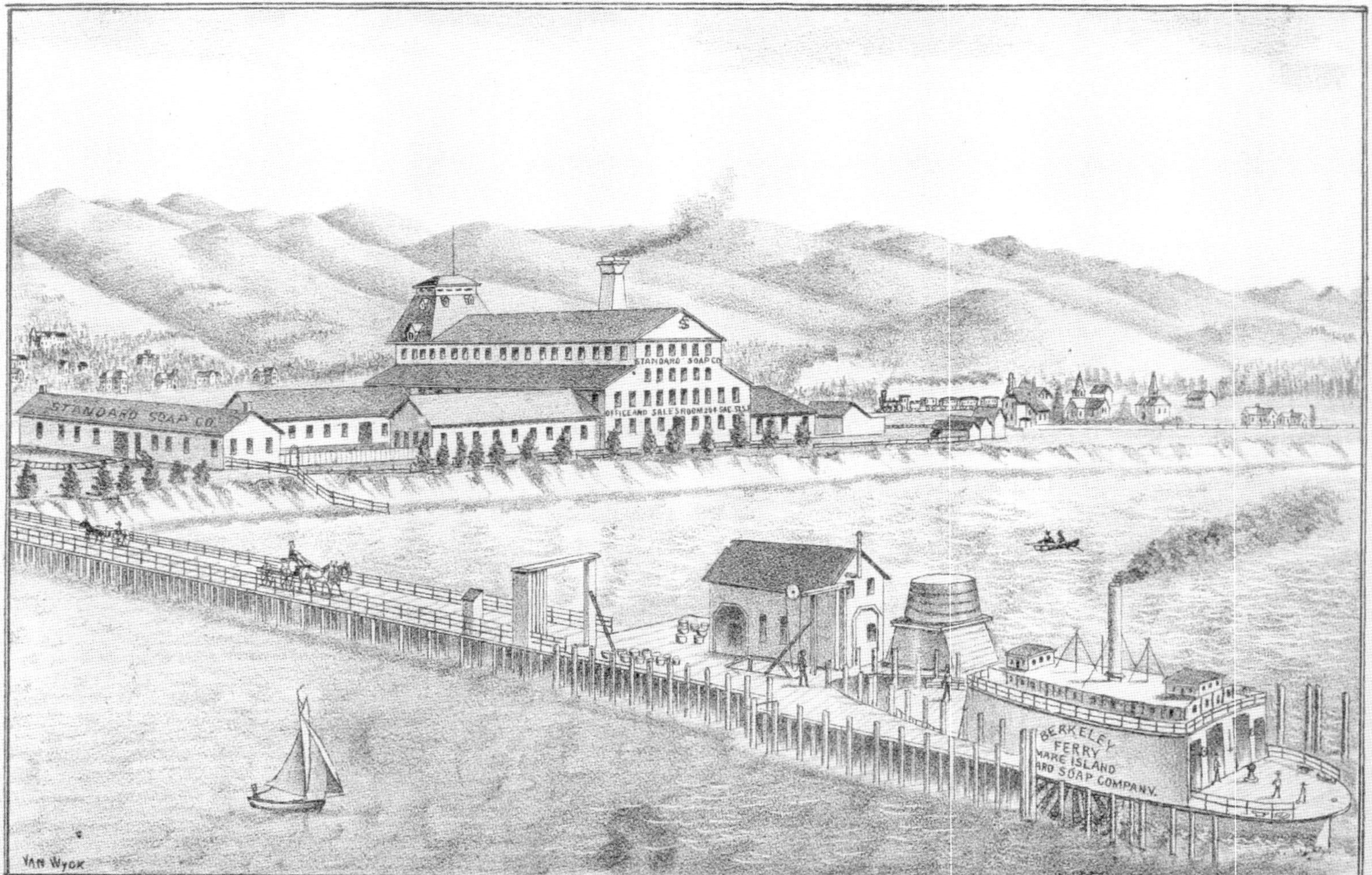

STANDARD SOAP CO.'S WORKS & FERRY LANDING, WEST BERKELEY, CAL.

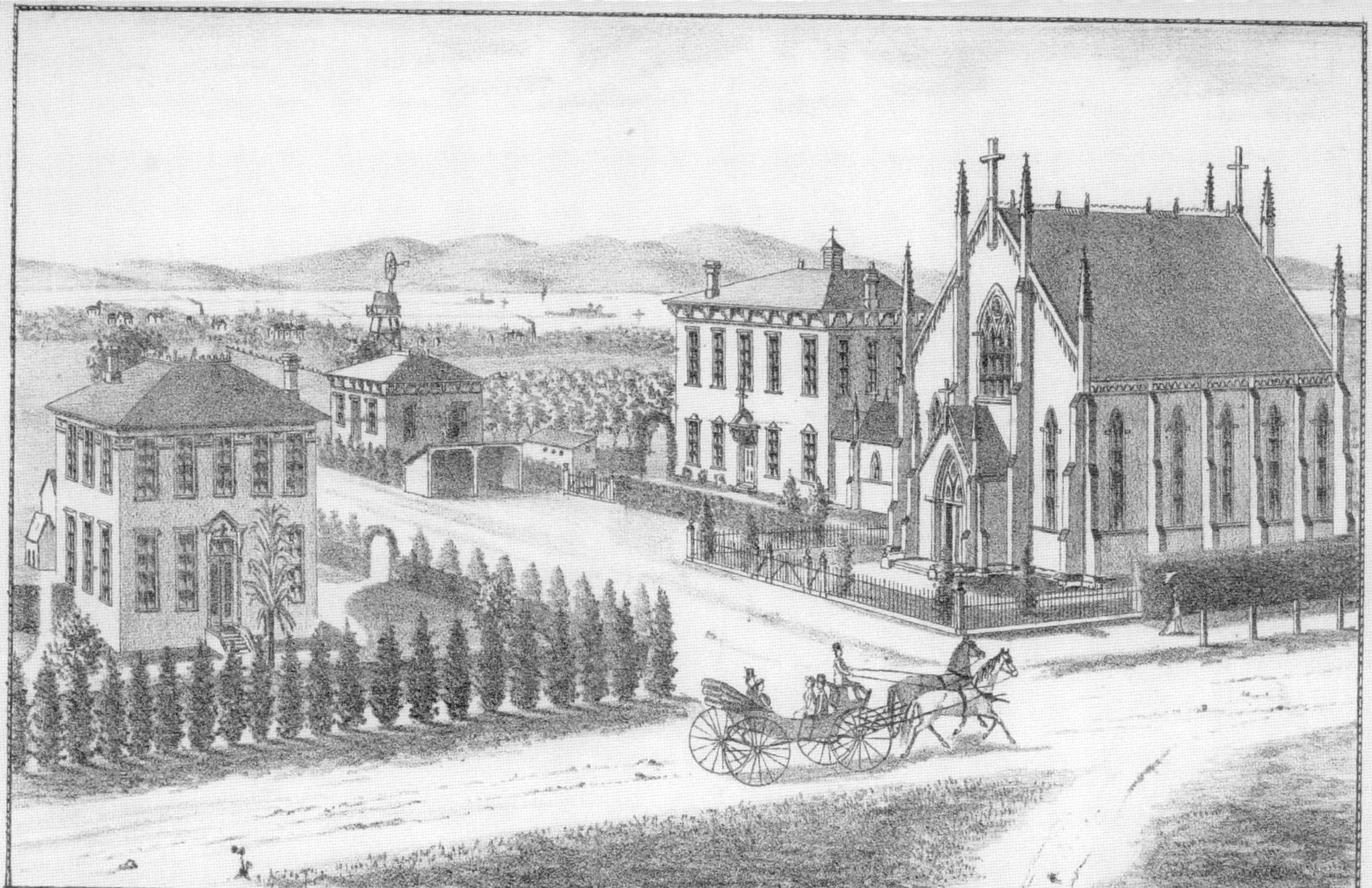

RESIDENCE OF THE VERY REV. P.M. COMERFORD. ST. PETERS BOYS SCHOOL. ST. JOSEPH'S PRESENTATION CONVENT. ST. JOSEPH'S CHURCH.

ST. JOSEPH'S CONVENT & CHURCH BERKELEY, ALAMEDA CO. CAL.

ELLIOTT, LITH, OAK, CAL

Among other pleasant homes, we may mention those of Mrs. M. Hillegass, Judge Philip Teare, C. K. Clark, F. H. Lawton, H. B. Berryman, J. K. and Robert Stewart, and many others.

The town is full of pleasant and beautiful homes. Every one here can sit down, literally, under his own vine and fig-tree.

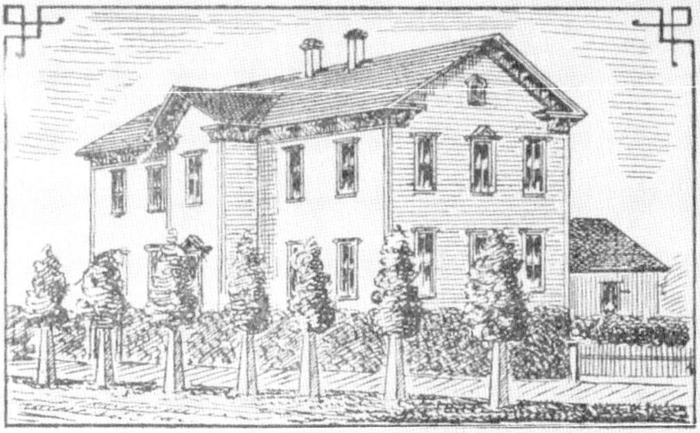

SAN PABLO SCHOOL, WEST BERKELEY.

The architecture of Berkeley houses is free and of great variety. It is not limited in regard to style. Touches of the renaissance are mingled with traces of the time of Queen Anne, outlines of the Swiss chalet, and ideas that are strictly modern and Californian.

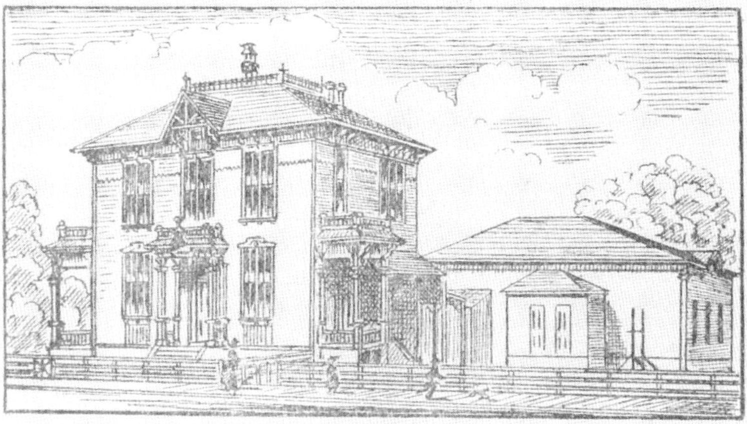

KELLOGG SCHOOL, BERKELEY.

Sewer System of Berkeley.

THE natural slope of the town location offers extraordinary facilities for a good sewerage system. Such a system has been adopted, and eight miles of main lines will soon be completed. The rate of grade in the mains for their whole length is *over 100 feet to the mile*, and the sewerage is discharged into San Francisco Bay below mean tide. Plans for the construction of several miles of lateral sewers are being prepared, and they will be built as soon as the mains are ready for connecting. The building of these will be continued till the system is completed, thus making Berkeley *one of the best sewered towns in this or any other State.* The sewers are constructed of the best quality of vitrified iron stone pipe, carefully laid and jointed with best Portland cement.

The capacity of the system adopted is sufficient for the needs of a population far greater than the area of the town could accommodate, their estimated capacity being ample for upwards of 80,000 persons, at the same time the expense for each lot of 50 feet frontage is insignificant compared with the benefits to be gained.

Early Settlement of Berkeley.

AT an early date in the history of Oakland came four men to Contra Costa for pastime, expecting soon to start for the East. They had been quite successful as miners. Being men of good judgment they took in at a glance the situation, and concluded to remain. They took possession of one mile square of land above Vicente Peralta grant which eventually made them all wealthy. These names are George M. Blake, F. K. Shattuck, William Hillegass, and James Leonard.

F. K. Shattuck is the only one living at this date. He has occupied a prominent position in the government of the county most of the time.

In 1868. the site of the State University was selected, and appropriately named Berkeley. At the nearest point to it on the bay was a small village called Ocean View, the name of which was afterward changed to West Berkeley. Hence came the distinction between East and West Berkeley. the former meaning the high and picturesque lands about the University, and the latter the western edge of the plateau near the shore of the bay. The two villages are under the same local government. They are connected by University Avenue, a broad and handsome thoroughfare, set with trees, of which the new town hall is one of the chief ornaments.

The town organization was effected in 1878. Its executive power is vested in a Board of Trustees, and a school board comprising six members, two of whom retire every year. The care taken in placing the best and most intelligent citizens in charge of school affairs indicates an earnest desire to keep the admirable system clean and perfect. The real life of the town dates from the location of the University.

Residences and Their Surroundings.

THE village of Berkeley, besides its educational attractions, is a most agreeable place of residence. It lies five miles north of Oakland on a plateau which slopes from a height of five hundred feet on the hill-side to the level of the bay. Every house, therefore, has a splendid outlook. Berkeley dates its origin from the establishment of the State University here in 1873. There were then scarcely half a dozen houses within its limits. Now over an area of eight square miles there is an unbroken succession of pretty cottages embowered in vines, rose-bushes, and fruit trees; churches, school-houses, and rising above them all the buildings of the University, grouped at the very base of the Coast Range on a terrace more than three hundred feet above tide-water.

The entire town has the advantage of altitude, good air, and the best of water drawn through tunnels from hidden reservoirs in the hills. San Francisco can be reached every half hour by the local trains which run till midnight. Property owners, whether holding land for sale or for homesteads, take just pride in the town, and are making systematic efforts to increase its natural beauties.

There is scarcely a vacant lot without its quota of evergreen and deciduous trees in the more compact portions of the town, which is rapidly becoming a forest from the south line at Shellmound and Oakland to the limits of Contra Costa County on the north. It is impossible to look in any direction without seeing groups of eucalypti and Lombardy poplars, masses of pines, spruces, cedars, and cypresses, interspersed with meadows, fruit-orchards, and nearly every variety of tree

Resources and Advantages.

BERKELEY is well supplied with water of the best quality. You can hardly penetrate the hills anywhere without finding it perfectly pure, and ready to burst forth at the touch.

The Alameda Water Company, which furnishes Berkeley with water, has two reservoirs, from which the town is supplied, sketches of which appear in this work. Reservoir No. 1 is located on the top of a hill south of the Asylum, cut out of the rock, which has a capacity of 2,500,000 gallons. It is supplied with pure mountain water, brought by a tunnel 3,000 feet in length. As it enters this reservoir through a four-inch pipe, under a full head, it throws up a column of water fully sixty feet high. Reservoir No. 2 is located in the hills back of Mr. Berryman's residence, and has a capacity of 23,000,000 gallons. It is also supplied by a tunnel 900 feet long from the mountain. The distributing tank forces the water into the main supply pipes, while the tower in the reservoir is connected with the main pipe, to supply when needed. The water is conducted through all the streets, and to West Berkeley, and Temescal.

Gas mains are laid, and a gasometer, placed by the Oakland Gas Company, for lighting streets and residences.

The town is as well supplied with churches as with schools, the Episcopalians, Presbyterians, Methodists, Congregationalists, and Catholics all being represented, and all having neat and commodious church edifices.

With schools of every grade, churches of every denomination, water and gas in every house, marvelous beauty of nature on every side, and a railroad to nearly every door, Berkeley certainly is rich in moral and physical advantages. What the country does not supply, the great city reaches out its generous hands across the water to liberally furnish.

Berkeley is popularly known as the "center of learning for California," and the title is not a misnomer. The refining influences which result from the presence of numerous State, public, and private institutions of learning; the healthfulness and peculiar charms of climate and scenery; its proximity to the city and the consequent facilities for travel and business, all conspire to render Berkeley a most desirable place of residence.

The location of the College of California, at Berkeley, was in part the result of liberal donations of land by owners of property in the vicinity. Mr. Geo. M. Blake made a donation of ten acres of land bordering on Strawberry Creek. Mr. Wm. Hillegass gave a deed for twenty acres, for a nominal consideration, on which the Agricultural College is now located.

F. K. Shattuck has some of the finest residence property in Berkeley for sale by the lot or acre. He can be found for the transaction of business at 467 Ninth Street, Oakland.

Charming Locations.

A RESIDENCE in Berkeley has in itself many peculiar advantages. To begin with, the town has an exceptional situation, lying on a gentle slope leading from the bay up to the Contra Costa hills, the upper portion being broken by picturesque cañons, pathways for limpid mountain brooks, whose natural beauties enhance the grounds of many elegant homes. Residences situated on this sunny slope, with a background of magnificent hills, com-

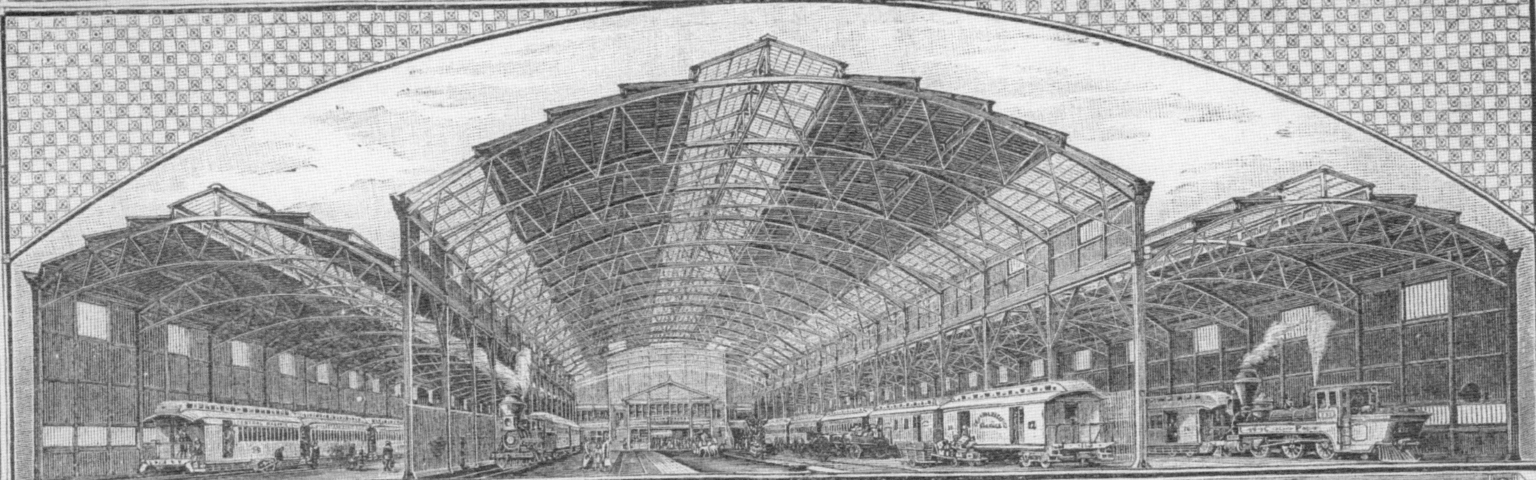

OAKLAND TERMINAL DEPOT C.P.R.R. • VIEW LOOKING WEST

The western, terminal station of the Central Pacific Railroad, shown above, is situate near Oakland, upon a pier of earthwork and rock running out into San Francisco Bay from its eastern shore a distance of 1¼ miles, having a wharf and ferry slip at its western extremity.

The building is constructed in three main divisions longitudinally. The central part is 120 feet wide and 60 feet high, and accommodates overland trains, and the divisions on either side of this are 60 feet wide and 40 feet high, being exclusively for suburban trains running to and from Oakland, Alameda and Berkeley, connecting with the San Francisco ferry steamers.

At the west end of the main or central division are two commodious waiting-rooms for passengers. The upper or main waiting-room, 120 x 120 feet, connecting by side aprons with the saloon deck of ferry steamers, and the lower waiting-room, connecting by end apron with the main deck of steamers, give quick and easy passage to and from the boats.

The building also contains a restaurant and various offices and apartments for railroad employees.

The structure, *1050 feet* total length, covers an area of over four acres, and is constructed mainly of wood and iron, the supports resting on concrete and pile foundations. The roof, covered with corrugated iron and glass, gives abundant light during the day, and at night the building is illuminated with electric lights generated by machinery on the premises.

ADVANTAGES OFFERED BY OAKLAND.

Trips to S. F. Half Hourly by Rail and Steamer.
Commodius and Elegant Steamers and Cars.
Delightful Climate and Charming Homes.
Educational Center of the Pacific Coast.
Fine Residence Locations Everywhere.
Numerous Fine Churches and Schools.

Hill, Dale, and Valley Scenery.
Splendid Drives and Rambles Without Limit.
Dells, Nooks, and Glens in Every Direction.
Flowers of all Varieties Bloom Perennially.
Ocean and Mountain Views Unsurpassed.
Delightful Views in Great Variety.

mand a most superb and diversified view.

There are so many pretty and pleasing views to be obtained from different points in Berkeley that one hardly knows which is the best. Perhaps one of the finest can be obtained from the residence of Judge York. His residence, which stands at a high elevation, commands a view of the entire town, reaching to the shores of the bay from the C. P. R. R. wharf to San Pablo, while the bay, with Alcatraz and the Golden Gate, are spread out like a panorama.

Many of the most charming homes have been located upon the slopes of the mountains in the warm belt, and flowers and shrubs have a wonderful growth.

Among the finest locations in Berkeley is that selected by Mr. W. Hillegass, one of its earliest pioneers, to whom reference has already been made. Over twenty years ago he selected here a beautiful tract adjoining the present site of the State University, and commanding a splendid panoramic view of the Golden Gate, the Bay of San Francisco, and the surrounding towns. Some of the choicest residence lots in town are offered for sale by the Hillegass Estate. These lots, which adjoin some of the finest improvements in Berkeley, are comprised in two beautiful tracts, aggregating about one hundred acres, and unsurpassed in the matter of view, elevation, location, etc. A view of Mrs. Hillegass' residence will be found on another page.

Among the many beautiful residences and grounds are those of Judge Garber, situated on Claremont Avenue on an elevated plateau, close to the foothills, and overlooking the town and bay and with a fine view of the Golden Gate in the distance. The grounds are laid out with taste and care, and, being so near the foothills, are above the reach of frost; hence, you find flourishing here tropical trees and plants. The orange trees, of which there are a goodly number, with their ripe fruit and the blossoms, form a pleasing feature of the landscape. This location is in a very sheltered spot, or warm belt, where the gardens have a tendency to run to rare and choice shrubs and marvelous flowers.

Berryman Station, the present terminus of the Berkeley branch of the C. P. R. R., was named in honor of Mr. H. B. Berryman, of Berkeley, a view of whose house and grounds will be found on another page. Mr. Berryman has large interests in Berkeley, and is a stirring, energetic citizen.

Progress of Berkeley.

BERKELEY is growing rapidly, says the *Advocate*. Improvements can be seen in all sections of the town, and yet the demand for houses exceeds the supply. Residence property here brings a better income from cash capital than when employed in usury or deposited in banks. San Francisco men are now learning that a much handsomer and more comfortable home may be made for a given sum of money in this town than in San Francisco, and that there is no material difference in the amount of time consumed in going to and from their places of business. They are learning, too, that in performing these journeys it is vastly more pleasant to travel on palatial ferries and luxuriously equipped trains, than work their passage by standing up and hanging on to the grip-straps in the San Francisco street cars.

Most far-seeing and intelligent men of either ample or moderate means, recognize the fact that choice business lots in Berkeley can now be secured for less money and on better terms

The Berkeley Village Improvement Association.

JULY, 1885.

DURING the past year great changes and improvements have taken place in the immediate vicinity of Dwight Way Station, and to the north and east of it. The Berkeley Village Improvement Association, of which Mr. Reuben Rickard is President, and Mr. Jas. L. Barker is Vice-President and Manager, having its office at Dwight Way Station, has been mainly instrumental in making the improvements which are so noticeable.

This institution has erected and nearly completed twenty dwellings in the above neighborhood—all of them good, substantial, tasteful residences, built to the order of their owners.

Mr. Barker, the Manager, was the prime mover in inducing the Central Pacific to extend their road to Berkeley. He now devotes all of his time and energy to the substantial and tasteful improvement of the town.

Real Estate.

JULY, 1885.

THE advantages of Berkeley, as a place of residence, have never been so fully presented to the outside public as during the past two years, and the credit belongs more particularly to the popular Real Estate Agents, Jas. L. Barker and Chas. H. McLenathen, who have been associated since January, 1884.

They have their office at Dwight Way Station with the Berkeley Village Improvement Association, of which Mr. Barker is Manager.

Mr. Barker is an "old resident of the town. Everybody knows him and he knows everybody"—he is authority on Berkeley Real Estate.

Mr. McLenathen gives all of his time and attention to the Real Estate and Insurance business. He is always on hand to show property and is an affable and courteous gentleman.

They make a specialty of Berkeley property, but are prepared to negotiate for outside property in exchange. They have lots of *all sizes* and to suit all purses, but *not one* in a *poor location*, either in point of healthfulness or outlook for scenery

They report that they have *yet to hear* of a customer who regrets having moved to Berkeley, on the contrary all are recommending and *urging* their friends to move over and share in their enjoyment.

Board of University Regents.

HIS EXCELLENCY GEORGE STONEMAN, SACRAMENTO, *Governor, ex-officio, President of the Board.*

HIS HONOR JOHN DAGGETT, OAKLAND, *Lieutenant-Governor.*

HON. H. M. LA RUE, SACRAMENTO, *Speaker of the Assembly.*

HON. W. T. WELCKER, SACRAMENTO, *State Superintendent of Public Instruction.*

HON. P. A. FINIGAN, 1248 CALIFORNIA STREET, SAN FRANCISCO, *President of the State Agricultural Society.*

P. B. CORNWALL, SOUTHEAST CORNER SPEAR AND FOLSOM STREETS, SAN FRANCISCO, *President of the Mechanics' Institute.*

W. T. REID, A. M., CORNER ELLSWORTH AND ALLSTON STREETS, BERKELEY, *President of the University.*

There are appointed, in addition to the above number other leading citizens from all parts of the State, which comprise the full Board.

Tuition in the Colleges of Science and of Letters is free to residents of California. Students from other States pay a matriculation fee of twenty-five dollars, and a tuition fee of fifty dollars a year. A small charge is made for chemicals in the Chemical Laboratory. This is often met by rendering services. Upon graduation, a fee of ten dollars is charged for a diploma.

Why He Liked Berkeley.

THE following is from a letter written by a physician, who, after experience in the army, and fourteen years' practice in one of the principal cities of New England, came to California on account of shattered health, in search of an equable climate, combined with the conveniences and refinements of easy and intellectual life. He says:—

"In climate, Berkeley leaves very little to be desired, having in fact one of the most temperate and equable in the whole State. Situated just opposite the Golden Gate, but separated from it by the width of the bay, and nearly three miles of gently rising land—about twelve miles in all—its summer temperature is moderated by breezes direct from the Pacific. And you must remember that these breezes not only bring the life and health-giving properties of the sea, but are cooled by passing over the descending Japanese gulf stream. These trades, which torment San Francisco as dust-rising winds, have generally, according to their violence, either died away or so slanted up (in their effort to get over the Contra Costa Range) that, by the time they have reached Berkeley, they are only welcomed as summer zephyrs. But their beneficence, both as health-givers and disease-destroyers, cannot well be over-estimated. The winter climate, too, is charming; the rain-fall averaging about twenty-five inches, while the cold is not often sufficient even to kill heliotropes.

"'The lay of the land,' also, is all that could be asked for. The Contra Costa Range, lying just to the east and north, protects us, in a great measure, from the desolating and irritating 'northers;' while, from this range, the land slopes gradually and beautifully to the bay three miles away. This slope gives ample facilities for drainage, particularly in this, the eastern part of the town, which is from two to three hundred feet above the level of the bay, and where 'hardpan' is from forty to fifty feet below the surface.

"The water supply, although not absolutely of the best quality, and in some need of further filtering, is ample, good, and reasonably free from danger of contamination. It is drawn from a number of springs near the crest of the hills to reservoirs, and thence distributed. The services of supply are therefore far above any risk from sewers or such like hidden dangers; and we may congratulate ourselves upon the fact that this water is almost universally used in this part of the town. From what I have said of the climate, the lay of the land, and natural drainage, you will see that malaria is an utter impossibility; and an epidemic of either of the zymotic diseases almost as much so. In the five years of my residence I have known of a few sporadic cases of typhoid and scarlet fever; but there has been no spread, because the vehicle of communication was wanting.

"I cannot do more, now, than touch upon the other only less important advantages of this as a place of residence: its magnificent views, exceeding anything I remember even in my wide journeyings in Europe and America; admirable educational facilities, and accessibility to cities, markets, shops, and libraries, although these are the very items that go so far to make up human ease and comfort. But I say to you, after a residence of five years, that I, as a physician, an invalid, and the father of a family, am *satisfied*, and beg you to make a trial of it. And, if you do, I prophesy that you will—stay."

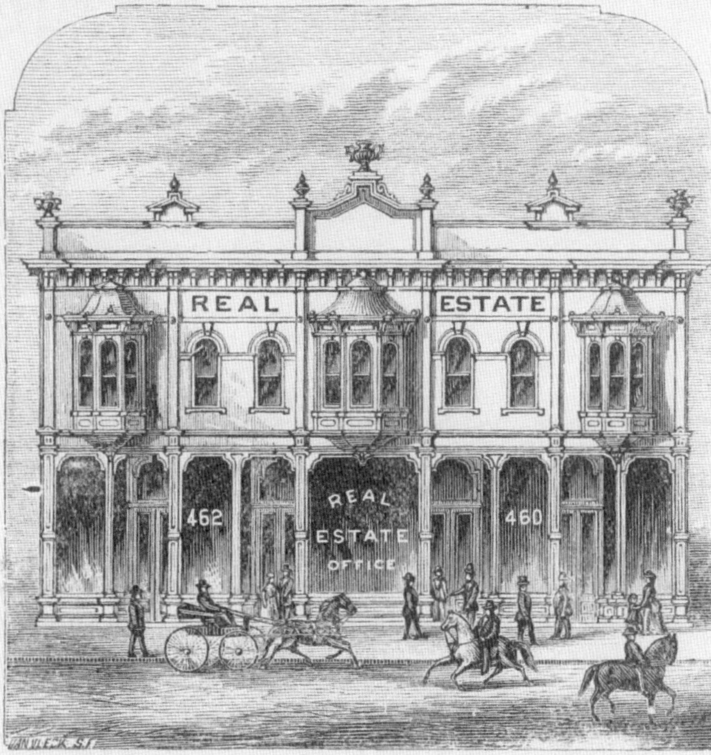

W. J. DINGEE REAL ESTATE OFFICE, EIGHTH STREET.

Real Estate.

PROPERTY in and about such a favored spot as Oakland naturally commands a good price. This is particularly so for choice residence spots; but when compared with prices elsewhere, residence property of Oakland will be found much below the average. There are always, in every place, some good improved places to be had.

Homes can be purchased at all prices, from the neat little tasty cottage at $1,500, to the more pretentious residence at $3,000 to $5,000, or the elegant mansion at $10,000 and upwards. Each can select a site according to his taste,—hotels, boarding houses, large or small cottages, or mansions in the crowded heart of the city. A little out one can climb a small hill and have a splendid outlook, or further off from a loftier perch can overlook the whole bay shore from Vallejo to San Jose. Lots can be selected and buildings erected to each one's taste. Lumber for building is cheap, and mechanics' wages is little if any higher than in the East. The cost of living and rents is as low as in other cities of same size. While suburban fruit and farming lands near Oakland are high, the adjoining county, Contra Costa, contains a large area of good land that can be obtained at from $20 to $150 an acre.

Reliable information about any kind of property in and about Oakland can be obtained of W. J. Dingee, who, having long resided in Oakland, can furnish information to parties East by letter, respecting property for sale, or on personal application will show the choicest residence grounds on improved places. He does a general real estate business. He is familiar with all the property about Oakland.

Oakland as a Manufacturing Center.

Oakland as a Manufacturing Center.

OAKLAND offers such facilities and advantages for manufacturing enterprises as can be offered by no other point on the Pacific Coast.

In support of this claim, says the Committee on Manufacturing, of which V. D. Moody, banker, is President, we state as follows: "We have a frontage within the city limits of over ten miles of railroad tracks, of which frontage at least eight miles are available for manufacturing purposes; enjoys a climate the most favorable for human exertion, being neither hot in summer nor too cold in winter.

"The mortality of this city is the lowest of any city in the world of its size.

"The cost of living and rents is as low, if not lower, than can be found in nine-tenths of the cities of the United States.

"Building materials are cheap. Mechanics' wages are about the same as in the Eastern States.

"Capital for legitimate enterprises is abundant, and the rate of interest is unusually favorable to the borrower.

"In conclusion, this committee would add, that the people of Oakland would welcome and assist, to the utmost of their ability, all persons who may possess the enterprise and knowledge which are needed to establish and maintain successfully manufacturing enterprises, and that all communications and inquiries addressed to the President of the Committee on Manufactures will be promptly answered."

We present a description of some of the prominent manufactories of Oakland, of such as would favor us with information.

Judson Manufacturing Co.

THIS is a stock company with a capital of $2,000,000. This important manufactory is located on the northern limits of Oakland.

The buildings have a frontage of 1,200 feet on the track of the Central Pacific Railroad, and extend westwardly to the bay. These buildings are twenty-eight in number, several of which have been built during the present year. A brick warehouse, 50x100 feet, built this year, stands on the northern line. In this are stored the more valuable of the products awaiting

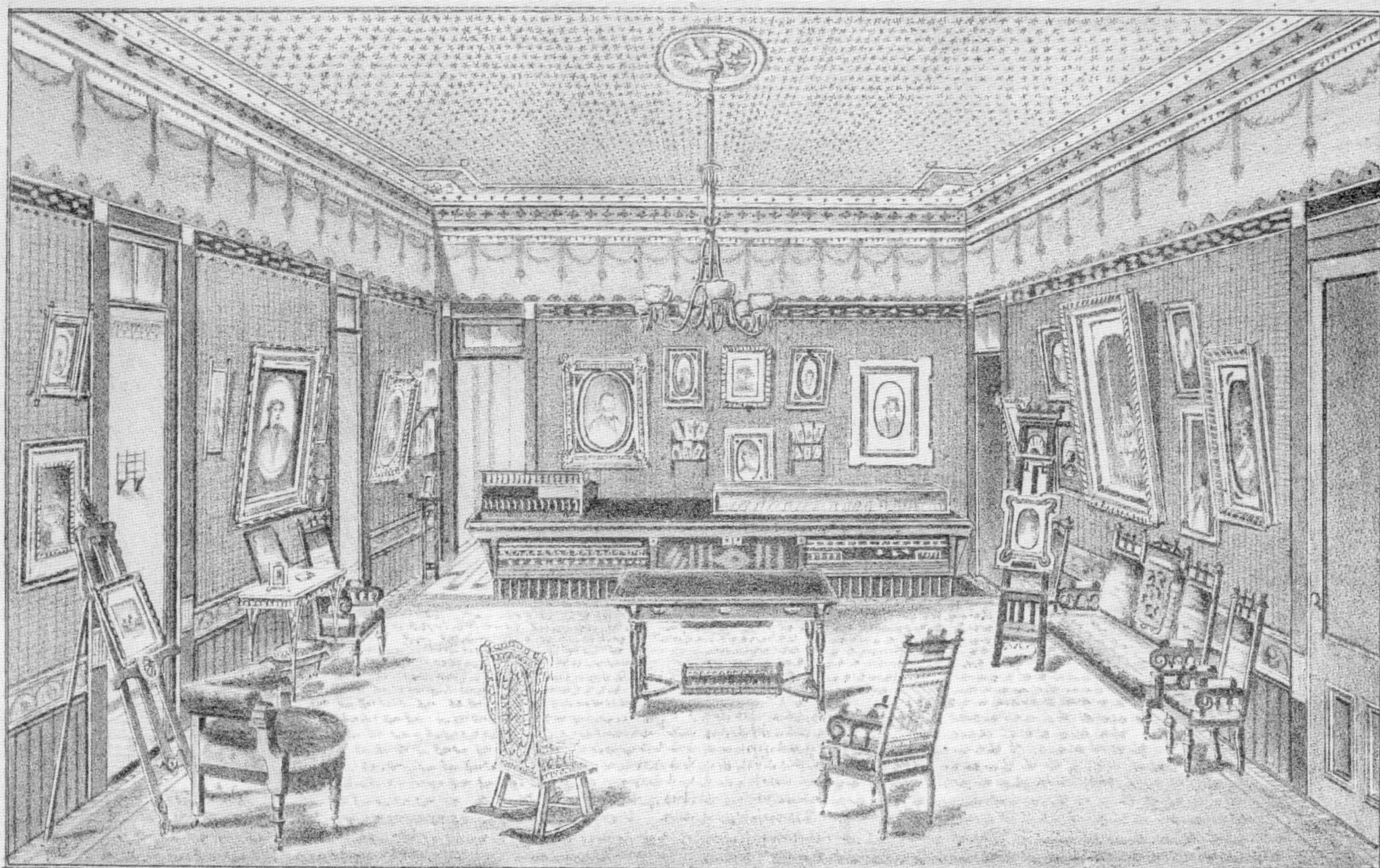

INTERIOR OF W.W. DAMES' PHOTOGRAPHIC GALLERY. 911 BROADWAY, OAKLAND. ELLIOTT LITHO.

shipment. The California Victor Mower is a prominent specialty of these works, and about two thousand five hundred are manufactured annually.

A labyrinth of shops bewilders the observer, in which are made finishing nails, horse nails, shoe nails, brads, and tacks of every size.

Here are the largest shears in the world, made on the spot, for the use of the works, and weighing eighteen tons. Scrap iron of every description from the slightest to five inches in diameter is severed readily by this iron monster.

The amount disbursed in wages is about $180,000 annually. The value of the annual product may be fairly estimated at one million dollars. The Victor Mower alone is manufactured to the value of over two hundred thousand dollars annually.

Pacific Iron and Nail Co.

THE Pacific Iron and Nail Company is a wealthy and enterprising association organized by merchants of San Francisco and Oakland, for the purpose of carrying on their special industry. They comprise three principal structures, at the foot of Market Street, the largest 100x160 feet, the second 100x130 feet, and the third 72x42 feet, besides smaller buildings. A wharf 1,000 feet in length extends to the channel, affording ample conveniences for receipt of material and the shipment of goods. The facilities of the establishment are unsurpassed in all respects. No nail works on the continent are perhaps so well equipped. The machinery is of the most perfect description, and includes recent inventions never used elsewhere. The present capacity of the works is 600 kegs per day, which will soon be increased to 1,000. The establishment will produce everything in the shape of a nail, from the smallest brad to the largest spike.

Other Iron Works.

OAKLAND BOILER WORKS are located on the corner of Third and Franklin Streets, Clark & Woolley proprietors. They manufacture to order steam boilers and do steam fitting, sheet-iron work, and repairing.

NORTHWESTERN MANUFACTURING AND CAR COMPANY is a branch of the factory at Stillwater, Minnesota, and is among the largest manufactories in the United States. The celebrated thresher, "Minnesota Chief," ranks high among harvesting machinery throughout the Western States and in California. The Oakland branch of this company occupies a large frontage on Washington, First, and Second Streets, and a force of fifty men is employed when the works are in full blast. The aggregate sales of this company, from the Oakland works, for the year, will reach $150,000, including threshers, feeders, and cleaners. The parts are made in Minnesota and shipped here and set up. They also manufacture horse-powers and portable engines. Mr. G. W. Morrison is manager of Oakland branch.

OAKLAND IRON WORKS of Ives Scoville & Co., on Jefferson and Second Streets, have been doing a good business during the year. All kinds of machinery, including steam engines and mining machinery, are manufactured here. About fifteen men are employed on an average.

Planing Mills.

WASHINGTON STREET PLANING MILL is located on the corner of Fifth and Washington Streets, and has a good local trade. Everything in the line of house-finishing, as well as sawing, planing, and shaping of every kind, is made here. McManus & Hanavan are the proprietors, and keep ten men employed.

PACIFIC COAST PLANING MILL is owned by A. Kendall & Co., the firm consisting of Alpheus Kendall and M. F. Henderson, and has done a good season's work. The firm are owners of lumber mills in Humboldt County, giving them peculiar advantages. They employ on an average thirty men. The factory is at the corner of Grove and Second Streets.

OAKLAND PLANING MILLS were built about twelve years ago, and have turned out a vast amount of mill-work in their time. Messrs. Burnham, Standeford & Co. (the firm consisting of O. H. Burnham, D. W. Standeford, and L. G. Cole) are among the oldest in the business in Oakland. Orders during the year have been nearly up to the average of the past six years. The number of hands employed varies with the season, but will average about fifty. Their manufactory is at the corner of Washington and First Streets.

PIONEER PLANING MILL COMPANY consists of eight practical men, namely, C. L. Lombard, J. E. White, F. S. Sanford, J. McCully, Geo. W. Smith, Geo. Carroll, J. Bannerman, and A. W. Peterson. They formed a company, with the above title, about February 1, 1883, and leased the buildings and machinery at the foot of Broadway, of the old Pioneer Planing Mills. The enterprise has been successful, and their volume of business is increasing. A force of fifteen men are at present employed, including members of the company, who are all mechanics. The company at present consists of J. E. White, F. S. Sanford, J. McCully, Geo. Carroll, and J. Bannerman.

EAST OAKLAND PLANING MILLS, Crist Galliger & Co. proprietors, are located on the corner of East Twelfth Street and Fourteenth Avenue. These mills have been fairly active during the year, filling orders not only for Oakland, but for interior points and San Francisco. Forty men are employed.

THE EAGLE BOX AND MANUFACTURING COMPANY was established in the spring of 1880. The factory is now located at Nos. 611–615 Market Street, Oakland.

The officers of the company are Richard Abbey, President; Geo. Roeth, Secretary; Alfred Abbey, Manager.

All kinds of fruit boxes, packages, crates, trays, canned goods, and other boxes for commercial use, are manufactured. Their lock joint boxes for dried fruit meet with a ready sale, being much neater than the ordinary package, and protecting the fruit from dust, worms, etc. The Lock Stript Egg Carrier is a specialty. Their goods have a market throughout this and adjoining States.

Oakland Brewery.

THIRTY-TWO years ago the Oakland Brewery was started by two enterprising men, on the northeast corner of Ninth Street and Broadway. Two years later J. C. Wilman became proprietor. He disposed of the growing establishment to Joseph Becht. In 1863 the brewery was burned to the ground. It was rebuilt on the same site. Lawrence and Fred Knauer, father and son, succeeded Mr. Becht, in 1867. April, 1869, the property was purchased by H. Mangle, John Bose, and Charles Kramm. That fall the new firm bought land at the present location and began erecting another brewery. It was completed in 1870. The building covered 100x50 feet. The business was then transferred to these premises. Horse-power was at once

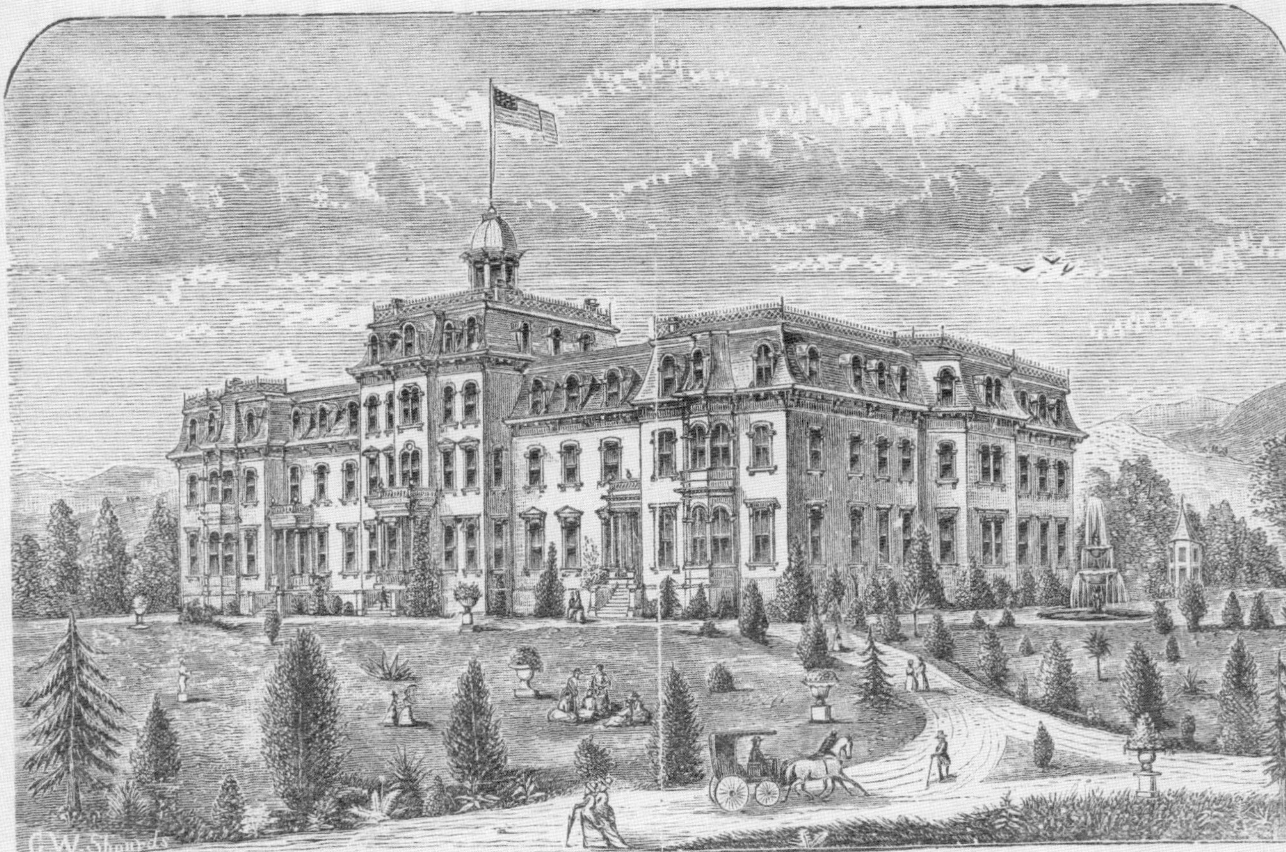

MILLS SEMINARY.

adopted. Joseph Dieves acquired Mangle's interest in 1870. Soon after, Bose died and Messrs. Kramm & Dieves became sole owners. In 1876 steam superseded horse-power, and the capacity of the establishment rose to 18,000 barrels per year. It was about 150 barrels per year in 1853.

The Oakland Brewery is situated on the northeast corner of Telegraph Avenue and Durant Street. Its premises are of considerable extent. The Telegraph Avenue frontage is 193 feet; the Durant Street, 125 feet, and the New Broadway, 93 feet. Messrs. Kramm & Dieves reside side by side on Telegraph Avenue, in houses adjacent to the brewery.

There is no building more notable than the Oakland Brewery in the northern part of the city. It is of brick and wood, two stories, with a superstructure of wood, one story. The offices are on the southwest corner.

Three articles, barley, hops, and moss, are the only ingredients, besides yeast and water, used by the Oakland Brewery. Beers are made of various deleterious substances, but Messrs. Kramm & Dieves refrain from utilizing cerealine, glucose, maltose, and so on through the list.

In a large tank on the second floor the process of beer-making is begun. It holds eighty sacks of barley, which are left to soak in water. From there the barley is conveyed by a pipe to two half floors, one under the other, each 65x55 feet. The wet grain is laid upon an asphaltum pavement, where it sprouts, "makes the sugar." Air enters through a number of small windows, each fitted with a wire screen. From here the barley is taken by an elevator to an upper room where it is spread out and subjected to a high temperature, and, when fully dried, is malt. We have not space to mention the various processes through which it passes before it becomes ready for use, but will say that no housewife could be cleaner about her work than are the employes of the Oakland Brewery. Every room is kept as sweet as a milk pantry should be. Returned casks are scalded with hot water and rinsed with cold water. There are no unpleasant odors about the place. Water and muscle are unsparingly used. Tidiness reigns all about.

The Oakland Brewery is one of the city's leading industries. Its annual coal bill is $5,000. Each month it pays out $1,000 in wages. It consumes annually about 21,000 pounds of hops and 15,000 sacks of barley. Its beer is consumed largely in Oakland and Alameda County, and is on sale throughout the counties of Contra Costa, Solano, Fresno, Tulare, Stanislaus, and Mendocino. Ed. Cloelen has for seventeen years been superintendent of the Oakland Brewery.

The Oakland Brewery from January, 1884, to January, 1885, gained 1,352 barrels over the preceding year, selling over 15,000 barrels. Following are the declared sales for that year of all Alameda County breweries:—

Oakland Brewery	15,285
Hofburg (Berkeley)	6,078
Washington	4,506
Brooklyn	3,051
East Oakland	1,163
New York (Haywards)	1,481
Lyon (Haywards)	577
Livermore	472
Alameda	418
Columbia (San Leandro)	379
Milwaukee (Mission San Jose)	244

Flouring Mills.

THE Encinal Flouring Mills are located on the corner of Washington and Fourth Streets, Gould & Williamson, proprietors. The mills are driven by steam power, and have all the needed machinery for grinding all kinds

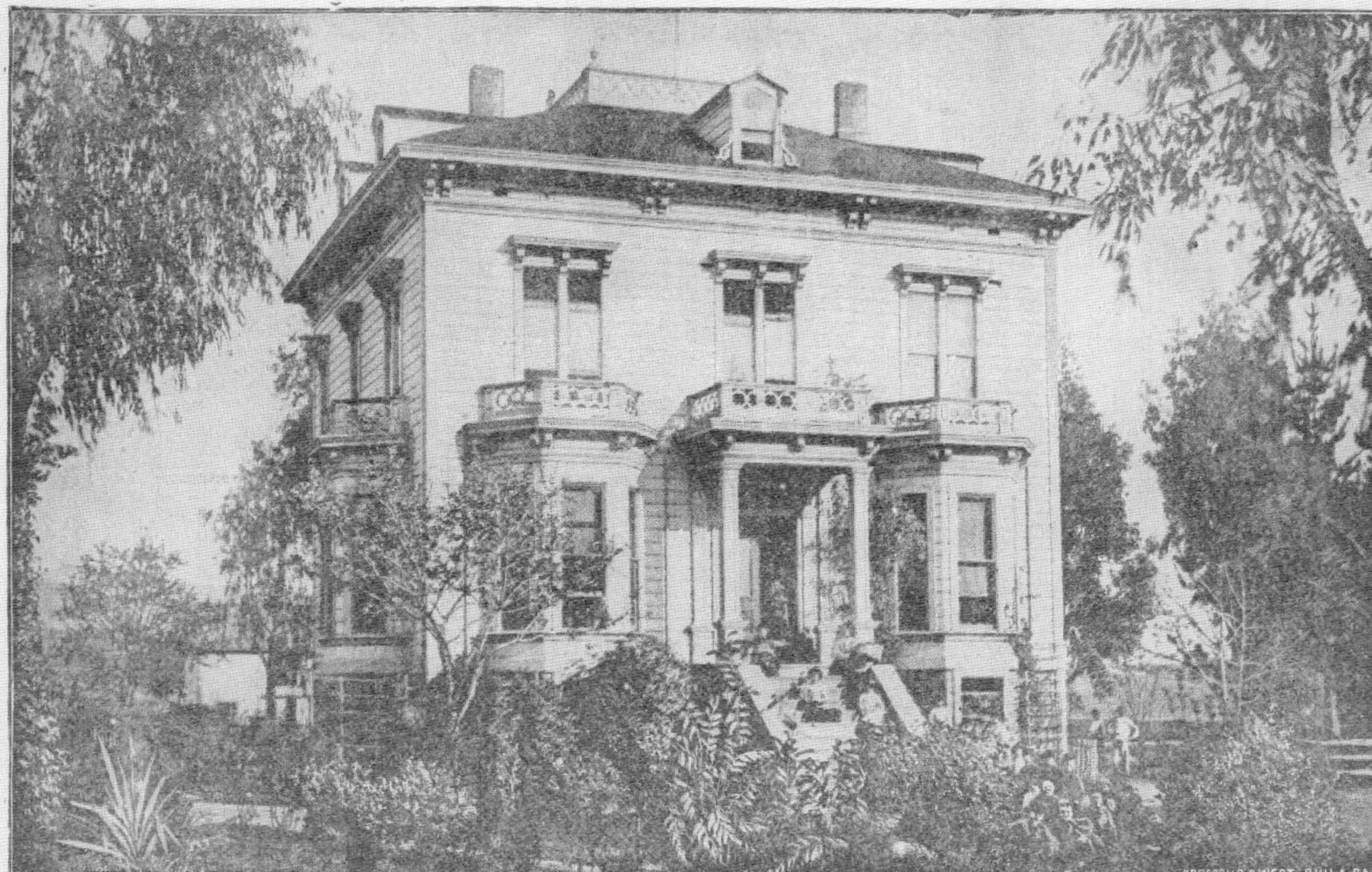

HOME FOR CHILDREN, LADIES' RELIEF SOCIETY OF OAKLAND, CALIFORNIA.

of grain. They make meals a specialty. Their business is growing, having steadily increased from the start.

THE GOLDEN RULE FLOURING MILLS, operated by Hickok, Schroeder & Co., have, since they were totally destroyed by fire, on the 3d of December, 1884, been rebuilt and refitted with all the latest and best improved machinery, and have been in full running order since the 1st of May, 1885. The output for the first six months has averaged 4,000 barrels of flour per month, which would indicate a total per annum of 48,000 barrels, but the actual capacity of the mills is over 60,000 barrels. The total number of men employed in the mills is sixteen, and the amount of small stuff and various kinds of feed manufactured by them, outside of the flour, amounts to between $40,000 and $50,000. Considering the great difficulties under which the flour industry on the Pacific Coast has been laboring during the last twelve months, the Golden Rule Mills have been among the most successful mills operated.

Alameda Furniture Factory.

WE would like to call attention of the people of Oakland to the fact that furniture of all descriptions is manufactured in our midst at the large factory on Encinal Avenue, Alameda, which is represented in our illustrations. It is hoped our citizens will give our home manufactured furniture a fair trial, as we are satisfied that, in style and price, it is equal to any. We represent in our views the sale-rooms of the Alameda Furniture Manufacturing Company in the Weber Block, 401 and 403 Twelfth Street, Oakland, where a full stock of their own manufactures, as well as Eastern furniture, will be kept, and offered at prices never known before. We also carry a full stock of Eastern wood mantels and make to order the same or any other patterns, and at Eastern prices; in fact we will duplicate any article of furniture or mantels at what they cost East, saving the cost of freight.

All our lumber is thoroughly kilndried, and we warrant all we make. All we ask is to come and look before purchasing. We offer special inducements for the holiday trade.

East Oakland Tanneries.

THE Oak Grove Tannery, East Oakland, was built twenty-one years ago, and came into the hands of its present proprietor, J. S. Derby, thirteen years since. The average yearly production of hides is 12,000, valued, on a good market, at $75,000. Boston and St. Louis have, of late years, been the chief market for the product. The number of men employed varies with the season of the year, the average being sixteen.

G. F. CRIST'S TANNERY, East Oakland, was established in 1871, by the present proprietor, who has conducted an extensive and uniformly successful business. San Francisco dealers take most of the product, the annual value of which is $120,000; men employed, 25.

California Pottery.

THIS industry was begun by James Miller in 1875, in a small room only 12x12 feet, where he followed modeling and moulding. From that small beginning the business has been increased to its present mammoth proportions. There are now 3 kilns, the largest of which is 28 feet long, 15 feet wide, and 15 feet high. The combined capacity of the 3 kilns is about $2,000 worth of goods. The buildings consist of a work-shop, 200x50 feet, two stories; a drying-house, 50x50 feet, two stories; a work-shop, 25x100 feet, one story; a grinding-room, 30x60 feet, one story; a jigger-shop, 30x100 feet, two stories; and a flower-pot shop, 30x100 feet. The premises include one and three-fourths acres of ground. There are three mills, with a capacity of fifty tons of clay per day. The following articles are manufactured at the works: Sewer-pipe, sewer-pipe fittings, ornaments and trimmings for buildings, chimney-tops, garden vases, fountains, antique urns, flower-pots, etc. The works are under the personal supervision of Mr. Miller, who is not only a master workman at his trade, but an artist of the highest order as well, many of his designs being almost imcomparable. The material used at the works comes from Michigan Bar. About fifty men are employed. The owners of the works are Messrs. Miller & Windsor.

The Cotton Mills.

THE new cotton mills at Oakland, the only ones on the Pacific Coast, have just been fairly started. The labor to be employed had to be trained. At present the number of hands is 150, but more will be needed by and by when the mills are run to their full capacity. A few skilled operatives were brought out from Scotland by William Rutherford, the Superintendent, and have been engaged in teaching the others the finer points of the trade. The goods made at these mills have met at once with a favorable reception wherever exhibited to the wholesale traders of the coast. One of the chief staples is twines, various in kind, including those used in sail and net making, and crash toweling, bags, and duckings. An admixture of jute is employed to add to the weight and strength of these goods. In some instances the Oakland mills have offered goods cheaper than they could be laid down in this market by Eastern manufacturers. The samples presented by the Oakland mills are said to excel the like grades of cotton made in New England. The mill company have purchased 500 bales that were grown in the San Joaquin Valley in the vicinity of Bakersfield, California, and they intend to derive the most of their future stock from this region and Texas. They find California cotton to be of very excellent quality.

California Jute Mills.

THIS establishment is located in East Oakland and has done a good year's work. At present about 225 white hands are employed, and 100 Chinese. White applicants, with a genuine desire to learn and become useful operatives, are given the perference in every case. Wages range from fifty cents per day to the novice, who merely looks on in order to learn, to $1.75 per day to the most skillful. In securing and teaching so large a proportion of white labor, the management has conferred a benefit upon the community.

Among the improvements is a brick warehouse, 50x85 feet, and a large one-story brick building, 106½x92½, to be used for an operating room. Sewing machines, to be operated by white labor only, have been introduced. The yearly product is three millions of yards of cloth annually for ore, bean, and coffee bags. Machines for working flax are being added, together with the latest improvements in machinery necessary to a complete factory which shall be able to compete with any other. The manager judges that fully 350 hands will be required when all contemplated improvements are perfected. Mr. John Robertson is Superintendent, and Mr. Benj. Northup, millwright and foreman of the mechanical department.

Standard Soap Company.

THE business and works of the Standard Soap Company, a picture of which appears in this work, are situated on the water front at West Berkeley, and connected with side track of the C. P. R. R., forming a connection with the network of the general railway system of the United States. The business of the present company was established in San Francisco in 1861, in one of the old original iron buildings, which came around the horn in 1849, and was located at the corner of Front and Broadway Streets, San Francisco.

This plant occupies the entire block of ground, No. 109, West Berkeley, being 300x300 feet. To give an idea of the size of the manufactory, we give the amount of material used in its construction: 2,500,000 feet of lumber, and 300,000 bricks for foundation and chimneys. No similar factory can be found in the United States which in appearance is more imposing than this plant, which when worked to its full capacity would be more than one million, five hundred thousand pounds of soap per month. This factory is systematically worked in departments, under the supervision of a competent foreman, such as Box Making, Cutting, Toilet Soap, Candle Making, Glycerine, etc. It also has a full Printing Department, where all labels, circulars, and the necessary printing for the Works is done. We question if any other Soap Company in the world has as complete a printing outfit as this factory. This company also owns the steamer, *Mare Island*, which makes daily trips from the works to San Francisco. A picture of the steamer is shown in the foreground of the illustration on another page.

West Berkeley Lumber Yard.

THIS extensive business, owned by the Mendocino Lumber Company and managed by Mr. Thomas Richardson, has been purchased by Messrs. Charles D. Ford and Henry W. Taylor. Mr. Ford has been connected with the yard for several years past, and is the son of the president of the Mendocino Lumber Company. Mr. H. W. Taylor is a gentleman of large business experience. Under their management the business cannot fail to increase rapidly. The West Berkeley Lumber Yard is one of the oldest in the State. Its location is admirable as a shipping point either by rail or by water, and its trade has become so extensive that many acres of ground are required for the accommodation of its lumber and material, the shipment of which represents hundreds of car loads during the year. In 1882 ship and car were brought together by means of rails being placed down to the end of the wharf, which is 1,500 feet in length, from the main line of the C. P. R. R. In addition to this the capacity for storing and drying lumber has lately been largely increased. It is the intention of the company to carry as full and well assorted a stock of building material as any other lumber interest on the Pacific Coast. Their shipments now extend to all parts of the State, and even as far east as Chicago.

A view of the yard and wharf is given in this work. Their sales the past year were of lumber, 9,000,000 feet; shingles, 5,000,000; and lath, 1,000,000. Some sixteen men are constantly employed. They also handle doors, sash, blinds, nails, brick, lime, cement, plaster, and plasterers' hair.

Why Called Berkeley.

THE founding of a seminary of advanced learning on the western shore of the American Continent, from whose windows could be seen the vast expanse of the Pacific Ocean, suggested to those engaged in the project the famous line of Berkeley,—

"Westward the course of Empire takes its way."

Hence, the site received the name of the author of the poetic prophecy.

Berkeley Planing Mill.

AMONG permanent fixtures of the place is the Berkeley Planing Mill, which was established in January, 1885, by Mr. Geo. C. Pape. It is located on the corner of Berkeley Way and Louisa Street. This little mill, a view of which appears on another page, is proving a great convenience to residents of Berkeley, as all kinds of work, such as mouldings, brackets, turning, wood carving, and scroll sawing, beside the ordinary work of a planing mill, is furnished to order. Mr. Pape by strict attention to business has built up a good trade. It supplies a long-felt want, and is appreciated by the citizens of Berkeley.

Leading Business Firm.

DWIGHT WAY STATION is the first station south of Berkeley. The buildings and lumber yard of the Berkeley Village Improvement Association, are located at this point. Stewart Brothers, the leading mercantile firm of Berkeley, have a large establishment here, and do a heavy business. As they do all their own freighting, and also run two delivery wagons, they keep constantly employed a number of men and teams. Beside the regular grocery business, they deal largely in green fruits and produce, as well as coal, wood, hay, and grain. A view of their business house and residences will be found on another page.

West Berkeley.

WEST BERKELEY bids fair to become a manufacturing center. It has already in operation a large Planing mill, Soap factory, Cement works, Guadalupe Mine Reduction Works, Lubricating oil works, Starch works, Glass works, Giant Powder Co.'s works, Acid works, and Paraffine Paint works. And last, but not least, one of the largest lumber yards and establishments on the bay. Robert Ingenlath has a neat store and residence combined, adjoining Mr. Bruns, where he not only attends to the plumbing business, but carries a large stock of tin and granite ware.

To give an idea of the business carried on at a single store at West Berkeley, we mention that of D. H. Bruns & Co., which carries a general assortment of groceries, provisions, boots and shoes, and hardware, and keeps in stock $20 000 worth of goods. He buys largely, and is able to sell at San Francisco prices, and has thus by fair dealing built him up a large and increasing business. He does the largest mercantile business of any firm in West Berkeley, his sales averaging $100 per day. Mr. Bruns began in a small way, and by strict attention to business and fair dealing, has built up a large trade.

Messrs. Schmidt & Schnelle have just erected a neat and commodious store on the corner of Ninth and University Ave.

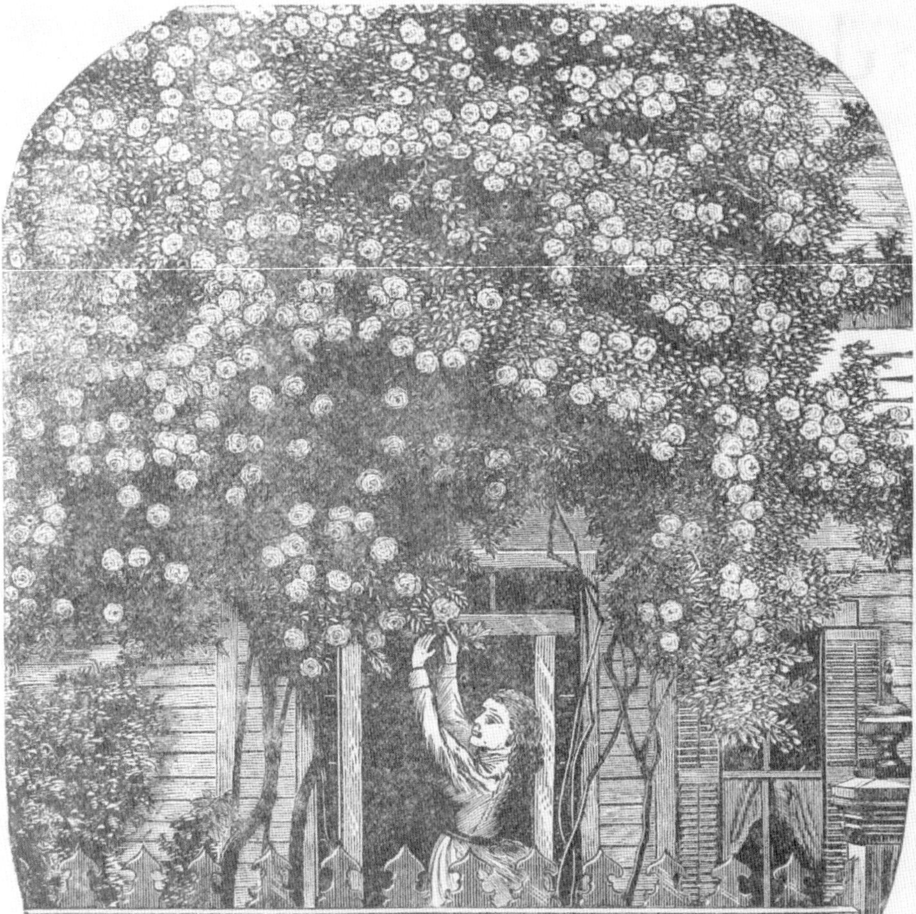

WINTER SCENE IN OAKLAND.

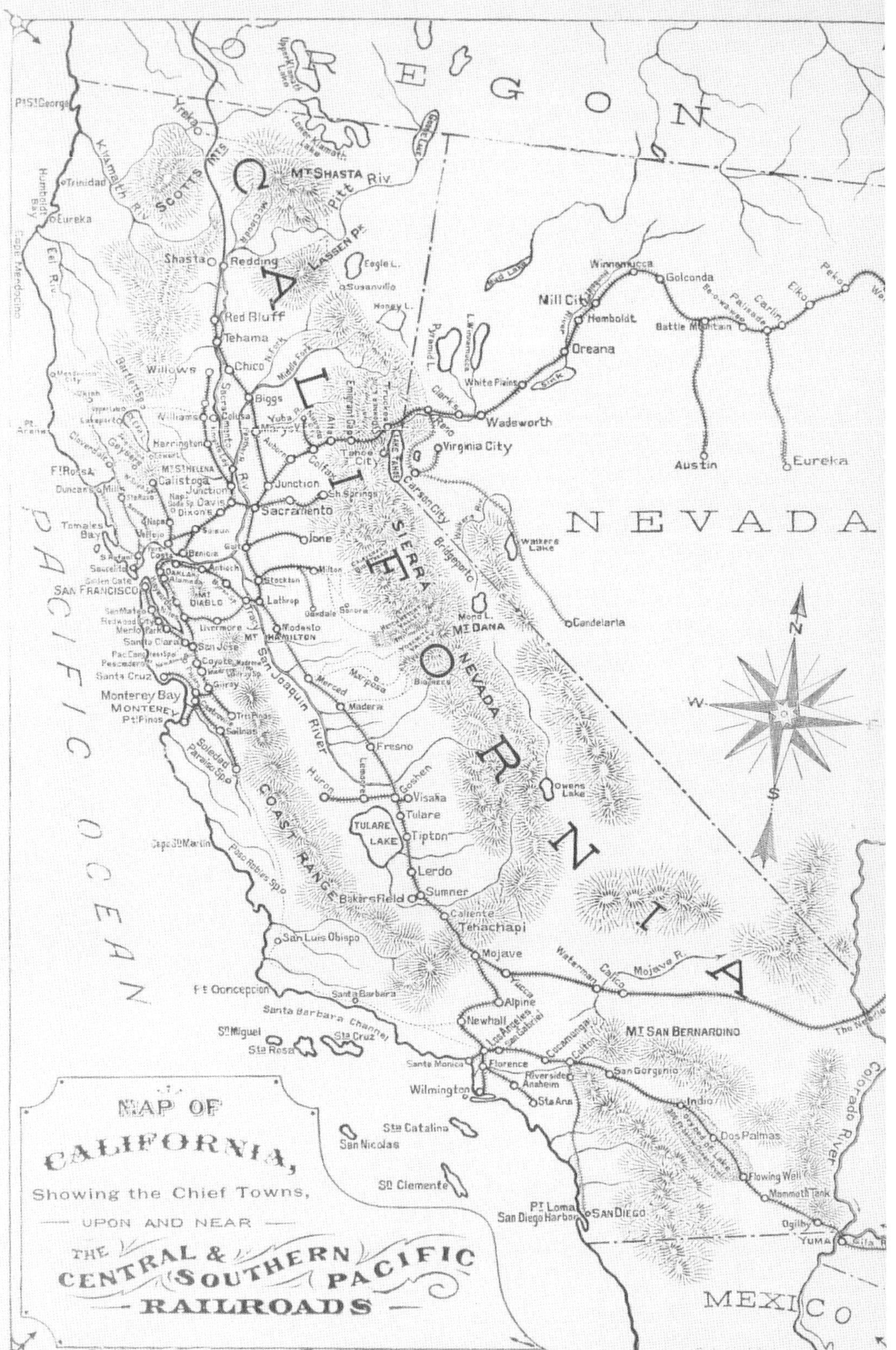
MAP OF
CALIFORNIA,
Showing the Chief Towns,
UPON AND NEAR
THE CENTRAL & SOUTHERN PACIFIC
RAILROADS
OREGON
CALIFORNIA
NEVADA
MEXICO
PACIFIC OCEAN
N
S
W
Upper Klamath Lake
Lower Klamath Lake
Goose Lake
Yreka
Pt St George
Klamath Riv.
SCOTTS MTS
Mt SHASTA
Pitt Riv.
Trinidad
Humboldt Bay
Eureka
Cape Mendocino
Eel Riv.
LASSEN Pk
Shasta
Redding
Eagle L.
Susanville
Honey L.
Red Bluff
Tehama
Chico
Willows
Biggs
Williams
Colusa
Marysville
Yuba
Emigrant Gap
Truckee
Reno
Wadsworth
Harrington
Colfax
Tahoe City
LAKE TAHOE
Virginia City
Carson City
Mt St HELENA
Calistoga
Junction
Davis
Dixon's
Sacramento
Napa
Vallejo
Benicia
Suisun
Galt
Ione
Tomales Bay
Saucelito
Golden Gate
SAN FRANCISCO
Oakland
Alameda
Antioch
MT DIABLO
Stockton
Milton
Lathrop
Modesto
Oakdale
Sonora
Livermore
MT HAMILTON
San Mateo
Redwood City
Menlo Park
Santa Clara
San Jose
Coyote
Gilroy
Santa Cruz
Monterey Bay
MONTEREY
Pt Pinos
Tres Pinos
Salinas
Soledad
SIERRA
NEVADA
Mono L.
Mt DANA
Bridgeport
Walkers Lake
Candelaria
Merced
Mariposa
Madera
San Joaquin River
Fresno
Huron
Lemoore
Goshen
Visalia
Tulare
TULARE LAKE
Tipton
Owens Lake
Lerdo
Sumner
Bakersfield
COAST RANGE
Cape San Martin
Paso Robles Spa
San Luis Obispo
Caliente
Tehachapi
Mojave
Waterman
Calico
Mojave R.
Pt Concepcion
Santa Barbara
Santa Barbara Channel
Alpine
Newhall
Los Angeles
San Gabriel
St Miguel
Sta Rosa
Sta Cruz
Santa Monica
Florence
Wilmington
Cucamonga
Colton
Riverside
Anaheim
Sta Ana
Mt SAN BERNARDINO
San Gorgonio
Indio
Dos Palmas
Sta Catalina
San Nicolas
Sn Clemente
Flowing Well
Mammoth Tank
Pt Loma
San Diego Harbor
SAN DIEGO
Ogilby
YUMA
Colorado River
Winnemucca
Golconda
Mill City
Humboldt
Battle Mountain
Palisade
Carlin
Elko
Oreana
Pyramid L.
L. Winnemucca
White Plains
Austin
Eureka